Silicon Valley, Women, and the California Dream

GENDER, CLASS, AND OPPORTUNITY
IN THE TWENTIETH CENTURY

Glenna Matthews

STANFORD UNIVERSITY PRESS
STANFORD, CALIFORNIA
2003

Stanford University Press
Stanford, California

© 2003 by the Board of Trustees of the
Leland Stanford Junior University

Published with the assistance of the Edgar M. Kahn Memorial Fund.

Library of Congress Cataloging-in-Publication Data
Matthews, Glenna.
    Silicon valley, women, and the California dream : gender, class,
and opportunity in the twentieth century / Glenna Matthews.
        p.   cm.
    Originated as the author's doctoral thesis, Stanford University, 1977.
    Includes bibliographical references and index.
    ISBN 0-8047-4154-9 (cloth : alk. paper)
    ISBN 0-8047-4796-2 (paper : alk. paper)
        1. Women computer industry employees — California — Santa
Clara Valley.   I. Title: Gender, class, and opportunity in the twentieth
century.   II. Title.
    HD6073.C65222 U56 2003
    331.4'81004'0979473 — dc21   2002004728

Designed by Janet Wood
Typeset by BookMatters in 10/14 Janson

Original Printing 2002

Last figure below indicates year of this printing:
12   11   10   09   08   07   06   05   04   03   02

To my dear friends Monica Loewi, Sandy Mahoney, and John Snetsinger

In memory of Larry Mahoney

CONTENTS

TABLES

MAPS

Every book has a history, but because this book originated as a Stanford University dissertation in the 1970s, its history is longer than most. To be completely accurate, my interest in the subject even antedated my graduate school experience. From late 1968 to early 1970, I hosted a weekly League of Women Voters television program devoted to public affairs in San Jose and Santa Clara County. Thus, it is not surprising that when I chose a topic of study at Stanford, I gravitated toward an area I had already come to see as fascinating — and that was before the area had become world famous as "Silicon Valley."

Another reason for my choice to study San Jose is the nature of the family in which I grew up. My late father, Glen Ingles, was a newspaper editor in various small California towns. Although I would not live in the Santa Clara Valley — Sunnyvale, to be precise — until adulthood, many of the issues with which this book deals, such as the conflict between development and resource preservation, were part of our nightly dinner-table conversation. Moreover, in the 1950s my late mother, Alberta Ingles, worked for the Coastal Area Protection League at an office in Laguna Beach. This organization tried to prevent the offshore drilling of oil. I learned many things from my parents; one of the most valuable was to care deeply about my native state.

For my dissertation, I chose to focus on the Santa Clara Valley during the Great Depression, because I had read enough of John Steinbeck to know that I wanted to discover if the historical record would verify his view of California as riven by class conflict during that turbulent decade. And, of course, it did. I published a number of articles drawn from the research but never a book. Then in the fall of 1992, I was teaching a class at the University of California, Berkeley, in which I teamed up with the anthropologist Aihwa Ong, a scholar who has written about female high-tech workers in Malaysia. The course was entitled "Comparative Gender Systems," and we devoted a great deal of attention to the situation of women workers. It came to me that I could compare and contrast two different groups of immigrant women workers in two different industries in the Santa Clara Valley, fruit and electronics, and perhaps develop a fresh way of looking at the subject. This book is the result of that decision.

Over time, I have accumulated a greater than usual number of debts to friends and colleagues. In thanking those who have been helpful, I must begin with my Stanford mentor Carl Degler. He has provided an outstanding model of scholarly engagement as well as valued personal friendship. I have long believed that the opportunity to work with him was one of the most significant turning points in my life.

Second, I want to thank the dozens of interview subjects whose cooperation made this research possible. I didn't rely only on oral history, but the book could never have been written without it, because the written record does not do full justice to a number of the people whose experiences I wanted to document. Moreover, as I worked on the dissertation and then the book, I drew upon many other people to recommend interview subjects or to put me in touch with them. The notes section acknowledges these individuals where possible. Because I received so many names and telephone numbers from him, Michael Eisenscher deserves special thanks.

I would like to say a special word, too, about Lenny Siegel, who dedicated himself to creating an archive of clippings about the Valley's high-tech industry and who has made it available to scholars. The value of his effort was manifest to me as soon as I heard about it. In researching the depression decade, it had taken me six months to read my way through the *San Jose Mercury-Herald* (as it then was called) to locate the newspaper articles that would endow me with a matrix of knowledge about that period. Thanks to the clippings files about high tech, I could get right to the meat of the very substantial coverage of the subject in the local press.

Speaking of the *San Jose Mercury*, I would like to thank two former employees of that publication, Phil Trounstine and Harry Farrell. Each has a tremendous knowledge about the area, and each generously shared his knowledge with me. Indeed, I came to believe that there was not much of public significance that went on in San Jose in the last half of the twentieth century that escaped the attention of one or both of these men. Another San Josean who deserves to be singled out is Craig Parada of the San Jose City Planning Department. He provided me with specialized maps of San Jose that show the impact of the plethora of annexations on that city.

Two social scientists who have studied high-tech workers in the Valley also provided generous help to me. Karen Hossfeld has interviewed hundreds of assembly workers, and I have been able to discuss the Valley's high-tech industry with her — as well as read her articles and her dissertation. Boy Luethje of Frankfurt, Germany, has insights and information about the Valley that are unparalleled. Not only has he shared them with me, but he has also read a number of chapters, sparing me from mistakes and enriching my own understanding. Moreover, it was Professor Luethje who told me that I had to talk to Dr. Joseph LaDou, a man with an extraordinary grasp of the occupational safety and health issues for high tech and someone else whose help must be acknowledged.

One of the most riveting interviews I conducted was in the fall of 1999, when I talked to Sam Kagel, an attorney and professional labor mediator/arbitrator who was then ninety years old and who had just signed a three-year contract with the International Longshoremen's and Warehousemen's Union (ILWU). Mr. Kagel told me of becoming interested in California labor when he was an undergraduate and of then serving on the Strike Committee of the ILWU in San Francisco in 1934. With an unexcelled perspective on California labor, he's a man to be listened to. I asked him how he explained the fact that seasonally employed, immigrant female workers in the canneries got a union in the 1930s. He fixed me with a piercing look and replied "the march inland," the name for the ILWU's plan to organize collateral industries after its success in 1934. In consequence, I strengthened my argument in that respect.

Over the years, I have presented my research to several audiences, an experience that has invariably been illuminating. Local audiences have included the California Studies Dinner Seminar, the Bay Area Labor History Workshop, the women and work study group, and the Institute of Urban and Regional Development. I have also spoken at the Claremont Graduate School; MIT; California State University, Fullerton; and the University of Central Florida. Thanks to one and all.

Several scholars, in addition to Professor Luethje, read the whole or a part of the manuscript, including Bob Cherny, Janet Flammang, Bill Issel, Dick Walker, and Charles Wollenberg. To each of them I extend profound gratitude. I am, of course, responsible for any errors that remain.

I also want to thank librarians and archivists at DeAnza Community College's California History Center, the Labor Archives at San Francisco State University, the Institute for Governmental Studies at University of California, Berkeley, the Bancroft Library, the National Archives, the AFL-CIO Archives in Washington, Stanford University Archives, the San Jose Public Library's California Room, and the San Jose Historical Museum, as well as personnel at Varian Associates, Intel, and Lockheed. Lynn Bonfield and Susan Sherwood of the San Francisco State Labor Archives deserve special mention, because they allowed me to examine the Sam Kagel Collection before it had been catalogued — I could assist them in evaluating its historical significance — and because of many other acts of kindness along the way.

One of the most crucial sources of help came in the form of a yearlong fellowship from the National Endowment for the Humanities in 1998–99. Not only was the financial assistance welcome, but also receiving the NEH was a wonderful validation for the project.

Norris Pope of Stanford University Press demonstrated interest in the book as soon as I presented the idea to him. Many thanks to him and to all the other people at the press who have helped usher the book into life.

Finally, to all of the friends and family who have lived with my passion for the Santa Clara Valley, there are no words to convey the depth of my gratitude. Sadly, neither of my parents is now alive to see the book, but they always displayed a lively interest in it, even in their nineties. My children, Karen and David, and my grandchildren, Monica, Margaret, and Justin, have done so much to sweeten my life; in the former case, they are two of my best friends as well as my offspring, and in the latter case, I have come to appreciate that none of the stereotypes about being a grandparent does the role justice. Thanks also to my daughter-in-law Maria Matthews and her mother, Sheila Lester. Others I want to mention include Deborah Gardner, Pat Hills, Greg Nolan, and Kevin Whitfield, my East Coast support group; Bob Darcy, Adelia Hanson, Lynn Murnane, Etta Perkins, and Dorothy Schrader of Stillwater, Oklahoma; Barbara and Fred Nash of Laguna Beach (and many other members of the Laguna Beach High School Class of 1955); and my friends in the Bay Area. Among the last-named are Dee Andrews, Dion

Aroner, Joan Bieder, Ann Chandler, Eli Leon, Karen Paget, Anna Rabkin, Jackie Reinier, Jennie Rhine, Kay Trimberger, and Catherine Trimbur.

The friends to whom the book is dedicated have been singled out because they have had so much tenure in office, so to speak, have been so loyal, and have listened to me beyond what is reasonable but not beyond their endurance. Monica Loewi was my roommate at Pomona College in the 1950s and has been an unflagging friend ever since. Though she lives in Canada, she has shown up for many of the "big" occasions of my life. Sandy Mahoney and the late Larry Mahoney of Sunnyvale, whom I first met in 1964, provided me with months of hospitality when I no longer lived in the Valley myself but needed to be there to conduct research. I should also say that Sandy — was there ever a better confidante! — has faithfully clipped appropriate articles in the *San Jose Mercury* for me over the years. John Snetsinger, fellow historian and friend since childhood, has given me heart since the days when I was a re-entry student at San Jose State University and wondering whether I could aspire to the doctoral program at Stanford. Clichéd though it may be to say this, these are the people who make my life worth living.

Glenna Matthews
Berkeley and Laguna Beach

Introduction

This book is about the social and economic history of California's Silicon Valley, with a particular focus on its women workers. Silicon Valley is an area slightly south of San Francisco that has been internationally celebrated for its abundance of high-tech wizardry, while also being poorly understood. The latter is because the mythology of high-tech success has been so powerful that despite many serious attempts to depict "the dark side of the chip," the Valley's aura of representing the culmination of the California Dream remained nearly undiminished until the dot-com downturn at the dawn of the twenty-first century.[1] Of course, no region could generate the kind of wealth produced by Silicon Valley without some portion of its inhabitants benefiting from it. But who, how much, and at what cost? How have regional characteristics shaped opportunities, especially for the most vulnerable — who often turn out to be immigrant women? How did the opportunities change over the course of the twentieth century? These are the issues I will explore.

Silicon Valley is, and has been for a generation, the world capital of advanced technology. In and around the Santa Clara Valley are thousands of high-tech firms, a plethora of venture capitalists, and one of the greatest concentrations of inventiveness and entrepreneurial energy in human history. As the technology itself has evolved, its Valley acolytes have continued to reinvent themselves and their products. They've gone from focusing on transistors, to microprocessors, to computers and computer software, to the Internet. Many people have become rich, and the area has experienced both the rewards and the problems of its massive growth, most acutely, the problem of an increase in jobs unmatched by one in housing units. The area has also grown in ethnic diversity simultaneously with its economic transformation. In short, the Valley has been the site of extraordinary changes over the course of the late twentieth century. It is my contention that the fate of women workers, who have been at the heart of various production processes throughout the century, offers the best test of the reality behind the glitzy image. I also argue that the lens of gender helps us understand the course of the transformation. In addition to focusing on the women themselves, however, I also document and explore the key moments in the Valley's history between 1900 and 2000.

Silicon Valley is world famous. Less well known today is the fact that earlier in the century, the Santa Clara Valley enjoyed wide renown for an entirely different reason. As the "Valley of Heart's Delight," the area contained the world's largest concentration of fruit-processing plants, set in a sea of thousands of acres of fruit orchards. So beauteous was it during the spring, when the prune, apricot, and cherry trees were in bloom, that people made pilgrimages to enjoy the sight of a seemingly unending expanse of white and pink blossoms.[2] Then, as now, the Valley generated prosperity, though not on the same scale as that produced by high tech. Within a single generation, the Valley of Heart's Delight had given way to Silicon Valley. Thus the extraordinary changes of the past few decades have been part of a larger pattern of ongoing transformation.

The Valley's Continuities

Clearly, so vast a change in the local economy as that from the Valley of Heart's Delight to Silicon Valley has brought about many discontinuities.

But there are also a surprising number of continuities as well, threads that can be followed throughout the course of the century. Most important of these is the role played by immigrant women in the production process for both fruit and electronics. In both eras and for both industries, women workers have constituted the bulk of the operatives at the bottom of the occupational hierarchy. In the early part of the century, these women workers tended to be from southern Europe. In the latter part, they have been Latina and Asian. In both eras, they have struggled with the problems of poor pay and difficult working conditions, as well as with the impact of intense racism. Put another way, in both eras, women's opportunities have been shaped by the realities of a segmented labor market in which "women's work" is devalued and underpaid. In the earlier era, however, the potential for exploitation was tempered by the cannery and packing-house workers' achievement of unionization in the late 1930s.

Another commonality lies in the role of the immigrant entrepreneur. Despite the presence of large, overweening firms in both industries, both have also been characterized by opportunities for small-scale start-ups, by the availability of capital for such undertakings, and by certain immigrants finding a way to take advantage of the situation. In neither era, however, has this necessarily meant that immigrant employers have been any more favorable to the interests of their co-ethnics than employers of native-born extraction.

A third commonality lies in the way that immigrant households in both eras have laboriously worked to get ahead. Although some of the particulars have differed, the need to come up with creative ways of keeping a household afloat has remained the same. Reminiscing about the early twentieth century, for example, my Italian informants recalled their mothers' inventiveness in providing food for the family and hospitality for guests. Speaking of a much later period, an immigrant from Vietnam told me about managing an apartment complex while working, going to school, and caring for her family. What these stories share is the theme of immigrant women's remarkable efforts on behalf of themselves and their families.

Another link between the two eras has been the reliance on international trade. Indeed, from the very earliest development by European Americans, the Santa Clara Valley has been connected to world markets, first for hides, then cattle, then wheat, then fruit, and then semiconductors — and beyond. In the 1930s, the impact of the Great Depression was exacerbated by the loss of the German market for Santa Clara Valley prunes, when Hitler instituted economic self-sufficiency. In the early 1980s, a downturn in the world market for semiconductors proved nearly as devastating to the local economy. But today, the Valley's relationship to the global economy is far more complex than it had been in the past, because the Valley is so much at the hub of information-age technology.

Finally, one can discern a link in the technical know-how required in the two eras. In the past, the dozens of canneries necessitated the presence of highly trained machinists to keep the complicated equipment running smoothly. Therefore, when Stanford University-trained engineers founded pioneering electronics firms in the 1930s and 1940s, they had a pool of skilled men to draw upon for their workforce of technicians. One firm in particular, what is now FMC (and no longer headquartered in the Valley), symbolizes the connection between the two eras. FMC started out as Food Machinery Corporation, and its original purpose was to manufacture capital equipment for use in orchards and canneries. In the early 1940s, the company obtained a defense contract to produce amphibious landing craft, thus beginning its metamorphosis to FORTUNE 500 giant.

The Valley's Discontinuities

Of all the discontinuities that could be enumerated — changes in the landscape, explosive inflation in the cost of housing, ever-more clogged freeways that make the drive to work torture for many Valley residents — none is more important than the change in the nature of capital. Always tied into world markets, the Valley is now home to the headquarters for some of the firms that have pioneered offshore production of electronics components. Where earlier workers struggled against recalcitrant and sometimes violent employers who even resorted to collusion in the attempt to keep out unions, workers must now contend with the knowledge that they are implicitly competing with workers in low-wage economies throughout the world. This has changed the rules of the game for workers in profound ways. In the days before a union brought a measure of job stability, a cannery worker knew that if she crossed a floor lady, she alone might be out of a job. High-tech operatives today have every reason to fear that the jobs themselves may vanish.

This book describes how the Valley has changed and how generations of workers have tried to cope with the barriers to their success and the opportunities that have been available. As a historian, I believe that my discipline can illuminate the current situation, especially given the commonalities between the two industries' workforces. An examination of the past is especially telling in this case: The historical record reveals the means by which the local labor movement lost the vitality it had possessed in the 1930s, thereby rendering high-tech workers more vulnerable to exploitation than might otherwise have been the case. Indeed, one of the most striking aspects of this story is the fact that seasonal women workers — not taken seriously by the mainstream, male-led AFL — nonetheless became part of organized labor in the 1930s. This was in part due to the extraordinary militancy of the Bay Area's "march inland" (led by the International Longshoremen and Warehousemen's Union). A generation later, many students of the subject have written off the Bay Area's high-tech workers as being impossible to organize. What had intervened between the two periods was the intense anxiety about radicalism that was a prominent feature of the cold war years. In the name of combating radicals, the opponents of militant unionism seriously weakened the strength of the Valley's labor movement. This development was occurring throughout the country, but it was all the more noteworthy in an area with such a powerful history of success for organized labor.

The Scope of the Book

A word about the scope. Although I am primarily interested in the most vulnerable, especially working-class, immigrant women, I will also explore the opportunities for other women. Indeed, in addition to the nicknames of "the Valley of Heart's Delight" and "Silicon Valley," the area has been called "the Feminist Capital of the Nation" because of the sheer number of women elected to office since the mid-1970s. It is important to look at the interplay between this electoral success and the fate of women workers. In this book, I argue that certain middle-class women leaders afforded the workers more reliable allies at first than did the male-led union movement.

As for the geographic scope, this is difficult to specify with complete precision. I focus primarily on San Jose, because in the first place it, the county seat of Santa Clara County and the biggest city therein, was clearly the capital of the fruit industry — though the orchards were scattered throughout much of the county. On the other hand, the high-tech industry originated to the north of San Jose in the area around Stanford University. Up until recently, the city could not plausibly have called itself the capital of Silicon Valley. But as the land farther north has filled up, San Jose has seen an increasing number of firms locate within its boundaries. It now bills itself as "the Capital of Silicon Valley," and its downtown contains the offices of the Silicon Valley Chamber of Commerce. Moreover, for a long time, many high-tech workers have lived in San Jose. Thus, it is impossible to confine the discussion to the jurisdiction of San Jose alone.[3]

A word, too, about my use of the term "California Dream" in the title and throughout the book. By California Dream, I mean the expectation that the good life will be even more available in the Golden State than in other parts of the United States, because of California's salubrious climate and abundant resources. For me, one of the most vivid depictions of this dream is in a W. C. Fields film of the 1930s called "It's a Gift." Fields plays a much-put-upon grocery-store-owner in an undisclosed small town elsewhere in the country who fantasizes about the fine life he might have were he to own an orange grove in California. By the end of the movie, he has realized his ambition to glorious effect.

From fruit-crate labels to promotional literature to movies and television to songs such as "California Dreamin'" by the Mamas and the Papas or "California Girls" by the Beach Boys, generations of Americans and those abroad have been schooled to believe that California is *the* place where dreams come true.

The Book's Structure

It is now time to outline the structure of the book and to sketch the lineaments of the argument. I begin with a discussion of the fruit industry and its workforce in the early twentieth century, setting this in the context of a discussion of community power. During the 1930s, seasonally employed, preponderantly female cannery workers would achieve a union in the face of very difficult odds. Chapter 1 prepares the way for understanding that feat by exploring ethnic patterns, analyzing the work itself, and delineating the stresses and strains in the business elite.

Chapter 2 deals with the fruit industry workforce in its moment of greatest success. The depression hit the local economy hard, growers and processors both suffered, and both were willing to take off their gloves — speaking both metaphorically and literally — to prevent their labor force from organizing. During the turbulent 1930s, San Jose saw multiple episodes of worker militancy and vigilantism to combat the militancy. This chapter explains how the unionization could succeed in spite of the obstacles. It also documents the reversal in the local fates of the Republican and Democratic parties: from a majority in registration for the former in 1930 to one for the latter in 1940. This is a change that held for the balance of the twentieth century.

The 1940s and 1950s saw the beginnings of explosive change, which was in large part brought about by events set in motion during World War II. At that time, the Valley became home to a defense industry employing thousands of workers. But the change was also enhanced by the actions of local leaders, in particular San Jose's legendary city manager, A.P. "Dutch" Hamann, who oversaw a growth in the city's physical boundaries of roughly 850 percent within the course of twenty years. Chapter 3 deals with this issue, as well as with paradoxical developments whereby Mexican Americans living in East San Jose began to organize politically at the same time that the cannery union, which represented thousands of primarily Mexican American women workers (they arrived during the war), lost its grassroots character. I argue that the crippling of democracy in the cannery union was a tragedy not only for workers but also for the long-term character of the regional labor movement.

Even before the war, the groundwork was being laid for an electronics industry in the Valley. Chapter 4, "Toward Silicon Valley," draws upon new research that illuminates the role played by Stanford University as well as the other forces conducing toward technological innovation, up to and including the birth of the semiconductor industry. The voluminous papers of the pioneering Varian Associates make it possible to learn a great deal about early presuppositions with respect to the high-tech production workforce. This chapter also includes a discussion of women workers in the defense industry, because this industry employed thousands of (unionized) women, as well as a surprising number of women professionals. Finally, it was during this era that reformers successfully filed suit against both processors and an undemocratic union, so that women cannery workers began to enjoy real advancement opportunities for the first time.

By an interesting quirk of destiny, Silicon Valley was evolving into a high-tech center just as the Immigration Act of 1965 and the conclusion of decades of fighting in Southeast Asia were bringing thousands of new immigrants to California, a significant portion of whom moved to the Santa Clara Valley. Indeed, San Jose's population went from being 7.6 percent foreign-born in 1970 to 26.5 percent foreign-born in 1990. Chapter 5 deals with this phenomenon and with the composition of the new working class produced by the massive immigration, with the types of jobs its members have filled, and with the strategies they have adopted to get ahead.

By another quirk of destiny, the ethnic transformation of the Santa Clara Valley and the burgeoning of high tech coincided with the flexing of electoral muscle by Valley women, both in Santa Clara County and in the city of San Jose. At one point in the 1980s, both jurisdictions were governed by female majorities. Chapter 6 assesses the payoff for women workers, as well as the progress of business and professional women in "the Feminist Capital of the Nation," which at the same time was developing a strongly gendered, and macho, work culture. In striking contrast to the macho work culture, however, as of 2000, the head of the local labor movement was a woman, Amy Dean, and the head of the largest and most prestigious local firm was Hewlett-Packard's Carly Fiorina, the first woman to run a FORTUNE 30 company.

Finally, Chapter 7 explores the local impact of the new way of doing business, from the origins of offshore production to the recent past. It encompasses the stories of the fierce competition with Japan that erupted in the 1980s, of failed unionization attempts, of bitter struggles over toxic hazards, and of the toll taken by the degradation of blue-collar employment, especially given the virtual disappearance of the unionized fruit industry. The chapter also includes an account of the initiatives being taken by the South Bay labor movement to fight back.

What it all adds up to is this: The Santa Clara Valley has always offered opportunities to get ahead to certain hardworking and enterprising individuals, including immigrants. This is true despite the very real barriers to immigrant success constituted by prejudicial attitudes and exploitative working conditions. In particular, once the fruit industry workforce achieved union-ization, it became possible for many workers to pass middle-class status on to their children. Because the defense industry developed with a unionized workforce, it, too, afforded immigrant workers who became naturalized the opportunity to move ahead. But over time, the opportunities for all working-class people have become constricted. The fruit industry is all but gone. The defense industry has shrunk. Home ownership, often the means of getting ahead, has become extremely difficult to achieve. And the least-skilled elec-tronics workers are in a very unfortunate bargaining position vis-à-vis their employers. Today, in fact, there is not a single large high-tech firm with a unionized workforce. Furthermore, firms are increasingly relying on tempo-rary workers to do their production work, a phenomenon that undercuts the possibility of making a good life on the basis of one of these jobs. Moreover, all the indications are that inequalities are growing.[4] Those who arrive in the Valley with education, with access to resources, or with an immense amount of good luck can make it big. Thousands of others are not so fortunate.

In addition to the growth in offshore production, there is another reason that capital wears a different face now than in the fruit industry heyday. The fruit industry employers fought hard against their workers, but they also fought one another. Growers and processors had divergent interests when it came to the price of fruit. There was even one attempt by dissident growers to ally with labor against the processors in the late 1930s. Social theory sug-gests — and I concur — that it is much easier for workers to develop an op-positional culture when capital is so divided.

The high-tech industry is, on the other hand, able to present a united front to its workers. Organized into both the American Electronics Associ-ation and the Silicon Valley Manufacturing Group, employers have success-fully shared information about the best means of keeping unions out. In ad-dition, the Valley's high-tech glamour has exuded an aura that has seemingly been as captivating to many of its denizens as to those around the globe who emulate the legendary success. Writers have referred to the Valley's go-go ethos as a religious system, so devout has been the belief in the high-tech gospel — at least among those in a position to benefit materially from it — and so willing have many people been to make the personal sacrifices neces-sary to keep in the game.[5] In such an atmosphere, it's very difficult for an op-positional culture to take hold.

There is a growing literature on immigrant women.[6] I see this study as contributing to the discourse by documenting the importance of regional culture and economy to the fate of women immigrants. From the mid-nineteenth century on, Europeans who arrived in the Santa Clara Valley found themselves in an environment that was very different from what they might have encountered in the East or Midwest.[7] In the late nineteenth and early twentieth century, those from Mexico and Asia built communities despite the hostile treatment at the hands of European Americans.[8] Southern Italians found they were treated in certain situations as somehow less than "white," but they also found themselves possessors of fruit-cultivating skills from the homeland that were highly valuable in their new community. Hence their consignment to the proletarian mudsill was less complete than it otherwise might have been.

In short, ethnic patterns in San Jose and in the greater Bay Area have been, if not unique, at least sufficiently unusual as to warrant careful scrutiny. Moreover, during the turbulent 1930s, the high level of worker militancy in the Bay Area — spurred on by the "march inland" in the mid-1930s — helps explain the successful unionization of seasonally employed women, while the dissipation of that regional militancy during the cold war years helps us understand the fate of high-tech workers. I agree with the urban historian Kathleen Conzen, who has said: "Historians too easily overlook the role still played by local cultures in a modernizing America. Heirs to the nineteenth-century American obsession with the spatially unifying and homogenizing forces of national development, we have sensitized ourselves to issues of ethnic and racial pluralism while neglecting the comparable pluralisms of place."[9]

I also see this study as contributing to a better understanding of the lives and jobs of women workers in general. Consistently undervalued by both employers and a male-dominated union movement, they are only now beginning to be treated better by scholars. More than one labor historian has constructed a typology of skill levels, for example, in which the categories of skilled, semiskilled, and unskilled turn out to overlap with male and female jobs. It has also been difficult for some to grasp that seasonally employed women may nonetheless have a real commitment to their jobs. The fighting spirit of the Valley's cannery workers is a wonderful legacy that gives the lie to those, whether in the labor movement or in the scholarly community, who deem the vulnerable high-tech workers to be unorganizable. But the forces arrayed against the latter are so powerful — as the following pages demonstrate — that it will take new strategies, new alliances, and new ideas to relieve their plight.

Finally, from my standpoint, the most important reason for this study has been to explain historically how it could be that the prosperity generated by Silicon Valley has been so maldistributed. We know that inequality is growing in American society in general. That this development could take place even in an area that had, at one time, a strong and vital labor movement — and that is known today for its openness and innovation — needs to be documented and the reasons understood. In an area that is celebrated around the world for its capacity to enrich some of its inhabitants, we need to acknowledge and try to understand why thousands of the Valley's working poor are presented with fewer and fewer opportunities to access the California Dream.

ONE

The Fruited Valley

Santa Clara Valley, known throughout the world as "The Valley of Heart's Delight" because of its scenic attractions, mild climate, and diversified agriculture, is located 32 miles south of San Francisco. . . . Horticulture is the leading industry of the county, and it is doubtful if there is a section of similar area in all the world that produces so many varieties or so vast a quantity of fruits. . . . San Jose, the county seat, is the industrial center of this productive area and has long been recognized as the most extensive canning and dried fruit packing center of the world.

— *California Blue Book,* 1928

The Santa Clara Valley is
To those who hold it dear
A veritable Paradise
Each season of the year.
One loves it best in April
When the fruit trees are in bloom;
And a mass of snowy blossoms
Yield a subtle sweet perfume.
When orchard after orchard
Is spread before the eyes
With the whitest of white blossoms
Neath the bluest of blue skies.
Nobody could paint the picture
No pen describe the sight
That one can find in April
In "The Valley of Heart's Delight."

— CLARA LOUISE LAWRENCE,
"The Valley of Heart's Delight" (1931)

Origins

As the first secular pueblo in Spanish California, San Jose is California's oldest city. In 1777, the Spanish government sent some sixty-six people to establish a civil settlement in San Jose to grow food for Spain's remote mission outposts in California. A few decades later, after Mexico threw off Spanish colonial rule, San Jose became a Mexican outpost. In 1848, after the Treaty of Guadalupe Hidalgo ended the war between Mexico and the United States, victoriously for the latter, the region became an American settlement — one that would very quickly turn into a city given the forces set in motion by the gold rush. San Jose grew steadily but unspectacularly — unlike, for example, late nineteenth- and early twentieth-century cities in Southern California — until the years after World War II. During the postwar era, the city's growth in physical size and population can only be described as explosive, increasing from approximately 17 square miles to 137 and from 57,651 people in 1930 to 445,779 in 1970.

In the first decades of its life as an American city, and for many generations thereafter, San Jose depended primarily on agriculture for its economic sustenance. With 4,579 inhabitants in 1860, the city's largest local enterprise was cattle-raising. By 1865, the cultivation of cattle gave way to wheat. By 1875, fruit cultivation and processing began to assume the preeminence they would enjoy for nearly 100 years. Not to be overlooked is the fact that the area contained a quicksilver mine, which provided the largest single source of employment in the city's early years. The coming of the railroad to the Santa Clara Valley in the 1860s also enhanced the region's economic growth.

Ethnic Patterns

The Late Nineteenth Century

Very early in its American-era history, the city showed signs of being an unusual destination for European immigrants, in particular Irish Catholics, who were frequently treated with contempt in the Northeast.[1] In the San Jose area, Catholics were community founders and institution builders: In 1851 in neighboring Santa Clara, Italian Jesuits established the College of

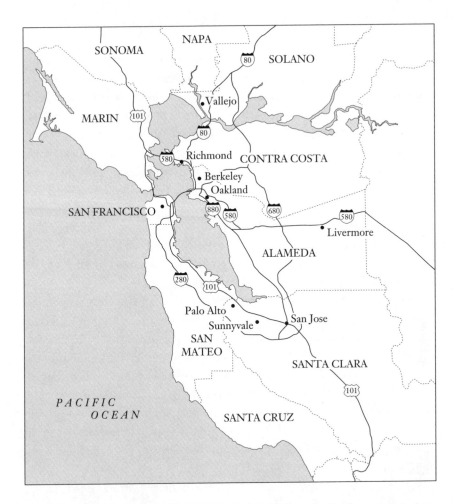

Map 1. The San Francisco Bay Area, including all the counties that touch the bay

Santa Clara, one of California's first institutions of higher learning. Even before the first substantial infusion of European Americans that came following the Treaty of Guadalupe Hidalgo and the gold rush, an Irish Catholic
family, the Murphys, had arrived and began to farm in the Valley. Thus they
were well established by the time native-born Americans started arriving in
significant numbers. By the late nineteenth century, the Murphys were the
Valley's wealthiest and most prominent residents, living on a scale that

Kevin Starr has called "baronial."[2] In 1870, one Murphy brother alone re-ported a worth of $500,000 to the census enumerator.[3]

But it was not only the Murphys who did well. Irish Catholic immigrants in general were prosperous in the region. A sample of 613 people drawn from the 1860 manuscript census produced 63 individuals born in Ireland. Ten years later, for those Irish-born still living in San Jose, there was no sta-tistically significant difference between their rates of occupational or prop-erty mobility and those of native-born Americans.[4] Because of this Irish Catholic success story, there was never a period of thoroughgoing Anglo Protestant hegemony in the Santa Clara Valley, a situation that echoed that of the region as a whole.[5] Anglo Protestants did not automatically become enlightened about those of another religion when they moved to the Valley, but they did necessarily find themselves dealing with Irish Catholics on a dif-ferent basis — more as peers — than might have been the case in their region of origin.

Although Irish Catholics enjoyed relatively more opportunity than might have been the case in the Northeast, there was another group of Catholics who had no such advantage: those of Mexican or Mexican/Indian descent, whose land it had been until 1848. Modern scholarship is documenting the wretched treatment that these Californios received at the hands of the in-vading Americans in many parts of the state.[6] Stripped of most of their land, they were subject to violence as well as discrimination. Indeed, the historian William Deverell has argued that the Mexican War did not actually end in Los Angeles in 1848, because throughout the succeeding decade there was a high level of brutality directed against Mexicans.[7]

Although less violent than Americans in Southern California, so far as we know, the Americans in San Jose were just as determined as their southern neighbors to control land ownership. In consequence, as of 1860, of the 47 people born in California in the aforementioned sample of 613, only 10.6 percent owned real property; the mean for the entire sample being 19.2 per-cent. Moreover, contemporary accounts tell of an occasion when American squatters paraded cannons through downtown San Jose to intimidate the au-thorities into validating their claims vis-à-vis the Californios.[8] Then, too, there was the impact of the California Land Act of 1851. Despite the fact that the Treaty of Guadalupe Hidalgo had guaranteed Mexican property rights in ceded territory, the Land Act placed the burden of proof on

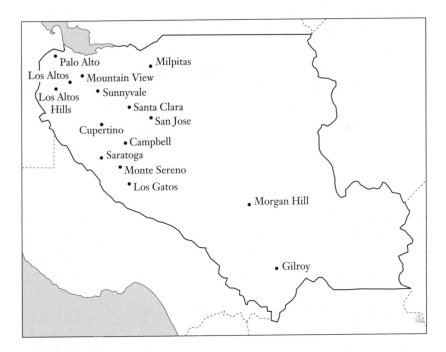

Map 2. Santa Clara County

Californios to establish their rights to the land. Because many Californios lacked the capital for extensive litigation, the land wound up in the hands of Americans.

Nonetheless, because the New Almaden quicksilver mine some fifteen miles south of downtown San Jose afforded employment for them, Mexicans/Californios continued to have a presence in the Valley. In the city proper, Mexicans lost land and political power during the 1850s, but at the New Almaden mines, they built mutual aid societies. They even went on strike during the 1860s.[9] As a consequence of the militancy of the New Almaden Californios, however, mine owners set out to "whiten" their workforce by bringing in Cornish and other European American miners. The net result was that the area's Mexican population dwindled from a high of approximately 2,000 in the 1850s and 1860s to only about 500 by the early twentieth century.[10]

By the 1870s, the burgeoning importance of the fruit industry was beginning to create a new ethnic mix in the Valley as well as to transform the land-scape and the nature of the local economy. It was a Frenchman who, in 1856, had made the single biggest contribution to the Valley's horticulture by im-porting scions of French prune plum stock and grafting them onto wild plum trees. When combined with the creative activities of other individuals, this laid the basis for vast orchards to come. By 1891, the county produced twenty-two million pounds of prunes.[11] Indeed, by 1930, somewhere between one-third and one-half of the *world's* prune supply came from Santa Clara County, and the prune plum was just one of the fruits grown there. The allu-vial soils and the Mediterranean climate proved ideal for fruit cultivation.

As the acreage in fruit grew, so too did the need for workers who could cultivate and harvest the crops. Among the first to be so hired were Chinese men, who had originally come to the area to work on the railroad built in the 1860s. By 1880 Santa Clara County had a population of 35,146, of whom 2,695 were Chinese (mostly male).[12] These immigrants had to contend with unique problems. Not only did they face the discrimination inherent in the Chinese Exclusion Act of 1882, but also they, like other Asian immigrants, were unable to become naturalized citizens until various legal changes of the twentieth century. Hence, the lives of these pioneering agricultural workers in the Santa Clara Valley were shadowed by their being especially vulnerable.

In addition to working in the fields, Chinese immigrants were employed as the first workforce in the growing number of canneries.[13] San Jose's first cannery came into being in 1871, and a small-scale operation it was at first. Opened by James Dawson, a physician from Maryland, it consisted that first year of a kitchen-table operation conducted by Dr. Dawson and his wife. In the Dawsons' first year, they processed 350 cases of fruit and tomatoes. Sixteen years later, with a workforce consisting mainly of Chinese men, the Dawson Cannery produced 140,000 cases of fruit.[14] The Chinese were so in-tegral to the early history of Valley horticulture that a Chinese man, Yen Chew, even founded the Bayside Cannery of Alviso in the late 1890s. The Bayside Cannery, which was the first major firm founded by a Chinese per-son, specialized in tomatoes and asparagus, and at its peak it provided em-ployment for hundreds of Chinese.[15]

By the late nineteenth century, another group of Asians — those from Japan — began to figure as an important presence in the Valley. Ironically, their arrival owed much to anti-Chinese feeling in the area, part of a larger phenomenon in Northern California that centered in San Francisco. As feelings against the Chinese came to a head with the passage of the Chinese Exclusion Act, local agriculturalists turned to the Japanese as an alternative workforce. The Issei, or Japanese immigrants, began to arrive in the 1890s, and by 1900 there were 284 people of Japanese birth in the Valley, with the number of Chinese having declined to 1,738.[16]

At about the same time that the Japanese started to arrive, a massive immigration to the United States began from southern Europe. Thousands of these new immigrants found their way to the Valley. By 1930, about 20 percent of San Jose's population was first- or second-generation Italian. A smaller percentage of Portuguese inhabitants also lived in San Jose, with the majority choosing to live in neighboring Santa Clara. Santa Clara County also was home to a colony of Spanish immigrants, many of whom lived in Mountain View, a town to the north of San Jose.

Whether the thousands of immigrants from southern Europe shared more with the people of color than with the Anglo/Irish/French/German residents is an interesting question, and one that yields to no easy resolution. Modern scholarship highlights the way in which certain Europeans were "in-between people" who would eventually become "white ethnics," but not without much pain and struggle along the way. At first, southern European immigrants were ranked "above" African Americans and Asian immigrants but "below" the older, established "white" population.[17] In 1891, for example, the *New York Times* editorialized that "[t]hese sneaking and cowardly Sicilians, who have transplanted to this country the lawless passions, the cutthroat practices, and the oathbound societies of their native country, are to us a pest without mitigation."[18] One thing southern Europeans did have was the ability to become citizens and, hence, to vote. This gave them a stronger position than that of immigrants from China and Japan. Nor were they officially discouraged from bringing women and families, as were the Asians. But they did confront many other difficult problems, as we will learn later in this chapter.

The Early Twentieth Century

Ten Years in Paradise, a book published in 1903 by a local society writer, provides a good picture of the area at the start of the twentieth century, both in its listings of resources and local notables and in its ellipses or silences.

Figure 1. The Valley of Heart's Delight circa 1900. Courtesy of the Sourisseau Academy, San Jose State University.

Worth noting is the fact that the author, Mary Carroll, had been born in Ireland. Thus the person functioning as arbiter was from a group unlikely to furnish social arbiters in the Northeast. Carroll describes the many beautiful homes in "the Garden City" (the area would not receive the designation of the "Valley of Heart's Delight" until around 1915); lists the clubs, including a Political Equality Club for women; and in general extols the benefits of living in "paradise." In an appendix, she provides a fifteen-page list of "society women" along with their addresses and "at home" days. The list contains one Latino name, Arques, a sprinkling of French and German names, Irish certainly, but none that is Italian or Portuguese, let alone Chinese or Japanese. Moreover, in writing about "What Santa Clara County Offers to the Capitalist," she says nothing about the Asian immigrants who were there by the hundreds and were performing much of the Valley's hardest work. Clearly, they were invisible to her.[19]

Contrary to Mary Carroll's depiction of the area, the early twentieth century saw significant changes in the ethnic mosaic of San Jose and Santa Clara

County. The number of immigrants from southern and eastern Europe increased (until the passage of immigration restriction in 1924), as did the number of Mexicans and Japanese. As each group moved into the area, they tended to cluster in particular areas of town, depending on their countries of origin. The groups of immigrants settling in the area gave the small city of San Jose some of the ethnic complexity and the residential patterns traditionally associated with larger cities.

One example of the ethnic neighborhoods involves the Chinese, a group that peaked in population in 1890 and then declined in size until growing again during the high-tech era. Like many places in California, San Jose was the site of anti-Chinese feeling that came to a head in the late nineteenth century.[20] Chinese immigrants, therefore, felt safer within the confines of their own community. Once outside it, they were fair game for harassment and even physical abuse. The infamous Dennis Kearney, leader of the anti-Chinese movement in San Francisco, even gave a speech in San Jose in June 1878 — but evoked nothing like the tumultuous response that had greeted him in the City by the Bay.[21]

Though San Jose never saw the same level of organized opposition to its Chinese residents as did San Francisco, the City Council did declare Chinatown to be a public nuisance in March 1887. Two months later, an arson fire destroyed the community. But at this point, the story had an unusual twist: A German immigrant by the name of John Heinlen cooperated with Chinese merchants in building a new Chinatown on land he owned, under his protection, and therefore less vulnerable to outside attack. Heinlen spent $30,000 on construction, hiring the same architect who had designed the new city hall, and then he rented the buildings to the Chinese. Several hundred Chinese settled in Heinlenville, as it was known, and the area remained the focus of the community until well into the twentieth century. With a disproportionate number of men, Heinlenville was a center of gambling and vice. Yet it also contained a traditional temple as well as a Chinese Methodist Episcopal Church, and it was "home" to the relatively small number of children, for whom it constituted a genuine community.[22] But even with this new community, the number of Chinese living in Santa Clara County continued to dwindle, until in 1940 the census shows only 555 people of Chinese ancestry.

As the number of Chinese dwindled, their place in local agriculture was taken, incrementally over a period of years, by the Japanese. Starting from a base of 284 residents in the county in 1900, the number of Japanese immigrants climbed to 4,049 by 1940. Like the Chinese community, the Japanese community began as a bachelor society, owing to restrictions on bringing Japanese women into the United States. In this instance, however, women began to arrive after the first few years. Also similar to the Chinese, the Japanese immigrants were unable to become naturalized citizens. But unlike the earlier arrivals, the Japanese often managed to farm their own land in the Valley — specializing in berries, rather than orchard fruits — despite the serious, but not insuperable, obstacle established by California's passage of alien land laws aimed at preventing this from happening. (The Japanese achieved access to land by a variety of arrangements.[23]) The Japanese community, or *Nihonmachi*, was located next to Heinlenville in an area just north of downtown. It included a Buddhist church and a number of small businesses, which gave the community a center, while the land under Japanese cultivation tended to be in outlying areas regarded as less desirable by the European Americans.[24]

With a strong and growing numerical presence in the area, the Japanese also constituted a visible presence at San Jose High School, the only public high school within the city limits. An examination of the yearbooks for the depression decade shows that there were dozens of Japanese students enrolled at San Jose High; that they belonged to various honors societies and sports teams, some of which they captained; and that, in a few instances, they were even elected to student body office.[25] This is not to gainsay the undoubted racism directed against the Japanese — the internment of the Japanese in the 1940s being proof of that — but rather to point out that neither were they so marginalized as to be unable to participate in the majority community.

Another group that established itself in the early twentieth century — one that is very significant in the Silicon Valley workforce today — came from the Philippines. As with other groups of Asians, the Filipinos came as a nearly all-male group, owing to the cruelties of U.S. immigration policy. They, too, faced massive discrimination even as they worked the fields of the Santa Clara Valley, picking tomatoes, beans, and fruit.[26]

Post-1900, the once-vibrant Mexican American community began to reestablish itself as an important component of the Valley — although its

Figure 2. Japanese children in San Jose in the early twentieth century. Courtesy of the Bancroft Library, University of California, Berkeley.

largest increase in population would not come until the 1940s. During the first decades of the twentieth century, the turbulence in Mexico resulting from the Mexican Revolution sent many Mexicans to California. Although most of these immigrants settled in the southern part of the state, the Mexican population of Santa Clara County had reached 912 by 1920, enough to sustain the old *mutualista* traditions from the nineteenth century. When World War II brought thousands of Mexican American immigrants into Santa Clara County, they arrived in an area with an unbroken Mexican presence.[27] Unincorporated neighborhoods to the east of San Jose began to be the Chicano domain. One such neighborhood, Sal Si Puedes ("Get Out If You Can"), is now well known as the home of Cesar Chavez in the days just before he cofounded the United Farm Workers.

Though the community's real-life Mexicans — those with the greatest claim to being the heirs of the Californio past — were both economically and geographically marginal, Anglo boosters briefly created a fiesta, the Fiesta de

Figure 3. Mexican migrant in field near San Jose, 1938. Photograph by Dorothea Lange. Courtesy of the Library of Congress.

las Rosas, which was based on a fantasy "Spanish" past of "dons" and "doñas." In 1925, they launched a celebration, complete with parade, of these fore-bears with their supposedly pure Spanish blood that was thought (incorrectly) to be unmixed with that of Indios. The celebration lapsed in 1933, owing to the financial exigencies of the Great Depression.[28]

Throughout this period, immigrants from southern Europe were steadily increasing in number. Although they did not have as hard a time as the Asians and Mexicans, they did face many problems of their own. In the first place, Catholics from Italy, Spain, and Portugal encountered a Church dominated by the earlier Catholic arrivals from Ireland, from whom the southern Europeans felt great cultural distance — and who frequently treated them with disdain. Not until they were able to construct their own churches were Catholics from southern Europe able to turn to their religion as an unequivocal source of emotional support and release.

In the late nineteenth century, the Catholic hierarchy began to realize that there was a problem for Italian immigrants to the United States, and in 1887, Bishop Scalabrini of Piacenza organized the Congregation of the Missionaries of St. Charles to propagate the faith in this country and to found Italian parishes. By 1930, San Jose contained three Catholic churches that served Italian parishioners, one of which owed its existence directly to Scalabrini's efforts.[29] For their part, the Portuguese built their own church, Five Wounds, in San Jose in 1914, and it has served as an important center of the Portuguese community ever since.

Even more devastating than a Church dominated by disdainful Irish was the widely held belief that immigrants from southern Europe were intellectually deficient, the dregs of their respective homelands. This view was articulated in many ways and by many Americans in the late nineteenth and early twentieth centuries, from the ravings of Madison Grant in *The Passing of the Great Race*, published in 1916, to workers who thought of their Italian coworkers as "white niggers," to school officials who deemed it appropriate to set up "dumbbell" classes for immigrant children. Grant, for example, maintained that the "new immigration" was composed of "the weak, the broken, and the mentally crippled of all races drawn from the lowest stratum of the Mediterranean basin."[30] As another instance of these prejudicial attitudes, one man referred to San Jose's Italian American city councilman, Charles Denegri, as "the whitest wop I ever knew."[31]

The Success of the Italians

These views were echoed by influential people in the Santa Clara Valley, especially by school officials. In 1919, a Stanford graduate student tested twelve-year-olds in San Jose and found that the incidence of "retardation" was positively correlated with the number of Italians in a classroom. He attributed his findings — which he insisted were based on innate mental capacity rather than the students' difficulties with English — to the Italians' being "of peasant type: patient, persevering, and mediocre." What's more, "these people are largely Mediterranean with a noticeably Negroid strain and other exotic mixtures."[32] As of 1921, San Jose had a new superintendent of schools, Walter Bachrodt, who agreed with these conclusions. In consequence, San Jose initiated a reform of its schools in 1922, with heavy emphasis on testing and on classification based on an invidious view of Italian immigrant youngsters.[33]

Thus we know that Italians, the largest single immigrant group as of 1930, suffered prejudicial attitudes that had a material impact on their well-being and, in particular, on the character of their children's education. Nonetheless, by the 1970s and 1980s, what was most evident about those of Italian descent in the Santa Clara Valley — some 101,000, or 6.8 percent of the county's population, according to the 1990 U.S. Census — was their stature in the community and their assimilation. For many families, the initial working-class ascription lasted for only a generation.[34] How did they achieve their mobility in the face of these difficulties? There are several answers to this question. In part, it was the fact that thousands of cannery and packing workers achieved a union in the 1930s, providing more job stability and more earning power, the subject of the next chapter. In part, it resulted from the employment opportunities that opened up during World War II and its aftermath. But in actuality, to understand fully the Italian success story — which parallels the Irish success story, except on a larger scale — we must start with an even earlier period.

The Italian immigrants came to an area where they could acquire land. The 1930 U.S. census discloses a rate of home-ownership of 68.2 percent for foreign-born white families in San Jose, with the national average being 51.8 percent for the same category. (Strikingly, if inexplicably, the proportion of homeowners among the general population of San Jose was 55.3 percent.) For Italian immigrants, ownership of a home meant not only the pride and

stability that come with this status but also the ability to use the land for intensive cultivation and thus as the basis for a household economy. Very
significantly, a contemporary observer, geographer Jan Broek, who studied
the Valley around 1930, noticed that many cannery workers were also small-
scale orchardists, a most unusual pattern, he thought.[35] A few of them even
opened small canneries, such as the firm of Filice and Perrelli.

A retired cannery worker of Italian descent, who was born in San Jose in
1914, explains how the household economy worked in his childhood:

> This is how people got by. They ate spaghetti with mustard greens
> [which grew wild in the fields] to save money. The grocery store was
> Italian-owned, and people there would extend credit if you needed it.
> There was a Sicilian doctor nearby: He didn't charge if you couldn't
> afford to pay. And my parents' house cost only $750.
>
> There were four of us kids, me and my three sisters. We all worked
> in the summer picking fruit. We were proud to bring our checks home,
> because we knew our parents needed the money. Part of what we earned
> would go to buy school clothes. [All of them attended high school, and
> three of them graduated.]
>
> My mother was the best cook in the world. . . . In the barn were bell
> peppers getting pickled, anchovies getting cured, barrels of snails being
> cured with corn meal. We put up our own tomato sauce and tomato
> paste, bottled it, and then we had it for the winter. . . . My mother lived
> to be 96, and she worked in a cannery till she was in her 60s.[36]

In short, even without growing crops for the market — the pattern that so
impressed Broek — an Italian household made its land work for it in a myriad of ways.

Repeatedly, informants spoke of how their parents decided to migrate to
San Jose because it resembled Italy. Moreover, the parents arrived with a set
of skills — such as how to prune fruit trees — that they had learned in the old
country and that could immediately be put to use in the new land. Some used
these skills in their own orchards, while others used them in the fields of
their employers.

It can truly be said that the local horticulture and the Italian population
grew in tandem. Indeed, two of the most significant people in the development of agriculture throughout the state were Italian American — Marco

Fontana and Amadeo P. Giannini. The success of these two men had a marked impact on their compatriots, because it enhanced the chance that Italian American orchardists could get credit. In 1899, Fontana founded what would become the Del Monte Corporation in San Francisco. In 1904, San Jose–born Giannini founded the Bank of Italy in San Francisco, which would become the giant Bank of America. Noteworthy is the fact that the Bank of Italy's first out-of-town branch was established in San Jose in 1910, where it provided loans to local growers.

Above all, when it comes to looking for an explanation for the Italians achieving considerable mobility within a few decades, one must look at the pattern of education; this despite the prejudicial attitudes they faced. In many parts of the United States, immigrants sacrificed the education of their children in order to buy homes, a pattern discussed by Stephen Thernstrom in his pathbreaking *Poverty and Progress*, a study of Newburyport, Massachusetts.[37] In Newburyport in the late nineteenth century, Irish immigrant children attended school at a lower rate than their native-born counterparts, and this held down the intergenerational mobility of the Irish population in that area. Other scholars have found early twentieth-century Italian American youngsters echoing the same pattern. Writing of Providence, Rhode Island, for example, Joel Perlmann says: "Like the nineteenth-century Irish before them, the Italians were far less likely than others to receive an extended education. In 1915, for example, slightly less than one tenth of the children of Italians, as compared with two fifths of the rest of the city's children, enrolled in high school."[38] This was emphatically *not* the pattern in San Jose and Santa Clara County (see Table 1.1). There the 1930 census reveals a remarkably similar pattern of attendance by native-born and immigrant youngsters.

There is a reason for this pattern: The parents' access to land and their ability to construct a household economy based on the fruit industry meant that immigrant young people could work seasonally, pitting apricots, picking prunes, or canning fruit, and then they could attend school during the year. Many interview subjects spoke of their pride in helping their parents financially with their earnings, while knowing that a portion of those earnings was earmarked for buying school clothes and supplies. They also spoke of the value their parents placed on education: "When I was a kid, the teacher was always right, not 95 percent of the time, but 100 percent of the time. I re-

TABLE I.I

School Attendance by Parents' Nativity
for Native White Persons 14 Through 17 Years Old
Selected Cities, 1930

City	Number Attending School	Total Number	Percentage Attending School
SAN JOSE, CALIFORNIA			
Native parentage	1,820	1,937	94.0
Foreign or mixed parentage	1,477	1,605	92.0
SACRAMENTO, CALIFORNIA			
Native parentage	2,900	3,101	93.5
Foreign or mixed parentage	1,427	1,616	88.3
SAN DIEGO, CALIFORNIA			
Native parentage	4,711	5,233	90.0
Foreign or mixed parentage	1,535	1,681	91.3
DENVER, COLORADO			
Native parentage	9,239	11,411	81.0
Foreign or mixed parentage	3,445	4,653	74.0
NEW HAVEN, CONNECTICUT			
Native parentage	2,354	2,982	78.9
Foreign or mixed parentage	5,506	8,848	62.2

SOURCE: U.S. Census, 1930, *Population*, II, p. 1152.

member a man — he was illiterate — explaining why this was so to a teacher. 'You straighten the tree when it's young.'"[39]

It is important that this relatively positive outlook toward — as well as the attendance in — schools not be seen as an artifact of San Jose's Italian immigrants being from northern Italy, because the majority were not. All the available evidence suggests that although northerners constituted a presence, they were outnumbered by those from the Mezzogiorno and from Sicily.[40] There has long been a distinction made between those from northern Italy and those from the south or from the island of Sicily. The distinction is still made in Italy today, and it has shown up in much scholarly writing in the United States. According to the generalizations, northerners are enterprising; southerners are amoral and fatalistic, place relatively little value on education, and are deemed to be hopelessly provincial.[41] In San Jose and the Santa Clara Valley, however, whatever the power of the southerners' values may have been, they were, in effect, trumped by the favorable material circumstances that permitted families to own homes *and* to send their children to school.

The anthropologist Micaela di Leonardo, studying the Italian Americans of Northern California, argued that Italian American culture has been shaped by the particular material circumstances encountered by immigrants in different regions of the United States. When we understand this, we can "see beyond the vision that many have read into [Herbert] Gans's *Urban Villagers*: that Italian-American 'family culture' creates an ambitionless, self-reproducing, urban working class."[42] The San Jose findings are a striking confirmation of her argument.

It must also be noted that the fabled provincialism — *campanilismo*, or the phenomenon whereby immigrants seek out those who have heard the sound of the same church bell, or *campanile* — did manifest itself in the Santa Clara Valley. Though the area is now home to an umbrella "Italian American Heritage Foundation," in the early twentieth century, it contained a plethora of mutual aid societies and fraternal organizations reflecting a variety of regional origins. Moreover, old-timers recall that there were regional enclaves within the Italian sections of San Jose:

> Now, the Calabrese from Calabria, or from the tip of the boot [of Italy] to about halfway up, those were all Calabrese; they all lived at Alma Street and First and Old Almaden. See, people from Trabia [in Sicily] about half of them lived around Ninth, Tenth, Eleventh; Thirteenth Street was the center of it. Thirteenth and Taylor was the corner of the Trabia area. Then the other half of the people from Trabia lived between Willow and Alma. . . . [Northern Italians] were located around Fifth.[43]

Though present, the campanilismo was not sufficiently divisive to interfere with collective action by cannery and packing workers during the Great

Depression. Moreover, there is evidence that Italian American *prominenti* worked to combat extreme provincialism: Marco Fontana, for example, made a point of hiring Italian Americans from diverse regions, and A. P. Giannini worked to combat the mutual aid societies' influence so that all Italian Americans would save in his Bank of Italy.[44]

The heart of Italian American San Jose was an area of modest homes known as "Goosetown," evidently because of a pond that attracted flying geese. As with Chinatown and Japantown, Goosetown contained a number of small businesses. Where it differed — and differed markedly from the rest of San Jose — lay in the fact that homes there featured vegetable gardens in the front yard, instead of lawns, and most also had outdoor ovens. Recalls one woman: "We had the oven outside the house. Go pick the brush [prunings from the fruit trees], put the brush in the oven, then put the bread in. . . . And we baked pizza all the time. Oh my God, I liked the pizza."[45]

As another instance of the survival skills of those from southern Europe, Dora Peregrina Ferri, a woman whose parents were born in Spain, remembers admiringly the way her parents coped with life in the United States. Part of a group that was recruited in southern Spain to work in the sugar cane fields of Hawaii — where she was born — Dora's parents immigrated to the Bay Area around 1912, by which time her father had fulfilled the terms of his contract to work in the Hawaiian sugar crop. Once living in Redwood City (slightly north of Santa Clara County), her father set up a small business cutting down trees, and her mother set up a shop catering primarily, but not exclusively, to other immigrants. "She was a real go-getter. She used to send off for clothes that she got at wholesale prices. Then she'd drive around in her buggy selling them. She also had a store. She never learned English, so when somebody came in the door who didn't speak Spanish, she'd work out the transaction using beans." Dora herself worked in a cannery before her marriage. In advanced old age, she still boasts of the muscles she developed from the cannery work.[46]

Prejudicial Attitudes

The immigrants from southern Europe had to contend with the same prejudicial attitudes that faced the Mexican Americans and the Asian Americans. After the passage of the Immigration Quota Act of 1924, southern Europeans suffered from prejudicial treatment by federal immigration policy, because the quotas for entrance to the United States were based on population percentages in 1890, a time before the mass immigration from southern and eastern Europe.

Only the people of color, however, had to cope with ethnically based violence. In 1930, for example, an American man was arrested in San Jose for blasting Filipino homes and meeting places with dynamite, part of a campaign to drive out Filipino workers. Furthermore, pear growers in a certain section of the Valley were warned not to employ Filipinos or else their trees would be destroyed.[47] The Santa Clara County Central Labor Council, a group that had earlier expressed concern about the presence of "Mexican peons" in the Valley, passed a resolution supporting the deportation of Filipinos.[48]

Even where there was no overt violence, people of color were faced with working conditions that were so much worse than those of the Europeans that they constituted a kind of violence. Many retired Italians speak fondly of their childhood in the fields. Often the owners were family friends. In contrast, the memoir of a man who was part of a Mexican American family of prune pickers describes extraordinarily harsh circumstances. Rudy Calles first accompanied his family from Pasadena to "Prune Heaven" in the Santa Clara Valley in 1925. There they lived in a shack with no running water and no outhouse, and they slept on the floor. Full of resentment about such treatment by the owners, the children would occasionally urinate on the picked prunes by way of getting even.[49]

This, then, was ethnic San Jose on the eve of the Great Depression. The Valley would be hit hard by the economic downturn, and the loyalties and capacity for solidarity of various groups, including ethnic groups, would be put to a severe test.

The Fruit Industry

The magnet that brought most immigrants to Santa Clara Valley was the area's horticultural development. This development was part of a larger story about the turn, throughout many parts of the state, to specialty-crop agriculture.

As early as 1868, John Muir had been struck by the beauty of the Valley's landscape and its flourishing orchards. A few years later, the opening of a

TABLE 1.2

Fruit Farms by Value of Product
Santa Clara County, 1930

Value of Product	*Number of Farms*
Under $600	778
$600–$1,499	1,107
$1,500–$2,499	810
$2,500–$3,999	690
$4,000–$5,999	426
$6,000–$9,999	375
$10,000–$19,999	220
$20,000 and over	114

SOURCE: U.S. Census, 1930,
Agriculture, III, pp. 418–19

transcontinental railroad and the subsequent development of the refrigerator car enhanced the market for California fruit. There was a concomitant growth in the acreage devoted to fruit growing in the Santa Clara Valley. One scholar estimated that by 1930 orchards covered 65 percent of the Valley's improved land, with 66,000 acres devoted to prune cultivation alone.[50] Although orchards were well-suited to the climate of the area, the water issues had to be dealt with. In the early decades of American settlement, cattle had been allowed to graze on land not under irrigation, and wheat had been dry-farmed; but orchards, berries, and vegetables needed systematic irrigation to promote healthy growth in the absence of enough rainfall. By the late nineteenth century, Valley growers had found the answer to their water needs: They sank wells into the aquifer and found abundant water for their crops. But it was an answer that would suffice for only a generation or so.

Because the crops were so valuable — and because there was as yet little mechanized equipment for fruit cultivation and harvesting, such as the reapers and combines used for wheat in the Midwest — holdings tended to be small (see Table 1.2). Indeed, a grower with only half an acre of fruit might well have been involved in the market while also holding down another job. Hence in the Santa Clara Valley, horticulture did not generate a way of life, as farming did in much of the rest of the country.[51] Nor were there rural districts per se — though the balance among orchards, residences, and commercial uses varied substantially in different parts of the Valley. What struck Jan Broek was how thoroughly the homes and the orchards were interspersed.

Despite the fact that most orchardists were operating on a small scale, they did need to employ farm laborers to tend the trees and harvest the crops. According to the 1930 census, there were 1,084 male farm laborers in San Jose, out of a male workforce of 17,745. No doubt this figure under-represents the total, because of the absence of migratory workers.

Parallel to the rapid development of fruit growing in the late nineteenth century was a growth in the fruit processing industry. Following the success of the Dawson cannery that had been launched in 1871, dozens of canneries were founded in the Santa Clara Valley, so that by 1930 there were thirty-eight, the largest concentration anywhere in the world. In 1918, a few years after the opening of the Panama Canal had magnified the world market for California fruit, state canners shipped more than seventeen million cases of their products; by 1928, the figure had risen to more than thirty million cases.[52] This volume meant that the canning industry was second only to oil in its economic import to the state. About 30 percent of the California pack came from Santa Clara County, according to a report published by the San Jose Chamber of Commerce in 1931.

For both growers and processors, growth brought heightened competition and that, in turn, brought organizational change and an impetus toward consolidation. As for the canners, in 1899 under the leadership of Marco Fontana, eleven pioneer companies representing nearly half of the California pack formed the California Fruit Canners Association. This concentration of capital fostered a greater mechanization of the industry, including such de-vices as capping machines and automatic cookers, a development that made it more difficult for small operators to start up. In 1916, there was a still big-ger merger that led to the formation of the California Packing Corporation (Calpak), which marketed canned goods under the Del Monte label, the in-dustry's first nationally advertised brand name. The nucleus of Calpak was the California Fruit Canners Association, but the newer corporation en-compassed sixty-one plants and received a significant infusion of capital from

Wall Street as well as from California banks.[53] Canners formed a trade association, the California Canners League, in the same period. Even with the consolidation, it should be noted, it remained possible for small firms to start up with capital from the companies that manufactured the cans themselves.

Consolidation occurred among orchardists more or less simultaneously. Like all farmers, Santa Clara Valley growers needed credit to pay the costs they incurred before harvest. Stretched to the limit, they frequently felt that they were at the mercy of canners and packers when it came time to sell their fruit. As a consequence, in 1916 a small group of prune and apricot growers in the Valley spearheaded the founding of a commodity marketing organization patterned after the recently formed Sunkist and Sunmaid (which marketed citrus fruit and raisins, respectively). Capitalized at $200,000 — mostly on the basis of growers' notes — the California Prune and Apricot Growers' Association came into being in 1917.[54] The Association's most severe problem was the reluctance of many local growers to join. Because it was necessary to sign up a sizeable percentage of acreage in order to create a workable cooperative, the organization employed professional canvassers. By the early 1920s, the Association was one of a number of California dried fruit cooperatives being widely publicized as a success story. By 1929, cooperative marketing accounted for 33.6 percent of the sales of all fruits and nuts in Santa Clara County.[55] An advertisement for the Association's Sunsweet brand in a trade journal boasted that "rigid standardization" had built the organization from a "growers' folly" to an annual production of thirty-five million pounds.

But although the Association was successfully launched, it experienced many difficult years, even before the 1930s. This is partly because old habits of making individual decisions died hard. Furthermore, many growers had unreasonable expectations. They wanted the Association's management to perform an economic miracle — to control the price of prunes and apricots irrespective of market conditions. Finally, processors employed a variety of arguments to undermine grower support of the Association, including the assertion that there was something socialistic about a cooperative.[56]

Ominously, the Association proved incapable of dealing with the biggest problem facing the industry: overproduction. Trying to win monopoly control of the prune supply by aggressive sign-up campaigns, Association leaders trusted this tactic and their advertising to maintain prices and ignored the number of new trees that were being planted. In Santa Clara County, the number of prune trees went up 58 percent between 1920 and 1930.[57] Many growers, it seems, saw organizational change as a panacea and ceased to worry about a potential oversupply of fruit.

The leadership for regional consolidation among prune and apricot growers came from the Santa Clara Valley. The leadership for consolidation among processors, however, tended to come from San Francisco. Major amounts of capital were required for processing, and San Francisco was then the financial center of the West. This does not mean that San Jose was a mere satellite of San Francisco, however. Because San Jose was incontestably the California center of fruit processing in 1930, the dean of California canners was Elmer Chase of Richmond-Chase in San Jose. A civic leader, Chase was also the president of the Canners' League for more than two decades, until his death in 1939.

With respect to consolidation and cooperation, a summing up for growers in 1930 is as follows: Despite the Association, there were many forces that militated against unity. The small size of the average holding meant that owning enough land to launch a commercially viable venture was accessible to large numbers of people. This was a surefire means of promoting competition. Moreover, as we have noted, orchards and their owners were dispersed throughout the Valley, so growers had no particular geographic identity. Finally, a sampling of the growers in the San Jose City Directory of 1930 revealed great ethnic diversity: about one-third had Italian surnames, about one-third had Anglo surnames, and about one-third had German or Slavic surnames. The main commonality among growers was their antagonism toward the processors, their natural enemies in the annual war over the price of fruit.

As for the processors, the thirty-eight canneries in the Valley in 1930 can be roughly divided into three categories. First there were those that were part of large corporate holdings, such as Libby's (with headquarters in Chicago), Hunt's, or Calpak. In the second place, there were those that were part of substantial firms smaller than Calpak but often owning more than one plant. Richmond-Chase, with canneries in San Jose, Mountain View, and Stockton, is a prime example of this type of firm. And finally, there were the marginal operations that would be especially vulnerable during the Great Depression. The thirty-eight canneries ranged in size of workforce from Garden City Canning Company, which employed 197 people during a peak period in August 1934, to Richmond-Chase, which employed 2,073 people during the same period. During the height of the season, the fruit industry employed from twenty thousand to thirty thousand women and men, with women predominating.[58]

One indication of the level of concentration in the canning industry on the eve of the depression is the fact that Calpak was beginning to assume an overweening role. The largest packer and distributor of California fruit, the corporation also owned seventeen fruit and vegetable canneries in other states, fifteen fish canneries in Alaska, a fleet of steamers, and a shipyard in Alameda, California. In 1927, Calpak marketed more than $70,000,000 worth of goods.[59] Given this size and geographic spread, the directors of Calpak would clearly feel less loyalty to any one community than would an Elmer Chase. This, too, would prove consequential during the depression.

Thus in 1930, San Jose's fruit industry represented a substantial interest, but one that was far from monolithic. Indeed, it was bifurcated, with both growers and processors representing significant income for the community. Certainly, local bankers needed to be responsive to the interests of both. Within each sector, there were countertendencies at work: Some promoting integration, and some promoting competition and diversity. Civic booster-ism and a desire to promote the market for Santa Clara Valley fruit could bring the sectors together, as could their common interests as employers. But the two had fundamentally divergent interests where the price of fruit was concerned. There would be times during the Great Depression when they would be able to band together and make common cause. There would be other times, however, when their differences would loom large indeed.

In discussing the fruit industry, we must also take note of its impact on the environment. By 1930, the agricultural wells, which had seemed the perfect solution to growers' irrigation needs in the late nineteenth century, had begun to create a serious problem. The wells were responsible for an over-draft of the subterranean water supply: The water table was discernibly dropping, the land was subsiding as a consequence, and traces of saltwater from the San Francisco Bay were beginning to show up in the Valley's aquifer. The full story of the Valley's water, so important in assessing the im-pact of both the fruit industry and high tech, has yet to be written.[60] Suffice it to say that a contrast between the "benign" impact of fruit cultivation and the undoubted pollution wrought by the fabrication of electronics components would be a distortion. Moreover, as early as the 1880s, the disposal of organic waste produced by the canneries had become a serious issue, and the city had constructed an outfall to San Francisco Bay to deal with it.

Laboring Women

Between the kitchen-table scale cannery launched by the Dawsons in 1871 and the Santa Clara Valley's emergence as the fruit-processing capital of the world by 1930, there were six decades of intense economic growth and the arrival of many thousands of immigrants to provide a workforce. By the eve of the Great Depression, the canning industry was not only the largest employer in San Jose but also, statewide, the largest employer of women. This was because, in an era when much of the actual preparation of fruit was still being done by hand, women performed most of the production work — the peeling, cutting, and slicing — at the height of the season. Knowing that 30 percent of the statewide output came from San Jose and its environs, we can derive a sense of how important the 1930s unionization of the San Jose industry was in the history of wage-earning women.

On the one hand, the achievement of an AFL local composed preponderantly of seasonal, female employees in the Valley during the depression seems to counter virtually everything we know about union organizing. Certainly no one in the national AFL believed it possible to organize "semiskilled" immigrant women who worked only part of the year, nor did the group commit resources to the effort until the rival CIO appeared on the scene in the mid-1930s. Yet Valley cannery workers had certain things going for them — things that were clearly manifest by 1930 — which can help explain this otherwise startling outcome.

What the immigrant women had, in the first place, was their proximity to San Francisco, a city with one of the most activist and militant traditions in the American labor movement. Though until 1930 the vast majority of organized workers in San Francisco had been male — as was the case everywhere in the country — there had been efforts to include women who worked in female dominant jobs, such as waitressing, in the years before 1930.[61] During the depression decade, the Santa Clara County Central Labor Council's willingness to defy its state and national leadership in order to "go

Figure 4. Children in the nursery of J. C. Ainsley Canning Co., Campbell, circa 1920. Courtesy of the Campbell Historical Museums.

after the women" no doubt owed a great deal to support from feisty San Francisco labor leaders. Indeed, the Valley's entire labor movement had been launched in the 1880s with material support from the San Francisco Federated Trades Council.[62]

In the second place, the ethnicity of the workforce constituted something else that the workers had going for them. In a community where white European immigrants were relatively well-off, the cannery workers were, as of a 1913 survey, 48 percent Italian, 23 percent Portuguese, 11 percent "American," and 18 percent "other."[63] In fact, people of color could not expect to find work in the canneries without great difficulty — except for the Chinese-owned cannery — until the 1940s. There is a well-established literature on the white working class of northern California and on the way in which these workers' solidarity was, sadly, purchased at the expense of ruthless exclusion of people of color from their ranks.[64] In the period before World War II, the fruit industry workers of the Santa Clara Valley fit this mold. Indeed, with nearly three-quarters of the workers being immigrants from southern Europe, there were relatively few ethnically based tensions when it came time to form a union in the 1930s, as we shall learn.

Another characteristic of this workforce that helps us understand the subsequent ability to unionize lay in the broad range of ages of the women employed in the canneries, from children aged 14 and up to young single women to mothers to grandmothers. Oral testimony, the evidence from photographs, and statistical data all reinforce one another on this point. Demanding though the work was, it was not reserved for young people alone. This fact had consequences of the utmost significance, for it meant that women could return to their work year after year and could experience it as a regular part of their lives and identities, despite its seasonal nature. They were able to develop that sense of being part of a shared work culture that many scholars have singled out as an important ingredient in sustaining an effort to unionize.[65] The women were also able to maintain friendships with coworkers over many decades. Finally, the workers had a real stake in improving working conditions.[66]

In the days before the union, and before the use of cold storage in the plants, the working conditions in canneries were quite arduous. Because workers were expected to stay until a given day's produce was all processed, so that no fruit would be lost, the workday might well have exceeded ten hours in length. This occurred despite the fact that women workers were under the protection of special guidelines for women that had been established by the Industrial Welfare Commission of California, created in 1913. Charged with protecting the "health and morals" of women and children in the labor force, the IWC had fixed maximum hours for female employees. But an exception had been made in the case of work involving "perishable materials." As a result, those interviewed about the pre-union days in the canneries recall extraordinarily long work days and weeks — as long as eighteen hours a day or ninety-six hours a week — at the height of the season.[67] Moreover the job could be physically punishing, with workers often being required to stand for many hours. Not surprisingly, because their hands were in contact with various acidic fruits, they were also subject to frequent infections.

Another reason for difficult working conditions lay in the nature of the hiring. Every morning, in front of every cannery, a crowd of people gathered to seek employment, what is known as a "shape-up." At the most, canneries would hire their employees for the duration of a single pack, so security of employment was far from guaranteed. Those who got on the bad side of their supervisors could be summarily dismissed with no recourse. Another important way in which the arbitrary power of superordinates over workers could be exercised lay in the area of quality control. Each can a worker filled had her number stamped on it. According to oral testimony, workers lived in constant fear of being summoned to the sample room, where cans were randomly opened and checked. The fruit inside the can had to be perfectly uniform, with the slices all aligned, or the worker would be reprimanded and perhaps dismissed. The firm's good name for quality rested on the efforts of these women, and they were never allowed to forget it.

As genuinely terrifying as the quality control checks were, they also point to a resource the workers themselves possessed: They had considerable responsibility, and over time on the job, they developed real skill. Clearly, this promoted a sense of craft among those who filled such jobs, thereby increasing their commitment to their employment and their willingness to fight for it. Repeatedly in the course of interviews, women spoke with pride about what they had done: "It was hand work, and you learned to be very good at it or you would never last." "Our fruit was just beautiful." "It was a very interesting job." "You had to learn to cut the fruit just so — on the seam."[68]

It is easier to appreciate female craft than in times past, because — the skills of women workers having been so undervalued both by male unionists and by labor historians — feminist scholars have begun to challenge the way that "craft" and "skill" have been defined. Writing about waitresses, for example, Dorothy Sue Cobble argues: "Their history demonstrates that for workers, *craft* and *skill* were flexible terms encompassing a wide range of ability and job know-how. The achievement of skilled status was based on workplace struggle, not simply on some 'objective' measure of expertise."[69] Writing about nineteenth-century women collar laundresses, Carole Turbin explicitly makes the gender connection:

In the past scholars underestimated women workers' expertise because they confused the designation of skill with workers' status. Although contemporary observers and scholars based hierarchies of skill on technological criteria, they judged the work of women, black Americans,

Asians, and many other ethnic minorities as unskilled, in part because of their subordinate place in the social hierarchy. Moreover, the term skill was usually restricted to apply to expertise acquired through training in formal settings. . . . Women were adept at industrial work based on household tasks precisely because they brought to occupations years of training at home.[70]

A generation of feminist scholarship has taught us to understand that women's work has often been invisible, especially when it has been performed in a domestic setting. Gainful employment in a cannery did not equate with being at home, but the production work *did* bear some resemblance to a domestic task, as in the pattern discussed by Turbin. Hence the work of women has been the easier to undervalue, both when it comes to scholars assessing the skill involved or when it came, in the old days, to employers determining the remuneration it should earn.

In fact, the fruit industry constituted a classic segmented labor market, with women's work being systematically paid less than men's. If women workers were advantaged by having a vested interest in their craft, this did not show up in their paychecks. Some male jobs, those that involved tending and repairing machines, were, in fact, highly skilled. But the bulk of the male jobs below the supervisor level consisted of warehousing activities, work that required strength but much less skill than precision cutting of fruit. Nonetheless, women were invariably paid less than men — a difference that survived into the union era, when gender differentials were built into the contracts.

Until the widespread use of mechanical devices in preparing fruit created the need for a different set of worker incentives, a transition that was fully manifest by the 1940s, the overwhelming majority of female cannery workers were paid according to the piece-rate system.[71] The Industrial Welfare Commission, charged with overseeing a minimum wage for women workers in addition to the aforementioned maximum hours, had established a complicated audit system for piece-rate employees so that its staff could determine whether women were being fairly paid. Though the regulations fell short of being fully effective, the net result of these efforts was undoubtedly beneficial to the workers. Testimony during the National Recovery Administration's (NRA) hearings of the early 1930s and letters written to the NRA by workers both attest to much grimmer working conditions outside California. One worker, for example, used the term *peonage* to describe her employment. All parties saw the California industry as relatively progressive.[72]

Finally, in drawing up a balance sheet of what a cannery worker's job was all about — long hours and poor pay, on the one hand, but the opportunity to take pride in one's work, on the other — we must note the power that floor ladies and other supervisors had in the days before a union. Where would a worker be placed along a belt, for example? (This would determine how much fruit she could process and ultimately how much money she could make.) Would the man who came to take her cases as they were ready arrive promptly so that the rhythm of her work could be steady? Such issues loomed large, and abuses of power were commonplace. Workers often felt constrained to donate a lavish sum as a present for the floor lady, so as to improve their chances of favorable treatment.

Early Unions

In 1917, even before the Great Depression precipitated widespread labor militancy — with the Santa Clara Valley seeing many turbulent episodes — the Valley's cannery workers had demonstrated their fighting spirit by forming a short-lived union, the Toilers of the World, and by going on strike. The first point to make about this group is to note its hybrid quality. Chartered by the AFL as a federal labor union, the Toilers nonetheless displayed many signs of influence by the much more radical Industrial Workers of the World, a group that had been trying to organize farm labor in California for several years. The Toilers recruited male and female workers with equal interest, for example, and reached out to the unskilled and to people of color. Moreover, their program was unusually ambitious. All these traits were much more characteristic of the Wobblies than of the AFL. It has proven impossible, however, for historians to ascertain the exact nature of Wobbly involvement with the Toilers.[73]

In May 1917, the Toilers held an organizational meeting in San Jose to which one thousand people came. Mostly Italian, the audience also included Anglos and Japanese, again a very unusual circumstance. Those in attendance listened to speeches in both Italian and English, including one by a

Catholic priest and one by the pastor of the First Methodist Church. By this time, the Toilers had become one of the largest unions in Santa Clara County, with ten delegates on the Central Labor Council.

In July, the Toilers launched a strike, the largest in the fruit industry before 1931 and the first to use mass picketing and mass demonstrations. The authorities promptly called in the National Guard to "keep order," and the *San Jose Mercury-Herald* hinted at complicity by German agents. On the other hand, the strike received favorable attention in San Francisco's two Italian language newspapers, *La Voce del Popolo* and *L'Italia*, especially in the former.

The strike was settled through mediation in late July, and the union obtained agreements with most of the area's canneries that lasted for about two years, agreements that included provisions for wages and hours. Significantly, these agreements covered only the male workers, because, according to the union's explanation, the women's interests were protected by the IWC. The most recent student of the Toilers speculates that this concession was necessary for the union to stay in the AFL.[74] The Toilers then disappeared in 1919, that year of reaction when, in addition to the Red Scare at the national level, the state legislature of California passed a criminal syndicalism law making it much easier to prosecute labor activists.

Indeed, the 1920s were lean years for Santa Clara Valley labor movements, as they were for so much of the country. Employers instituted a local variant of the anti-union American Plan, and many service unions, such as the Retail Clerks, folded. A Central Labor Council that had been robust and had included many trades shrank in size and consequence.[75]

Nonetheless, an incident in 1929 testifies to the continuing militancy of the Central Labor Council — as well as foretells events of the decade to come. Elizabeth Nicholas, a Communist organizer who would work tirelessly in the fruit industry throughout the depression, went to see John J. Anderson, secretary-treasurer of the Central Labor Council. She asked if she would receive cooperation from the Council in trying to organize cannery workers; he replied in the affirmative.[76] One has to believe that neither the Communist Party, then launching its program of dual unionism, which called for creating an organization distinct from the AFL, nor the AFL leadership would have approved of this exchange. What is clear many years later is this: Not only were the Valley's mainstream labor leaders dedicated to organizing the canneries; they were also prepared to be quite ecumenical in achieving that goal. That attitude would subsequently prove enormously beneficial to cannery workers.

Local Government/Local Politics

As the twentieth century opened, San Jose was governed by the Mackenzie machine, consisting of regular Republicans with a more-than-cozy relationship with the Southern Pacific Railroad. In 1902, the machine fell victim to the Good Government League, a creation of two brothers, J.O. and E.A. Hayes, who used the League as a vehicle for taking control of the local Republican Party. In organizing what was the first such victory in the state, the Hayes brothers made a splashy entrance into Santa Clara Valley politics. In 1913, they bought two newspapers, which they then merged to form the *San Jose Mercury-Herald*. In addition, E.A. ran successfully for Congress in 1904, where he served seven terms.

There followed a seesaw battle between contending forces for control of the Valley's Republican Party, a prize made especially valuable by the fact that the Democratic Party was virtually moribund and would remain so until the 1930s. All the evidence indicates that the Hayes brothers were back in the regular Republican fold by 1906. Two years later, a surprising development saw the Union Labor Party capture a majority of the city council seats.

And yet this development was not so surprising. In the first place, the Valley possessed a vibrant labor movement in the early twentieth century. Although the thousands of fruit industry workers were not organized, the Central Labor Council encompassed, in addition to the traditionally strong building trades, the following groups: bakers, barbers, brewers, bartenders, cigar-makers, coopers, cooks and waiters, engineers, grocery clerks, gas workers, horseshoers, horticultural workers, laundry workers, leather workers, musicians, machinists, pressmen, retail clerks, streetcar men, stage employees, teamsters, typographers, and tailors.[77] With so many unions in operation, organized labor could exert political clout.

Then, too, there was the influence exercised by San Francisco, where the Union Labor Party controlled the municipal government between 1901 and 1911. Indeed these were years of general working-class political strength, in-

cluding a lively socialist movement in Northern California. The Oakland socialist newspaper reported regular meetings in San Jose during this period,
though it is impossible to state with certainty how strong a socialist movement there was in the Santa Clara Valley.[78]

Finally, San Jose labor had the benefit of a local leader, Walter Mathewson, business agent of the Building Trades Council, who would play a vigorous role not only in the community, but also at the state level. Elected to the
city council in 1906, he later went on to serve on the state Industrial Welfare
Commission.

All these elements came together to produce a stunning victory for the
labor movement in 1908. Led by the incumbent Mathewson, the Union
Labor Party swept all but one of the municipal offices; the vote was the heav-
iest in the history of San Jose. Moreover, the new officeholders immediately
announced their intention of employing only union workers on all city projects.[79] Those who opposed these developments blamed labor plus the Italian
vote, both of which were concentrated in two of the city's four wards. Hence
it is not surprising that the business elite's counteroffensive came in the form
of an attack on representation by ward, an initiative that culminated in a new
city charter in 1915.

But even before the destruction of the ward system in the charter of 1915,
there was an electoral setback for the labor coalition. In the 1912 election, 80
percent of the registered voters went to the polls, and, although the labor
candidate won, he was elected by a plurality of only 39 percent.[80] That year,
the electorate contained a new component, women voters who had gotten
the franchise in California in 1911. The Hayes brothers and other opponents
of the Union Labor Party effectively cast the issues in moral terms, with a
vote for labor being equated with a vote for gambling, liquor, and immoral-
ity. That this resonated with the new women voters can be, tentatively at
least, inferred from the results.

The next years saw dedicated work on behalf of a reform charter spearheaded by three groups in particular: the San Jose Chamber of Commerce,
the Women's Civic Study League, and the Merchants' Association. Elmer
Chase, leading local canner, rallied support for reform. Thomas Reed, a professor of political science from the University of California, played a key role
in drafting the charter, which established citywide elections and provided for
the first orthodox city-manager government in California. Members of the

labor movement, on the other hand, held themselves aloof from the process of drafting the charter. Moreover, many workers must have abstained from voting altogether, because the charter was adopted in an election that brought out only 40 percent of the registered voters.[81]

The adoption of the new charter and the election that put Chase and a solidly pro-business slate into the city council marked a watershed in San Jose politics. Despite the dominance of the Republican Party, workers had mobilized outside the two-party system and had controlled local government for a few years. After the destruction of the ward system, this would never again happen. When labor fought back in the 1930s, it would be not only at the ballot box — after registering Democratic — but also in mobilizing to unionize.

Growers versus processors; working-class political strength versus that of the business elite; segregated housing patterns featuring not only ethnic enclaves, but even provincially based subenclaves within the larger ethnic whole — many forces conduced to divide San Jose in the early years of the twentieth century. But within the city limits proper, there were things that brought the population together. There was only one public high school — San Jose High. Almost everybody's kids went to school together — except for migrant farm workers — and cheered for the same sports heroes. And all who lived in the Santa Clara Valley had a stake in a healthy market for fruit. The Great Depression, however, would deliver a nearly mortal wound to that market, and it would unleash a level of unimaginable turbulence, even violence, among people who often knew one another. It would also produce a wave of worker militancy that would carry cannery workers into the ranks of organized labor.

The Fruit Industry Workforce at High Tide:
A Wave of Militancy Hits the Valley

It is perfectly true that the depression has created havoc in the cannery cities in California.

—NATIONAL CONSUMERS LEAGUE,
National Recovery Administrations Hearings

The Great Depression of the 1930s had a profound, destabilizing impact on Santa Clara Valley's status quo — an impact that went beyond the changes wrought by the legislative legacy of the New Deal. The most obvious effects were that the Valley developed a pattern of being more Democratic than Republican in registration, a pattern that has substantially held ever since, and that the largest group of workers, those in the fruit industry, obtained a union. But the depression also set in motion a turn away from the fruit industry as the mainstay of the local economy. The growing and processing of fruit proved too unreliable, too volatile, to sustain prosperity. By the end of the decade, growers began to uproot trees, and local leaders began to turn their attention to alternative sources of economic vitality. Indeed, a significant portion of the original impetus for creating Silicon Valley came from the profound despair about the state of local horticulture during the 1930s.

When attempting to characterize the ways in which the Valley changed during the 1930s, it is impossible to portray a straightforward trajectory of either progress or decline. For our purposes, it is important to emphasize that this was the moment at which the California Dream of prosperity began to lay within the grasp of the Valley's cannery workers, because their jobs became more stable and more remunerative. A vital part of the story is that these workers lived in a region animated by the militancy of San Francisco's victorious waterfront workers.

Economic Collapse

The Great Depression devastated Santa Clara Valley's fruit industry, because when times are hard, people will still eat bread and buy other basic necessities, but they can eliminate canned fruit or dried prunes from their diets. Moreover, Valley growers simultaneously lost their biggest single foreign market for prunes — Germany. Before Hitler came to power and instituted economic self-sufficiency, Germans had imported 85,000 tons of prunes annually. After 1934, the German market virtually disappeared. This was a blow from which the prune industry could not recover until the advent of World War II, especially given the fact that California exported nearly 50 percent of its prunes before the depression hit.[1] Throughout the 1930s, the thousands of acres of Santa Clara Valley fruit trees still blossomed in the spring and bore fruit in the summer, but the prosperity that the fruit had brought to the area vanished.

Each segment of the industry had its own problems stemming from the depression. Growers, in addition to their diminishing markets, faced a steep decline in the price of fruit. Further, their tax burden proved especially onerous. When the depression began, California had no state income tax, which meant that the property tax collected by the county was the principal means of paying for the escalating cost of relief occasioned by the thousands of unemployed. After New Deal programs came into being and the state legislature adopted a moderate income tax, the burden on local property owners was somewhat eased. Yet it did not altogether disappear. In effect, this meant that throughout the 1930s, growers, whose income had shrunk substantially, sustained the highest expenses in history. Dewey Anderson, a man born in San Jose who went on to serve as head of relief for the state of California in the late 1930s, estimated many decades later that about one-third of the local farms had been in "serious trouble."[2] By this he meant that the local farms had been at risk of foreclosure until the New Deal's Frazier-Lemke Act of 1935 offered them the possibility of obtaining a three-year moratorium on the foreclosure process.

Times were also hard for the processors, especially early in the decade. The trade journal *Western Canner and Packer* reported gloomy figures, even for the biggest operators. For example, Calpak's earnings were more than $6 million in 1929 and less than $100,000 in 1930.[3] In 1931, the journal reported a "heavy loss" for Calpak, with the firm's executives all taking a cut in pay. Eventually, in response to the depression, the entire industry reduced production by approximately one-third.[4] In addition, many of the smaller operators went under at this time.

Faced with a shrinking market for their already marginal services, cannery workers obviously had the toughest time of all. Not surprisingly, given the dimensions of the collapse, processors tried to reduce their expenses as much as possible. A major means of achieving this goal was to reduce workers' wages. The average weekly wage for a cannery worker in Northern California dropped from $16.33 in July 1929 to a low of $8.04 in July 1933.[5] There was also a concomitant deterioration in working conditions. To reduce labor costs, owners allowed male workers to pile boxes and trays of fruit in such a way that women had to expend more energy in *their* work. To add to the problem, the Industrial Welfare Commission repeatedly allowed the minimum wage to go down. During the summer and spring of 1932–33, the Commission even suspended its weekly piece-rate audits, because the cannery owners maintained that they could not bear the expense involved.[6] For the workers, the situation was rendered even grimmer by the throngs of job seekers outside each cannery. If a worker protested about the low pay, he or she could easily be replaced.

If the fruit industry suffered, then the whole community suffered. The figures in Table 2.1 reveal the severity of San Jose's reduction in bank debits (a rough gauge of business activity) and home construction in the early 1930s. The best estimate is that at the depth of the distress, in 1932, about 20 percent of San Jose's population was unemployed.[7] Before the state and federal relief programs were put in place in 1933, the human misery created by this level of joblessness strained every local resource.

In the earliest period of the depression, the two principal private agencies

TABLE 2.1
Bank Debts and Home Building
San Jose, 1925–1934

Year	Bank Debts	Home Construction Expenditures	New Housing Units
		(THOUSANDS OF DOLLARS)	
1925	$308,575	$1,526	504
1926	327,360	2,162	670
1927	321,439	1,464	355
1928	361,203	1,217	378
1929	386,439	1,174	335
1930	331,687	714	185
1931	287,676	763	147
1932	188,230	203	63
1933	172,031	153	46
1934	207,067	139	37

NOTE: Bank Debts represent the total amount paid out by banks to cover customer checks, loans, and interest.

San Jose Mercury-Herald, February 15, 1935, and March 9, 1935.

that tried to give relief to those in need were the Salvation Army and the Volunteers of America, both of which had annual budgets of less than $20,000 — a sum that was wholly inadequate to the dimensions of the problem. In consequence, people made a number of ad hoc arrangements, including bartering and teachers who subsidized school lunches out of their own pockets. Eventually, the county set up a rudimentary relief program.

Beneath the surface manifestations of distress — the already low wages in further decline, the new homes not built, the desperate people looking for work — there lay another manifestation: Many of the accommodations within the fruit industry that had been forged in the early twentieth century collapsed quickly at the onset of the depression. For example, by 1931, the California Prune and Apricot Growers' Association's share of the prune tonnage went from 75 percent to 30 percent, as thousands of growers began to market their own crops independently and to engage in price competition. In the end, only massive and continuing federal aid saved the prune industry from ruin. (Between 1933 and 1937, the U.S. government bought nearly 97 million pounds of prunes and extended substantial loans through the Commodity Credit Corporation.[8])

Among the processors, however, the story took a different turn. From the informal trade association, the Canners' League, the processors moved to increasing consolidation and more formal organization, under the impetus first of the National Industrial Recovery Act and then of the Wagner Act. Thus they became an even stronger adversary for the fragmented growers.

Stirrings of Militancy

The economic collapse was a necessary precondition for the explosion of labor activism and related turbulence during the depression decade, but it does not sufficiently explain what went on in San Jose and its hinterland. The explosion also required the presence of a local culture of dissent sustained in part by a small group of bohemian, politically radical intellectuals who encouraged, either covertly or openly, the struggles of organizers and workers. As in the case of the mainstream labor movement, proximity to San Francisco meant that people in San Jose who were trying to bring about social change had certain advantages not available in an agricultural center in, say, California's Central Valley.

Santa Clara Valley's bohemians were part of the same cosmopolitan regional culture that centered in San Francisco but that extended as far south as Monterey and Carmel. The people who were part of this circle had access to publishing in national media, such as *The Nation*. They also enjoyed connections to people of influence in the wider metropolitan Bay Area, if not necessarily to the men on the San Jose City Council. Of independent means for the most part, and thus not beholden to the business interests, the intellectuals provided dissenting voices even before the economic downturn.

Best-known of the local bohemian intellectuals were a married couple, Colonel Charles Erskine Scott Wood and the poet Sara Bard Field Wood. The Woods owned a large estate in Los Gatos, a town adjacent to San Jose, where they entertained such people as the muckraking journalist Lincoln

Steffens, the poet Robinson Jeffers, and First Lady Eleanor Roosevelt. Colonel Wood had long been a political activist and possessed a special interest in the American Civil Liberties Union. Sara Wood was well known for her advocacy of birth control and other feminist goals. Legendary California author Carey McWilliams conveyed something of the Woods' style when he reminisced about his first meeting with them. McWilliams was startled to find that Colonel Wood greeted him while wearing a toga, and then Mrs. Wood "floated down from her aerie in the treetop."[9] Caroline Decker, leader of San Jose's Communist Party labor organization in the early 1930s, recalled the Woods with special gratitude, because they took her into their house and sheltered her when the labor struggles were at their peak.[10]

Another noteworthy aspect of the local culture of dissent is the fact that San Jose had its own version of London's Hyde Park. Located across from the courthouse, St. James Park provided a forum for radical speeches and rallies. Even Wobblies, unwelcome visitors in many parts of California, were able to give speeches in the park. Dewey Anderson remembered delighting in the atmosphere there as a young man. He could enter an argument as soon as he set foot within its boundaries, and "sometimes I'd argue both sides of the same issue in one evening."[11] Because of St. James Park, San Jose enjoyed an excellent reputation in regard to civil liberties. In 1933, the city council, alarmed by agricultural strikes in the Santa Clara Valley, took up the issue of banning meetings in public parks. In response, the ACLU sent a telegram of protest to the president of the council. San Jose, the telegram noted, had an enviable record and was, in fact, "an example for less progressive cities" because of the free speech in the park.[12] Thus, even before the depression struck, cannery workers had access to the free discussion of radical ideas.

The Strike of 1931

Wretchedly paid, with the heritage of the short-lived Toilers of the World only a decade in the past and with a venue for discussing how to mobilize against owners, cannery workers went on their first strike in 1931. That year's strike was especially noteworthy for two reasons. In the first place, it took place before the passage of the key New Deal legislation that first encouraged and then legitimated union organization (discussed later in this chapter). The date of the strike, therefore, is proof of how ready San Jose's cannery workers were for action.

In the second place, the strike marked the first visible role of the Communist Party in the Valley's labor struggles. As early as 1928, the Communist Party had begun to lay the groundwork for playing a role in organizing California's cannery and field workers. That was the year when the Third International mandated the formation of independent revolutionary unions under the Trade Union Unity League. Eagerly awaiting a chance to organize in Santa Clara County were about eight or nine local Communist Party members.[13] These women and men would play an important role in union activity throughout the decade — a much more important role, in fact, than their tiny numbers might suggest. From time to time, outsiders were sent in by the party to reinforce their efforts. But when the outsiders left, the locals remained and kept going with their determined efforts to organize the fruit industry. One former party member who was sent in to help, Dorothy Ray [Healey], has recalled her participation in the 1931 San Jose strike. She was a high school student in Berkeley and a Young Communist League member when, early that summer, the party sent her to the Santa Clara Valley. She obtained a job paring peaches at Calpak and began to talk to the other women about a union.[14]

While party members prepared themselves for leadership roles in a projected union, there were rank-and-file cannery workers who began to display dissatisfaction with the status quo. A few months before the strike, a number of Italian and Spanish workers had organized an independent union, the American Labor Union, with a membership at its peak of approximately one thousand. Although it didn't last long, the American Labor Union took part in a few small protests and prepared the way for the strike by dramatizing the harsh working conditions.[15]

Cannery working conditions may have been an underlying cause, but the workers had a more immediate grievance. In late July, employers cut wages between 20 and 25 percent. In a spontaneous reaction to the wage cut, hundreds of workers walked off the job.[16] Communist Party members gained leadership of the strike and declared the formation of the Cannery and Agricultural Workers' Industrial Union, a potent if short-lived organization that in 1933 alone would lead strikes involving some forty thousand farm workers throughout the state of California.

Not surprisingly, given the politically committed nature of the strike's leadership, the strikers' demands revealed broad social aims. The CAWIU asked not only for the restoration of 1930 wages, time and a half after eight hours, and union recognition but also for equal pay for equal work, regardless of age or sex, and free transportation to work for women.[17] Toward these ends, the CAWIU mounted picket lines at several canneries. Employers promptly brought in scabs and protected them with armed guards. As a result of the ensuing melee, the authorities arrested eight picketers.[18]

On July 31, 1931, two thousand strikers met at St. James Park and decided to march to the city jail to demand the release of the arrested picketers. When they reached the jail, the strikers met law enforcement officers who were prepared to do battle. Sheriff's deputies and police used tear gas bombs and blackjacks to drive the strikers back. The workers themselves employed brick bats.[19] At this juncture, hundreds of others who opposed the workers and had heard about the conflict converged on the jail, ready for a fight.[20] In a community so dependent on fruit processing, a strike jeopardized the prosperity of many in the community, besides the owners themselves — or so they thought. In the Valley, as in other parts of California, those who felt threatened during labor strife would show up to do battle on behalf of the owners.[21]

What transpired on July 31 proved to be the worst riot in the city's history. It ended only when firemen turned hoses on the strikers and police fired shots in the air. The twenty people who were arrested were strike leaders, despite the fact that the arrival of the others had done so much to increase the level of violence.

The day after the riot, the International Labor Defense, a Communist Party organization that was formed to secure legal help for those who were arrested or imprisoned, placarded San Jose with handbills announcing a meeting at the Italian Benevolent Hall. On the night of August 2, some seven hundred people attended the meeting, braving the scrutiny of the police surrounding the hall. Organizers took up a collection for the defense of the arrested leaders. By August 4, however, the strike was over, with none of the demands granted.[22] The workers' support had been far from solid, the federal government had not yet entered the picture as it would during the New Deal years, and the employers had stood very firm. Not only had Richmond-Chase (one of the companies involved) displayed machine guns at its gates, for example, but also a spokesman for Calpak had announced: "If we should have to close our plants here, we will simply ship our fruits to other plants the company has elsewhere in the state. The ones who will suffer will be the 1,700 or 1,800 workers we have on our payrolls here."[23]

Biased contemporary reporting and a dearth of documentary sources from the union make it very difficult to determine how many workers were involved in the 1931 strike and how close they came to success. Attempting to minimize the strike, the *San Jose Mercury-Herald* grudgingly gave it space, while emphasizing its alleged weaknesses, such as its failure to close the canneries. After the strike ended, the *Mercury-Herald* did acknowledge that for a few days two of the canneries had only 50 percent of the workforce in attendance.[24] In contrast, the *San Francisco News*, a liberal metropolitan daily, played up the strike with front-page treatment; one banner headline proclaimed: "U.S. Aid Asked by San Jose in Riots/Barricades Up."[25]

So what had been accomplished? In the short run, very little. Never again would the CAWIU make any inroads among cannery workers; its big success before its disappearance in 1935 came among field workers. But the strike did galvanize a small core of activists so that there were five or six in each cannery who would talk to workers after hours and visit them in their homes unceasingly until a union took shape in 1937. I. G. "Slugger" Ficarrota, for example, was only sixteen years old when he took part in the strike. Nonetheless, it changed his life. He subsequently dedicated himself to talking up a union in his neighborhood of Goosetown. He would later go on to serve as the cannery union's business agent for thirty-two years. The strike also laid the groundwork for cooperation between the Communists and others who, although they did not share revolutionary goals, were willing to work with Communist Party members if that was what it took to secure a cannery union.

The Strikes of 1933

In the two years that elapsed before the outbreak of new strikes — this time among field workers — an important development took place: The CAWIU chose San Jose as its headquarters, from which it would launch organizing drives throughout the state. With some of the largest processing plants in the world located in the Santa Clara Valley, the city seemed to be a logical choice.[26] The union established itself at 81 Post Street and began to charge dues of twenty-five cents a month for the employed and five cents for the unemployed. This meant an even greater concentration of energy and resources for organizing cannery workers and their colleagues who worked in the fields or the packing plants.

In February 1933, an event took place that demonstrates the level of local

Figure 5.   Children of the Ficarrota family in a San Jose orchard circa 1920. Courtesy of I. G. "Slugger" Ficarrota.

anxiety about radical activity. Two of the Valley's Communists, Elizabeth Nicholas and Matt Huotari, led a march to protest the poor quality of relief food for the unemployed. About 150 strong, the crowd proceeded down a major county thoroughfare, shouting, "Will we fight? Yes, we will fight!" Members of the American Legion — who provided protection for scabs on a regular basis and were, in effect, antiradical shock troops — met the crowd and engaged in a street fight in which one man was allegedly stabbed in the back. The authorities arrested Nicholas and Huotari. In the trial that followed, the district attorney argued that the defendants had been fomenting a revolution and hence constituted a threat to the public good. A witness for the prosecution testified that Nicholas and Huotari had harangued the crowd in a foreign language. In her defense, Nicholas, who was of Slavic descent, specifically denied that she had addressed the crowd in Italian. One can infer that she realized an Italian language appeal would have seemed especially threatening, inasmuch as Italians then constituted the largest group of foreign-born in the community.[27]

But if local authorities thought that the arrest and conviction of Nicholas and Huotari might contain or deter either the radicals or the workers who

Figure 6. Migrant Mexican laborers on the highway near San Jose, January 27, 1935. Photograph by Dorothea Lange. Copyright the Dorothea Lange Collection, Oakland Museum of California, City of Oakland. Gift of Paul S. Taylor.

were listening to them, they were sorely mistaken. In fact, 1933 proved to be the most explosive year in the history of San Jose, with three field worker strikes, the arrival in the city of full-time Communist Party operatives, and a brutal lynching in St. James Park. By the end of 1933, San Jose was nationally infamous for the violence that had taken place there during this turbulent period.

The Valley was not alone that year when it came to striking workers. The year 1933 saw the biggest outbreak of agricultural strikes in the nation's history: sixty-one actions in the United States, of which one-half were in California. It was the year in which farm wages reached their lowest point of the depression decade. It was also the year in which the power of the federal government seemed to be arrayed on behalf of workers, given the June passage of the National Industrial Recovery Act — including section 7(a), which stated that employees have the right to organize. All over the country, workers were mobilizing.[28]

The sequence of events in the Santa Clara Valley's labor strife was as follows. In April, two thousand pea pickers struck for higher wages, their leaders were arrested on vagrancy charges, and the strike ended with no gains. Shortly thereafter, Caroline Decker and Pat Chambers, two seasoned (if young) Communist Party members, arrived in San Jose to devote themselves to the CAWIU. Decker was acquainted with Lincoln Steffens, through whom she received introductions to the Valley's liberal intellectuals.[29] Decker and Chambers had not been in town long when, in June, 1,000 cherry pickers struck for higher wages, and a picket line of 250 people surrounded one cherry orchard alone. Meeting with the most violence of any of the field worker strikes — Sheriff William Emig of Santa Clara County armed special deputies with pick handles and authorized them to patrol the orchards — the cherry strikers nonetheless won a 50 percent raise, from twenty cents to thirty cents per hour. Finally, in August, pear pickers staged a strike that constituted the CAWIU's greatest local success.[30]

Years later Caroline Decker recalled with gratitude those who had helped bring about the pear strike's success.[31] Before the CAWIU launched the strike, Decker had written a letter to the president of the Palo Alto Democratic Club, setting forth the reasons for the strike; namely that pear growers were being paid more for their fruit and yet were cutting the wages of their own workers. She also asserted that the San Jose press was "perverting every bit of truth about the various strikes."[32] In return, the club president replied that, "Such letters written in the spirit of fairness will go a long way to help solve the so-called labor problem." He also said that he had forwarded her letter to Hugh Johnson, head of the newly established National Recovery Administration.[33] In addition, San Francisco newspapers with a liberal bent had bestowed much unfavorable publicity on the brutality directed against activists during the cherry strike, so there was beginning to be some level of public sympathy for workers in the greater Bay Area.

Armed with this kind of support, the CAWIU leaders decided to pursue a bold line of action during the pear strike. Although the growers had obtained injunctions against a picket line (a dramatic change from the usual violence and intimidation), the union ignored them and launched mass picketing. The day after the strike began, the appellate court in a nearby county handed down a decision that substantiated Decker's claim that the strikers had the right to picket.[34] And a new rally at St. James Park escaped police intervention. An extant handbill advertising the rally proclaims: "Roosevelt has told the workers to ORGANIZE!"[35]

Not only did the pear strike force the growers into the courts, but it also set another precedent: For the first time, the CAWIU gained the recognition of the California Bureau of Labor Statistics, and a representative of that agency came to San Jose to arbitrate the strike. In consequence, the workers gained an important objective. Although growers refused to recognize the CAWIU, one of the strikers' chief demands, they did grant a substantial increase in wages. In a letter written to the national Communist Party leader Earl Browder in late August 1933, Sam Darcy, organizer for District 13 (which encompassed California, Nevada, and Arizona) said: "If we can do in marine, RR, & oil what we have already done in agriculture, I would venture to say that we were launched."[36]

There was optimism in other branches of the labor movement, too. The August 18, 1933, issue of the *Union Gazette*, the house organ of the Central Labor Council, announced that for each week of the previous month, a new local had appeared. Brewery workers, beer-drivers, cleaners and dyers, retail clerks — all were organizing. The fact that many of these locals represented groups that had been within the labor fold until the ultraconservative 1920s, and then had disappeared, made this development all the sweeter.

The Disappearance of the CAWIU

The mainstream labor movement would continue to grow throughout the decade, but the CAWIU would never again conduct a strike in San Jose, let alone win gains for the workers. Immediately after the pear strike ended, Communist Party members rushed to the San Joaquin Valley, where a protracted cotton strike was taking place. By the time the CAWIU was through with the cotton strike, there was a compelling reason for avoiding San Jose.

In late November 1933, a lynching took place in San Jose. Although the lynching had nothing overtly to do with labor, it had important consequences for those who were trying to organize in the Valley. As the event unfolded, it demonstrated that the local law enforcement officials had little commitment to due process, a lesson that activists were quick to learn.

Brooke Hart was a popular twenty-two-year-old son of a local department store owner and a recent graduate of Santa Clara University. When he was kidnapped and nominally held for ransom — he had actually been murdered within hours of his capture — San Joseans were heartsick. A few days later, two men were apprehended in the act of making a ransom call to Hart's parents. The men quickly confessed, telling of killing Hart and then dumping his body in San Francisco Bay. The crime was especially shocking, because the kidnappers themselves came from respectable local families. Even before Hart's body was recovered, there were rumors about a proposed lynching. Duck hunters found the body on the morning of November 26, ten days after the arrests, and that night a mob of about two thousand people, including women, stormed the county jail and hanged the kidnappers from trees in St. James Park. Local authorities did nothing to protect the two men in their custody until such action was too late, despite the fact that the intention to lynch the men as soon as the body was found was a matter of public discussion in the press.[37]

Most shocking of all was the role played by the Republican governor of California, James Rolph. Rolph had been a popular and generally successful mayor of San Francisco for nineteen years before his election to the governorship of California in 1930. But dealing with a state in the grips of a devastating depression had apparently been too much for him. Even before the recovery of Hart's body, Rolph began to make inflammatory statements. On a trip to Los Angeles, for example, he told the press, "Why should I call out the troops to protect those two fellows? The people make the laws, don't they?" He thus implied that if the people wanted a lynching, they were entitled to it. After the lynching, he praised the people of San Jose and noted his own role. He had postponed an out-of-state trip, because "[i]f I had gone away, some one would have called out the troops on me." He further pledged that he would pardon anyone who might be convicted of a crime connected with the lynching.[38] Protest meetings in several parts of the country and strenuous efforts by the ACLU to shame the authorities into taking legal action against the mob ringleaders produced nothing but hostility toward outside interference.[39]

Decades later, it is clear that the most important catalyst for this tragic episode was the March 1932 kidnapping of the Lindbergh baby in New Jersey, an incident that provoked widespread public outrage. But even factoring in the Lindbergh case, it is difficult to fathom how such savagery could have taken place in San Jose.

The lynching in St. James Park, with its quasi-official approval, was part of a series of official decisions and unofficial events that together created a new, much chillier climate for labor in the Valley. In the spring of 1934, a new organization called the Associated Farmers (which was substantially funded by large corporate interests, such as Southern Pacific Railroad and the Canners' League) appeared in rural areas of California, with the clear aim of combating any prospects of farm labor organizations. In addition, representatives traveled around the state to lobby for the passage of antipicketing ordinances.[40] In March, the Santa Clara County Board of Supervisors passed such a measure, followed a few months later by a similar one from the San Jose City Council. The county's ordinance provided against loitering or standing on public highways, prohibited parades except for those connected with a funeral, and allowed no assemblages without a permit — all this applying in unincorporated territory.[41] That the space consecrated to speech-making, St. James Park, had been the site of a lynching no doubt constituted a strong deterrent to radical activism in itself.

"The Terror in San Jose"

Organized opposition to labor then took a more ominous turn, evidently triggered by the San Francisco general strike in July 1934.[42] In San Jose, there was vigilantism proceeding on two levels: one public and formal, the other covert and informal. On July 17, there was an announcement in the *Mercury-Herald* that three hundred leading citizens, including Ed Richmond of Richmond-Chase Cannery and someone from the San Jose Chamber of Commerce, had met to plan a drive to combat Communism. To this end, a "virile" organization was needed.

On July 18, the paper carried a large advertisement for the Committee of Public Safety of Santa Clara County. All good Americans were urged to come forward to sign the oath, which would be administered at the Chamber of Commerce. That day, two hundred men reportedly filed application for membership. Also that day, the remaining local radicals vacated Communist Party headquarters at 81 Post Street. (The state leaders of the CAWIU had long since departed, but others had continued to work out of this building. The landlord, alarmed by reports emanating from San Francisco, had requested the radicals' immediate departure.) In an article about the departing Communist Party, the *Mercury-Herald* noted that people from this address had been responsible for the "orchard riots" of the previous summer.

It seems more than coincidental that vigilantes took action the next day. In the words of a reporter for the *Mercury-Herald*, it happened this way:

> Armed with bright new pick handles, their faces grim, eyes shining with steady purpose, a large band of "vigilantes" composed of irate citizens, including many war veterans, smashed their way into three Communist "hot spots" here last night, seized a mass of red literature, and severely beat nine assorted radicals.

The *Union Gazette* presented a less heroic account, asserting that the vigilantes' leaders had assembled what hoodlums they could, armed them with bad whiskey as well as the pick handles, and set to work.[43]

Despite the excited prose that its reporter used to describe the incident, the *Mercury-Herald* editorially condemned the vigilantism as the "Wrong Way." Sheriff Emig, for his part, publicly deplored what had happened and announced an immediate investigation. Nonetheless, as in the case of the lynching, no one was ever brought to trial for having participated in the raid. Emig, who was developing a public relations flair for denouncing vigilantism while doing nothing to combat it, did manage to convince a reporter for *The Nation* that he was personally appalled.[44] Many people in the labor movement, however, remained unconvinced of his sincerity.[45] The episode, with its *Nation* coverage in an article entitled "The Terror in San Jose," served to confirm the image of the Santa Clara Valley as a hotbed of what today would be called "redneck reaction."

That the events in San Jose were part of a coordinated effort to smash agricultural unionism is borne out by the fact that these events exactly coincided with the arrest of the CAWIU's top leaders in Sacramento, whence they had fled after the lynching. Eight people were eventually convicted under the state's criminal syndicalism statute, and they served up to two years in state prison. Not surprisingly, this loss of leadership dealt a fatal blow to the CAWIU.[46] By 1935, the union was defunct, a victim both of repression and of the party's decision to end dual unionism and to work within the structure of the existing labor movement.

Thus in late 1934, the outlook seemed grim for the prospects of unionizing the fruit industry in the Santa Clara Valley. Dedicated organizers had been driven out of town, local law enforcement had winked at — if not colluded in — several episodes of vigilantism, and the Valley had developed an unsavory national reputation for brutality. The workers' considerable courage and militancy had produced no lasting results. Yet within three years, there would be a cannery local. To understand that development, we must begin by looking at the fissures between growers and processors at the local level.

Growers Versus Processors

On the eve of the Great Depression, both the growers and the processors had organizations to strengthen their respective bargaining positions. But with the economic downturn, the growers' organization proved pitifully weak, as mentioned earlier. The Canners' League, on the other hand, grew stronger under the impetus of the 1933 National Industrial Recovery Act, which encouraged nominally competing firms within an industry to cooperate.[47]

During the early 1930s, the growers and the processors, who had been bitter enemies in the annual war over the price of fruit, had a shared interest in staving off the threat of unionization. Indeed, the highly effective, antiunion Associated Farmers was the direct result of that shared interest and consequent willingness to work together. But the passage of the National

Figure 7. Cannery workers in San Jose circa 1935–40. This photograph demonstrates that there was a considerable range in the ages of the workers. Courtesy of History San Jose.

Labor Relations Act (Wagner Act) in 1935, which established rules for fair labor practices and placed the power of the federal government at the disposal of workers who wanted to unionize, drove a wedge between them. Because cannery and dried-fruit workers came under the jurisdiction of the act but field workers did not, processors and growers would have different ground rules for dealing with their workforces. In effect, growers could assume a more intransigent stance than processors could, because the power of the state would not be invoked to protect field workers.

Once their reason for working together had diminished and given the desperate circumstances for Valley growers, whose markets continued to be anemic at best, bitter strife broke out between growers and processors. The growers proved virtually unable to work together among themselves. Their frequent public meetings would usually degenerate into name-calling, and the various state and federal programs aimed at shoring up their prices turned out to be mere palliatives, rather than offering genuine solutions.[48]

On the other hand, the processors, in particular the canners, continued to cooperate closely, even after the U.S. Supreme Court struck down the National Industrial Recovery Act in 1935. Following the Supreme Court's decision, the Canners' League announced that its members would carry on as if there had been no Supreme Court action and would maintain the same trade practices as they had previously followed. Indeed, in the latter part of the decade, the cooperation among canners went even further than it had during the NRA period, with the Canners' League adopting a uniform cost-accounting system. In 1941, federal grand juries indicted the Canners' League and its eighty-three member companies for violation of the Sherman Antitrust Act. Though the case was eventually dismissed for lack of evidence, the fact that it was brought at all indicates how relatively monolithic the canners were during this period.[49]

Grower frustration with the situation came to a head in 1939, when those who raised apricots took militant, direct action against processors and against those who would sell at the processors' price. In May 1939, eight hundred apricot growers attended a mass meeting and unanimously endorsed a plan to form a union. The "union" that emerged was a strange hybrid indeed, because it was, to a large extent, sponsored by the local business community, while at the same time it employed the rhetoric of the labor movement. Certainly San Jose bankers had reason to be concerned about the condition of the Valley's economy. The *Mercury-Herald* reported that about 90 percent of the apricot orchards were heavily mortgaged and that apricot growers in the Valley had debts of approximately one million dollars on the merchants' books.[50] No doubt, this indebtedness accounted for the fact that, from the earliest mention of a union, Bradley Clayton of the First National Bank was one of the leading spokesmen. Another leader was Leon Jacobs, president of the Chamber of Commerce.

At the initial meeting, Clayton outlined a program for the new organization, including the stipulation that an advisory committee should negotiate prices on behalf of the entire group. Clearly this was an attempt to end the destructive price competition, from which the processors had been able to benefit mightily. Responding to the appeal for support, the Santa Clara County Central Labor Council gave the "union" a sweeping endorsement.[51]

Figure 8. Cannery workers and growers joining in a protest against food processors, Sunnyvale, 1939. Courtesy of the Sourisseau Academy, San Jose State University.

For a while, there was talk of a joint organization, with equal representation from growers and labor, that would bargain with canners on behalf of both groups. After a few days of negotiation, however, growers rejected this proposal. Nonetheless, the lines of communication between growers and organized labor had been opened. In addition, on at least one occasion, the growers' union used the county labor temple for a meeting.[52]

Eventually a committee of local businessmen was able to negotiate a compromise with processors over the price of fruit and thereby save the perishable apricot crop. But this was not before sporadic acts of violence against property had taken place, as well as grower blockades of cannery entrances (in cooperation with cannery workers) to prevent delivery of cheap fruit. Eight locally owned canneries led the way in the eventual compromise, with the absentee-owned firms being much tougher about price, because they had less of a stake in the Valley's prosperity. Two years later, a group of unhappy growers went so far as to approach the California CIO about receiving a charter. A member of the Associated Farmers stated, "[S]ome growers are beginning to feel that in order to get any place they must use labor union tactics and maybe eventually tie up with labor."[53] Highly unrealistic, this idea soon died, but it reveals the full depths of grower frustration.

Before the Great Depression, power in the fruit industry had been divided because of the fierce struggles between growers and processors over the price of fruit. In the early part of the decade, the struggle diminished, because both sectors wanted to combat unionism. The divisions wrought by the Wagner Act and the turbulence of the "Apricot War," however, reinvigorated the battle. But by 1939, the struggle was becoming lopsided — it was "a mere legal fiction" that the largest firm, Calpak, had a market relationship with its suppliers. Owning 21,500 acres of California farmland outright, the firm also had crop purchase contracts with 4,313 California growers, involving the produce of an additional 82,000 acres.[54] Grower unionization, the last desperate, albeit unrealistic, attempt to resist this trend, had failed, and the larger processors would henceforth have a very substantial voice in setting prices. Happily for the growers, World War II introduced enough prosperity to the fruit industry that they were spared the worst effects of their new powerlessness. That so many were eager to convert their orchards to other uses in the postwar years, however, may well have been related to their new position.

The Birth of a Cannery Local

That seasonally employed, vulnerable women workers formed a cannery local in the Santa Clara Valley in the face of so much difficulty can only be understood if we take account of developments at three levels: the national, the regional, and the local. At the national level, there was the passage of the Wagner Act and, shortly thereafter, the founding of the CIO, which provided a rival for the AFL and spurred the latter to display an interest in the cannery workers for the first time. At the regional level, there was the vitality that had been breathed into the labor movement by the successful 1934 strike of the San Francisco longshoremen led by Harry Bridges, followed by the "march inland."[55] Finally at the local level, there were the aforementioned stresses and strains within the business elite, as well as the ongoing attempt since the unsuccessful 1931 strike to organize cannery workers.

Before the passage of the Wagner Act, we can visualize the instruments of employer dominance as a series of concentric circles, with the shop floor at the center of the circle. There, control over workers could be exercised via the arbitrary prerogatives of floor lady, foreman, and supervisor. The next ring of control consisted of the legally constituted law enforcement officials, whose willingness to wield pick handles on behalf of employers was clearly manifest. Moreover, when there had been episodes of violence, only those connected with the labor movement had been subject to arrest. Beyond the officials were the Associated Farmers, the American Legion, and the vigilantes; no doubt groups with overlapping membership. Any of these might provide the manpower to crush a strike or to intimidate the organizers, as happened in the raids of 1934. The final ring was made up of community members who might be mobilized against striking workers, as in the riot of 1931. But the passage of the Wagner Act unequivocally placed the power of the federal government at the disposal of workers who wanted to organize, sending a message that due process would be enforced by the National Labor Relations Board, if not by local law enforcement. Employers did not suddenly cave in and become hospitable to unions — indeed, the LaFollette Committee documented much resistance in the Santa Clara Valley[56] — but the ground rules had changed, and everyone knew it.

Though San Jose's cannery workers wound up in the AFL fold, they benefited mightily, not only from the pathbreaking Wagner Act but also from the founding of the CIO. At both the national and the state levels of the AFL, leaders had made it very clear that they had little interest in organizing California's food industry, either field workers or processing workers. In 1934, for example, a group from the Associated Farmers went to see Paul Scharrenberg, then secretary of the California State Federation, to sound him out on the group's position with respect to farm labor. Scharrenberg told the group:

> The American Federation of Labor has spent a considerable sum of money during the past years in attempting to organize agricultural laborers. In my opinion, it cannot be successfully done. May I offer you the full cooperation of the American Federation of Labor in opposition to the subversive wave that is sweeping over California?[57]

In speaking of a "subversive wave," Scharrenberg was no doubt referring not only to the CAWIU but also to contemporary events in San Francisco, which appalled the old-line unionists of the AFL, such as the militant longshoremen's strike and then the general strike. Scharrenberg had even gone so far as to appear before a convention of the American Legion and declare that the Legion and the AFL had much in common.[58]

The passage of the Wagner Act—Roosevelt signed it on July 5, 1935—triggered a number of developments outside the Santa Clara Valley that would have a profound impact on the course of events inside the Valley. In the first place, canners decided to organize themselves and then make their peace with unionization—as long as they could control the nature of the union. In fact, we can learn a considerable amount about what lay behind the canners' decision from the candid interview granted by J. Paul St. Sure, the attorney for the emergent employers' group, California Processors and Growers.

According to St. Sure, canners representing almost 80 percent of the canning capacity in California north of the Tehachapi Mountains joined California Processors and Growers upon its formation in 1936. These canners had decided not to resist unionization but to find a "responsible union" with which they could work. They then contacted both the Teamsters Union and the State Federation. At first, the latter held back from full-scale cooperation with employers, but the Teamsters seemed relatively open to cooperation from the start.[59]

The fact that the Teamsters were contemplating cooperating with an employers' group owed much to another chain of events set in motion by the passage of the Wagner Act. Between 1936 and 1938, this chain of events culminated in the founding of the CIO. With its avowed intent of organizing workers who had been ignored by the AFL, the CIO challenged the status quo of industrial relations in unprecedented ways and caused spasms of anxiety among both employers and mainstream labor. In California, that anxiety was especially acute among the Teamsters because of the actions of Harry Bridges and the International Longshoremen's Association (which was soon to quit the AFL, join the CIO, and become the International Longshoremen's and Warehousemen's Union). Following the passage of the Wagner Act, Bridges and the ILA had launched what they called "the march inland," an attempt to organize workers in collateral industries, such as food processing. Dave Beck, head of the Teamsters Union, feared that too many ILA victories would place his members in the untenable position of taking direction from the ILA, which already controlled the waterfront. To the Teamsters, thus, the canneries were beginning to look like a good place to stop the march inland.[60]

During the mid-1930s, there had been three distinct groups trying to organize Santa Clara Valley canneries: warehousemen with loose ties to the ILA, Communists, and the Central Labor Council. One of the warehousemen, Slugger Ficarrota, recalls how much effort he put forth during this period: "Young talent made the cannery union go. Only young people could have put in the hours we did. Why, an eighteen-hour day was nothing to me — that was the only way to keep my job at the cannery and go to all the house meetings, too."[61] Communist Party member Elizabeth Nicholas had been blacklisted in the canneries since the strike of 1931 and was consequently unable to talk union on the job. Instead she devoted herself to endless home visitation.[62] Finally, the two top officers of the Santa Clara County Central Labor Council, President Earl Moorhead and Secretary John J. Anderson, were also dedicated to organizing the food industry, despite the attitude of their own State Federation. None of the three groups had any animus against Bridges, industrial unionism, or the march inland. All three were, therefore, running the risk of offending the crafts-oriented State Federation.

The turning point for the State Federation was the moment when Edward Vandeleur, who had replaced Paul Scharrenberg as secretary of the Federation, decided to cooperate with California Processors and Growers. This turning point occurred in the spring of 1937. In Stockton, a militant union had organized cannery and field workers along industrial lines and, in April, called a strike with ILA support. The threat to AFL jurisdiction over the food industry posed by these left-wing insurgents convinced Vandeleur to cast his lot with employers. Thus the Stockton local found itself facing the opposition of not only employers but also the State Federation and the Teamsters. Not surprisingly, given this coalition, the strike was unsuccessful.[63]

St. Sure has left an account of the lengths to which cooperation between Vandeleur and California Processors and Growers proceeded after Stockton. The employers' group hired someone to put out a newspaper, nominally in the name of cannery workers. This publication specialized in broadside attacks on the ILA. According to St. Sure, "The paper was really a dilly." Vandeleur himself had a secretary who was on the payroll of Safeway Stores. In fact, according to St. Sure's account, the canners' principal concern about Vandeleur was that he might become too flamboyant in his red-baiting attacks on the ILA to be credible.[64]

Shortly before the Stockton strike, the AFL had chartered Federal Local 20325 in San Jose. (A federal charter local was the format used by the AFL for new jurisdictions where there were no existing crafts international, such as the brotherhood of machinists or of carpenters.) The new local had Elizabeth Nicholas, with her well-established reputation as a radical, as its vice president. Several of the other officers were students at San Jose State College and members of the Young Communist League.[65] In addition, it was well known that there had been contact between the members of 20325 and the San Francisco ILA. Clearly Local 20325 was one of those incipient unions most likely to be suspect to Vandeleur, who was empowered by the national organization after Stockton to revoke the charters of locals thought to be dangerously sympathetic to the ILA.[66] In fairness to Vandeleur, one need not have been preternaturally suspicious to have supposed CIO leanings among leaders of Local 20325.[67]

The campaign for achieving an AFL cannery local in Santa Clara County proceeded at an accelerated pace. The Committee for Agricultural Organization of the Central Labor Council launched an intensive program of radio broadcasts, leaflets, and mass meetings, with speeches in both Italian and English.[68] The Council also supported a constitution for the local that gave control to the rank and file, united field and cannery workers into one union, and prohibited racial discrimination, none of which could have pleased Vandeleur.

The actions of the Central Labor Council are intriguing. How much did its leaders know of the subterranean maneuvering between the State Federation and California Processors and Growers? Were the leaders aware of the coalition that had emerged in Stockton? In other words, were they being openly defiant, or were they proceeding on the basis of happy ignorance? It is doubtful that we will ever know the answers to these questions. What can be asserted with certainty is that the Council would have been highly unlikely to have adopted this course of action for whatever reason without the support of its militant co-unionists in San Francisco, the march inland resembling an irresistible prairie fire at this juncture.

On the very eve of Local 20325's entering into negotiations with canners, another cannery local suddenly appeared, whose petitions for membership were being circulated with the evident approval of the employers. Indeed, the *Union Gazette* charged that workers were being required to sign the petition for a new union as a condition of employment.[69] The officers of Local 20325 fired off telegrams to Vandeleur and William Green, the national head of the AFL, and at first received assurances that the two knew nothing of the petitions.[70] Before long, it became clear that Vandeleur was, in fact, sponsoring the new union. In late June, he revoked the charter of Local 20325 and issued a charter to a new group, Local 20852.[71]

Outraged, the Central Labor Council resolved to back Local 20325 to the fullest, even going so far as to contact its counterparts around the state to rally opposition to Vandeleur's tactics. But it was an unequal struggle. The combined strength of the state and national AFL, as well as the influence exerted by employers, overwhelmed 20325. By late July, Local 20852 had signed contracts with a number of San Jose canneries. These contracts followed the terms of a master contract worked out in areawide "negotiations" between California Processors and Growers and a committee headed by Vandeleur. The master contract would become standard throughout Northern California. Helpless to prevent these developments, the Valley's Central Labor Council admitted Local 20852 to its ranks within a few months and dropped its rebellious stance toward the State Federation.

The master contract was a cynical document in that California Processors and Growers "conceded" a small raise of two-and-a-half cents an hour so that the union could claim a victory, while addressing none of the other issues of concern to workers.[72] The workers were not fooled. The first time they were asked to vote on the contract, two thousand people at a meeting at San Jose Civic Auditorium turned it down, because they wanted an end to Sunday work.[73] Yet when the same contract was presented to them the following week, they accepted it. In the intervening week, floor ladies had allegedly exerted pressure to effect this reversal.

In a decade filled with improbable events, nothing is more improbable than what happened next to the cannery local, which had clearly originated as a company union. Simply put, the warehousemen/leaders, forced to swallow Local 20852 and Vandeleur, found a way to redeem the local and to create one that served the interests of its members. The best evidence for this contention is the fact that they launched a successful strike in 1941.

Years later, two of the warehousemen recalled the feelings they had had in 1937. Said Slugger Ficarrota: "I've always remembered what an old man said to me when I was just a kid: 'Even a bad union is better than no union at all. Militancy can rescue a bad union.'" Another, Don Sanfilippo, was more expansive:

> The AFL essentially got handed the cannery union membership on a silver platter. We had done all the preliminary work for years, and then all of a sudden there's a backdoor deal and a company union. We never had much of a chance. I held out about a month, but if you wanted a job, you had to join the union [20852]. Slugger and I and our group decided to go along for the time being, and then try to take control of it. Remember, at that point, the AFL union was the only legal union.[74]

This note of defiance is not merely the bravado of older people retrospectively coloring their attitudes with militancy but a realistic assessment of what the two men and many other people set out to do.

One of the most important stumbling blocks workers faced was the fact that California Processors and Growers granted a de facto closed shop in contracts that soon covered virtually all of Northern California. Hence, the CIO was effectively frozen out of the canneries.[75] Therefore, it was difficult to obtain the intervention of the National Labor Relations Board. In fact, charges were filed with the NLRB against California Processors and Growers but not by dissidents within the existing AFL union. Rather the challenge came from a group that had virtually no foothold in the Northern California canneries at this point—the CIO-affiliated United Cannery and Agricultural and Packing and Allied Workers of America. After Vandeleur revoked the charter in 1937, the officers of Local 20325 joined the newly emerging UCAPAWA. But in Northern California in the late 1930s—unlike the southern part of the state—UCAPAWA represented a structure with a quite small membership. Hence, after two sets of hearings, the NLRB rendered a decision that left the AFL union as the exclusive bargaining agent in the canneries.[76]

Thus if a counterattack were to be mounted to redeem Local 20825, it had to be from within. Between 1937 and 1939, there was a seesaw battle between Vandeleur (and his San Jose allies) and another group that included Ficarrota, Sanfilippo, Myra Eaton (the only woman in the group), and others. One member of the group, Walter Jones, describes a dramatic and perhaps decisive occurrence:

> At one of the regular monthly meetings, our group was heckling those first officers — the company union ones. They got disgusted and walked out. We knew enough about parliamentary procedure to figure out what to do next. We just took over the meeting. I guess that's one thing the Communists taught us — parliamentary procedure. [Jones had belonged to 20325 and had come to know Elizabeth Nicholas and other Communists.] We elected new officers. . . . Then we had to guard the union office night and day to protect the records.[77]

Contemporary correspondence between dissident leaders and the San Francisco law firm consulting with them — a firm that also represented the ILWU — documents a pattern of intrigue by the company union officers, with the reformers seeking counsel about how to respond. For example, there is a hastily scrawled note from Myra Eaton, in which she states that the company union "phonies" sent "stooges" to accept a contract, which the rank-and-file officers accepted under protest. How should they proceed?[78]

The next fight, which came to a head in July 1939, was nominally about representation for Local 20852 on the Central Labor Council; but more basically, it was a conflict between Vandeleur and the new cannery local officers over who should issue work permits (necessary for employment) and whether they should go to migratory workers. Ficarrota says simply, "We were too militant for Green and Vandeleur, and they were trying to get rid of us." Because Local 20852 had been issuing the permits on its own authority and without including the national office in the bureaucratic procedure, Vandeleur decreed that 20852 would forfeit its voice in a Central Labor Council election. At this juncture, the new cannery local officers picketed their own labor temple to protest their exclusion — although, in fact, the

Central Labor Council was on their side.[79] Having supported the cannery local, the Central Labor Council then found itself in the awkward position of having its own charter revoked by Vandeleur. With a Superior Court restraining order, the Council was able to proceed with the election despite the lack of a charter. The election was conducted peacefully (under the gaze of four policemen), a progressive slate won, and the Teamsters — who had recently announced plans for absorbing the cannery unions statewide — boycotted the proceedings.[80] Two months later, the State Federation restored the charter to the Council.

The summer of 1939, then, not only saw the labor temple being used by the apricot growers' union, as we have learned, but also saw the rank-and-file cannery leaders picketing that same edifice to dramatize their conflict with Vandeleur. Although the two events were not related in a direct way, they were, in fact, connected: Dissident cannery workers and militant growers were angry about what they took to be the unfair manipulations of canners. Indeed, surviving photographs of the apricot war show both cannery workers and growers demonstrating together outside of selected canneries. Thus, the effort to combat Vandeleur and company unionism could be mounted by cannery workers who were no longer at the margins of the community, an enormous change from earlier in the decade.

Given these circumstances — and with their own resources of ethnic community, of relative interethnic harmony, and of shop-floor camaraderie developed over years of working together despite the seasonal nature of the employment — the workers were able to stage a successful strike in 1941. The cannery council (composed of federal locals throughout Northern California, but with San Jose playing an especially big role because it was so much the largest) began negotiations by asking for a 33⅓ percent increase in wages. Rejecting a compromise proposed by the federal government, it launched an industrywide strike that lasted for twelve days. Governor Culbert Olson, the first Democratic governor of California in the twentieth century, lent his support to the union by suggesting that the canners meet the union's demands.[81] The strike ended when the canners offered a 25 percent raise.

Recalls Ficarotta:

We surprised a lot of people by that strike; the AFL officials weren't expecting it. [William Green did sanction it.] And people outside the union didn't anticipate the solid rank-and-file support we got. I remember that a reporter from the *Mercury-Herald* told me that we'd be lucky if we got 50 percent of the workers to walk off the job on schedule. We really showed him.

Thus, there was solid accomplishment for those who had fought Vandeleur: The twenty thousand-plus cannery workers in the Santa Clara Valley achieved a real union. Another victory in the early years was an end to the hated shape-up — in 1938, Northern California cannery workers had secured seniority hiring.[82] Moreover, many of those interviewed expressed satisfaction about having achieved a de facto industrial union. "It wasn't organized around any one craft or skill," Sanfilippo emphasized. "I think that John L. Lewis [United Mine Workers leader and CIO founder] was right about industrial unionism," Walter Jones said. Perhaps the most telling statement about the union's impact came from Dadie Lorente, a rank-and-file member. "I still have my first union card," she said in 1974.[83]

Ballot Box Mobilization

As cannery workers mobilized for the decade-long process of achieving a union that would defend their interests, they simultaneously mobilized at the ballot box. This phenomenon helps us to understand and assess their unionization struggle, because it confirms that the struggle was part of a conscious political awakening.

As of 1930, the triumph of the Union Labor Party in San Jose seemed remote indeed. The 1920s had seen the Republican Party enjoy much success, at both the state and the local levels. In the state, Democratic candidates won only 25 out of 555 electoral contests in the 1920s.[84] In San Jose and in Santa Clara County, officeholders were uniformly Republican; not surprisingly, given the fact that in 1930, for example, 78.4 percent of the registered voters were Republican.[85] In Santa Clara County, not a single Democratic candidate for the presidency was able to win a majority of the vote between 1896 and 1936. Yet by the end of the decade, the city of San Jose and the county of Santa Clara had become consistently Democrat in registration, if not always so in voting.

We can infer that cannery workers played a big role in this political transformation. They had the lowest rate of registration at the beginning of the decade, and the county's growth in number of registered voters (67.9%) greatly exceeded its growth in population (17.3%) during the course of the decade. Given this disparity in the two rates of growth, it seems evident that the group that had the lowest rate of registration in the early 1930s was the likeliest group to have furnished the major component of the new voters.[86]

It is likely that the biggest growth in registration came from the working class, owing to the nature of the political campaigns that generated the most passion during the decade. There is a well-established literature on the transforming impact that Franklin Roosevelt and the New Deal had on American politics for at least a generation — with Al Smith having played the role of John the Baptist, so to speak, because the election of 1928 began the reinvigoration of the Democratic Party. Less well known is the impact of the gubernatorial election of 1934 on the electorate in California.[87] This is the campaign that pitted the conservative incumbent Frank Merriam, against Upton Sinclair, the muckraking novelist who switched parties from Socialist to Democrat shortly before he captured the Democratic nomination for governor. Sinclair called his campaign "End Poverty in California," or EPIC. Although Sinclair lost the election, his candidacy brought thousands of new voters onto the rolls.

Taken together, Roosevelt in 1932 and Sinclair in 1934 had an extraordinary impact on Santa Clara County, where the number of Democratic registrants rose from 10,695 in 1930 to 32,639 in 1934. (See Table 2.2 and note that Republican registration declined by only 3,420 during this period. This means that the Democratic growth necessarily came from people new to the political process.) We can infer that campaigns focusing on issues with a clear-cut class dimension convinced workers to register. In fact, though Sinclair lost in Santa Clara County as well as in the state as a whole, the election of 1934 saw eight thousand new voters register in the county.

The new voters brought into the process by the EPIC campaign helped carry the Democrats to a resounding victory in Santa Clara County in 1936, the year of the Roosevelt landslide. Franklin Roosevelt got 58.5 percent of the vote, as opposed to 40.4 percent for Landon. This proved to be the high-water mark of countywide Democratic voting strength during the Roosevelt years.

TABLE 2.2

Party Registration of Santa Clara County

Year	Republican	Democratic	Other	Total
1922	31,165	7,678	3,664	42,507
1926	37,411	8,908	2,648	48,967
1928	43,210	13,498	2,236	58,944
1930	47,205	10,695	1,739	59,639
1932	44,964	23,404	1,874	70,242
1934	43,785	32,639	1,860	78,284
1936	38,181	38,767	1,994	78,942
1938	40,914	45,133	2,753	88,800
1940	45,005	52,780	2,357	100,142

SOURCE: Dewey Anderson and Percey E. Davidson, *Ballots and the Democratic Class Struggle* (Stanford: Stanford University Press, 1943), p. 357.

When one examines particular sections of the city of San Jose, however, a different pattern emerges. Although there are extant precinct-level records for only a few of the decade's elections, these records are very telling. In the Fourth Ward, where Goosetown was located, the Democratic Party continued to grow in strength throughout the decade. Indeed, the late 1930s — the years in which the cannery local was taking shape — were the very years in which Democratic strength crested in the Fourth Ward, with FDR getting 74 percent of the vote there in 1940.[88] In short, the support for unionism and for the Democratic Party grew in tandem. And San Jose, which for decades was more suburban than urban, would continue to manifest a surprisingly Democratic voting pattern throughout the balance of the twentieth century, a phenomenon that no doubt affected the subsequent fate of women in politics in the feminist 1970s and 1980s.

As we shall learn in the next chapter, there were a few halcyon years for the cannery local during the early 1940s, years of real rank-and-file involvement and control. Yet the defeat of the radicals, and with them the freezing out of the CIO, had serious long-term consequences. It was the radicals whose emphasis had been on racial inclusiveness and on equal wages for men and women.[89] When they were defeated, no one else took up these issues. Moreover, glad to get their dues, the national AFL was never willing to grant the cannery workers the status of being an international, which left them very vulnerable to raiders, as we shall learn. How the labor history of the Valley might have evolved had the mainstream labor movement taken immigrant women workers as seriously as it took male workers during the 1930s and 1940s can never be resolved. This much seems certain: The unorganized female production workers in high-tech jobs have suffered some of the consequences, in ways and for reasons that will be explored in the chapters to come.

But to quote Ficarrota, "Even a bad union is better than no union at all." Despite the unrealized possibilities, the cannery local gave thousands of workers — often immigrants and often women — and their families a chance to get a foothold on the ladder of ascent to building decent lives over the course of the twentieth century.

THREE

War and Cold War Shape the Valley: The Birth of a Metropolis and the Death of Union Democracy

Few cities in American history have undergone the kind of transition that saw San Jose grow from 68,457 in 1940 to 445,779 in 1970, just before the Valley was dubbed "Silicon Valley." Part of the growth came as a result of the forces set in motion by World War II — San Jose had reached a population of 95,280 by 1950 — and part came as a result of the military build-up in the cold war years that saw Santa Clara County become home to large defense contractors. Then there were the aggressively progrowth decisions by political leaders. And, finally, there was the flowering of electronics in the Valley, the goal of several key people in the business world and academia — and the subject of Chapter 4.

Not even the most visionary political or business leaders of the late 1940s, however, could have foreseen how potent an economic center this modest-sized fruit capital with the turbulent history would develop into. Nor could they have predicted how diverse its population would become: During the eventful midcentury years, the city and the area were transformed not only by sheer growth but also by the fact that a goodly number of the newcomers were people of color. Hence, it would no longer be possible to keep people of color at the margins of the community, as had been done in the past. The extent of the growth also meant that new means of governance would need to be crafted, that much new infrastructure — sewers, roads, water systems — would need to be built, that schools would need to be constructed on a massive scale.

At the same time that San Jose was exploding in size, another, darker phenomenon was taking place. The nascent cold war and the ensuing military build-up not only led to economic development but also furnished an opportunity for the opponents of militant unionism to roll back the tide of union democracy, inasmuch as they could draw upon cold war–induced anxieties to advance their cause. Going so far as to impugn the loyalty of members of the National Labor Relations Board staff, these opponents — who included both conservative unionists and California Processors and Growers — managed to turn the cannery union over to the Teamsters, with a consequent loss of grassroots governance. In effect, the events of the 1940s served to attenuate the energy created by the march inland of the 1930s with its potent regional impact.

The War Years

Even before World War II, civic elites in the Bay Area and in other parts of California were looking to military spending — the federal dollar for new bases — to help their cities grow.[1] From the standpoint of military planners in Washington, D.C., the West, with its good resources, good access to hydroelectric power, and elbow room for military bases, was appealing.[2] Although less successful than such big cities as Los Angeles, San Francisco, and San Diego in the quest for federal investment, Santa Clara County was able to attract Moffett Field, originally designed to be a dirigible base in the early 1930s. Moffett Field would become the home of Ames Research Center, an important building block for the later high-tech development.[3] In April 1940, the *Mercury-Herald* announced that Lockheed Aircraft (at that time a firm located only in Southern California) was recruiting workers in the Valley.[4] On November 15, 1940, the paper announced that Food Machinery

Corporation had just received a big arms contract, totaling $3 million.[5] Shortly thereafter, the Chamber of Commerce launched a concerted effort to secure defense work for local industry.[6]

Another major building block of what would eventually be Silicon Valley, and one that also preceded the war, was the turn toward sponsored research by Stanford University officials. As the Valley's fruit industry lay in near ruins during the Great Depression, there were disquieting symptoms of economic distress at its leading educational institution, Stanford. In common with kindred universities in other parts of the country, Stanford saw a decrease in giving during the 1930s and a consequent need to cut costs. The possibility of faculty conducting research commissioned by industry or by the federal government seemed to offer hope for a new source of funding at a dark time.[7] Thus as desperate growers were beginning to tear up fruit trees and certain bankers were endorsing the idea of a growers' union to give this component of the community a chance to defend itself more adequately against the economic might of canners, some Stanford leaders were also looking for new approaches, a development that is more fully explored in Chapter 4. In sum, only a thorough grasp of how hard the depression hit the area will enable us to understand how such dramatic changes could have occurred during the midcentury decades: The depression opened the minds of many to new ways of doing business.

World War II also proved to be a potent source of change for the state of California. The state's share of federal revenues rose from $15.1 billion in 1942 to $50.2 billion in 1945, and federal spending rose from $1.3 billion in 1940 to $8.5 billion in 1945.[8] By the time the war ended, California's economy was profoundly dependent on defense spending, with aircraft being built in Southern California and ships in the north.

Because the Northern California specialty of shipbuilding took place along the Bay's waterfront, the cities located directly on the water—San Francisco, Oakland, Richmond, and Marin City—felt the biggest impact of the federal dollar spent in the Bay Area.[9] Nonetheless, the effect of wartime spending on Santa Clara County was far from negligible. The two largest contractors there, Food Machinery Corporation and the Joshua Hendy Iron Works, received military contracts totaling $289 million.[10] Moreover, in 1943 IBM decided to locate a punch card factory in San Jose. Though this development did not stem from a military contract, per se, it seems likely that the company's move to the Valley was a response to the overall regional attraction fueled by military spending in California.

New Opportunities for Women Workers During the War Years

Sunnyvale's Hendy Iron Works produced engines and weapons parts for Navy ships. Originally founded in San Francisco in the 1850s, Hendy Iron Works moved to Sunnyvale after the 1906 earthquake. Hard times during the depression led to its virtual demise, but it was bought out in 1940 by a group of construction tycoons, including Henry J. Kaiser and members of the Bechtel family, who geared it up for defense production.[11] Before the war, Hendy had employed about fifty or sixty men in a job machine shop. With its new leadership, the company began to expand very early on in response to wartime exigencies. In 1942 and 1943, its employees grew in number from 3,000 to 7,677. By war's end, the number of employees had grown to about 12,000. As of August 1945, Hendy had built 754 massive engines for Liberty ships in three and a half years, each engine being two stories tall and weighing 137 tons.

Hendy is especially noteworthy because it employed a substantial number of women in previously male jobs — as "Rosie the Riveters," in effect. Although no complete list of company employees currently exists, it is possible to deduce that there were, at the very least, hundreds of women workers. Old newsletters, for example, report that Hendy fielded a women's basketball team. The blade shop, which was the two hundred–person division with the largest percentage of women employees, was 60 percent female in late 1944. In a picture of a group building a generator, there are fifty people, nine of them women. It seems reasonable to infer, therefore, that if one group was 60 percent and another was 18 percent female, then at least 10 percent of 12,000 employees — or 1,200 — were women.[12] Another reason for believing that Hendy had its share of "Rosies" is that the plant manager, Charles Moore, had found ways of transmuting the work of skilled machinists into less-skilled labor. He met the critical need for person power "by combining jigs, fixtures, and specially adapted machine tools" so that highly skilled workers could establish patterns for less-seasoned hands to follow.[13]

Lola Vaughan, who went to work for Hendy in 1942 as an engraving machine operator, was proud to be a part of the war effort.[14] She arrived in the

Figure 9. Joshua Hendy Iron Works women install blades in high-pressure turbine wheels in 1945. Courtesy of the Iron Man Museum.

Valley from Nevada, not knowing whether she would take an office job or work in a plant. She opted for the latter, because she had always liked machinery. After her brother and sister got jobs with Hendy, their mother moved to the Valley, too. Because of a shortage in housing, the entire family spent a year living in a trailer in an orchard.

Vaughan and her female coworkers benefited from the first substantial opportunity outside of the canneries for women to be employed in industry. They also benefited from being union members — along with the female cannery workers — since those who worked for Hendy were represented by the International Association of Machinists.[15] According to Vaughan's testimony, the union at first resisted having the women join, but the women persevered and were eventually not only accepted but also well defended in salary negotiations. Vaughan also recalls that the men were "fantastic" about teaching the ropes to their new female coworkers.

Figure 10. Lola Vaughan, an engraving machine special machinist for Joshua Hendy Iron Works during World War II, wears the early version of the approved shop uniform for women. Courtesy of the Iron Man Museum.

With such a large workforce at one major contractor, Sunnyvale applied for and received special permission from the federal government to grant permits to build housing for defense workers. As a "national defense area," the city was entitled to receive an allocation of scarce building materials. On a former pear and apricot orchard, a San Francisco developer built 55 (of a planned-for 250) modest homes in a tract known as Victory Village. Those not lucky enough to buy in the Village were sometimes able to camp out—or perhaps park a trailer, like the Vaughan family—in a nearby orchard.[16]

The story of Hendy Iron Works and Victory Village encapsulates what many of the long-term consequences of World War II would be for the Santa Clara Valley. In the first place, orchard land was used for housing, a scenario that would be repeated again and again during the ensuing decades. In the second place, the sharp growth in the number of employees at just one defense contractor—with jobs for both men and women—was part of a larger pattern whereby the fruit industry faced stiff competition for a workforce. Henceforth, the canneries would need to cast a wider net for employees. By the same token, the earlier arrivals from southern Europe, marginalized when they first arrived, enjoyed their first large-scale employment opportunities outside the fruit industry. Indeed, partial lists of wartime employees at Hendy reveal many Italian and Portuguese surnames.

Ethnic Changes in the Workforce

The war years and the area's military build-up brought about a dramatic transformation in the ethnic composition of the fruit industry workforce. For the first time, Mexican Americans, many of whom arrived in the Valley from Texas, began to get jobs in the fruit industry on a significant scale. By 1948, Mexican Americans constituted the largest single ethnic group among cannery women workers.[17] Concurrently there was a spurt in the region's Latino population: In 1940, the San Jose city directory listed 5,337 people with Spanish surnames; in 1950, the number was 16,874.[18] These newcomers were all the likelier to work in fruit, because many of them were not U.S. citizens, hence they were not able to work in the defense industry.

Another reason for the increase in the Latino population of the Valley was the result of the 1942 *bracero* program. Under the terms of an agreement with Mexico, Mexican nationals were allowed to enter the United States as contract workers, usually for a year and usually to perform farm work during the wartime labor shortages. The federal government had pledged to guarantee decent treatment to the tens of thousands of braceros who arrived during the duration of the program, which lasted until 1965. But, in fact, the braceros often encountered low wages and harsh working conditions. Though figures for this program are elusive, we know that in a peak harvest period in August 1954, there were about one thousand braceros employed in Santa Clara County.[19]

Taken together, the new arrivals responding to opportunities in the canneries and the farm laborers arriving under the bracero program gave Santa Clara County its first substantial Mexican population in a century. As with many other groups, there were stresses and strains within this community, occasioned by its members' arrivals at many different times and in many different circumstances.[20] In fact, as had happened with the Italian immigrants to the Valley and their campanilismo, the Mexican and Mexican American newcomers organized their social worlds at first around their communities of origin, whether those be in Texas, southern or central California, or Mexico itself.[21] This organization resulted in stress among the communities. Moreover, most Mexican Americans initially opposed the bracero program, because Mexican immigrants seemed to threaten the already precarious position of Mexican Americans in California society.[22]

As the Mexican American population grew, most of the newcomers settled in the preexisting barrio in unincorporated land east of San Jose. Here they were close to the cannery and agricultural work, and here too they were able to avoid the restrictive racial covenants governing certain other neighborhoods.[23] The barrio in East San Jose was starved for municipal services. Unpaved roads, the stench of rotting fruit, the lack of adequate sewers — all of these characterized what became known as the Mayfair district. Further, as had happened to earlier Catholic immigrants, the Mexican American newcomers came to an area that at first lacked a church that specially served its residents. Mexican Americans worshiped at Five Wounds, the Portuguese parish, where they got a better reception than what they encountered at Holy Cross or Sacred Heart, the Italian parishes.[24] All the difficulties notwithstanding, however, the East San Jose barrio had the elements of a vital community-in-the-making; one capable of inspiring loyalty in its inhabitants.[25] One journalist commented about the area in 1949: "San Jose was more like a Mexican pueblo than a typical U.S.A. town."[26]

Unions and the War Years

The years in which the ethnic composition of the cannery workforce was in transition from predominantly Italian to predominantly Mexican were also years of high rank-and-file involvement with Local 20852. One of the officers later recalled about the period from 1941 to 1945: "We were very democratic in those days. . . . We had annual elections — even the business agent ran, which is very unusual. I had opposition every election. We officers made pretty much the same as the workers."[27] When looked at in detail, the contracts from those years show evidence of a union that was fighting to advance interests dear to the hearts of the female workers. For example, the union sought to guarantee to piece-rate workers that in situations when one's position on a line could confer an advantage, the workers would rotate daily.[28]

One glaring inequity, however, accepted by the union at the time but remarkable to a later age, was the wage scale for male and female jobs. In a contract that went into effect in January 1942, for example, the lowest paid male job was pegged at 77 cents an hour, while the highest female piece-rate wage possible was pegged at an audit base of 65 cents an hour. As mentioned in Chapter 2, some of the female work required considerable skill, whereas the poorly paid male jobs included such work as stacking cans — a matter of muscle rather than the kind of skill that went into cutting and grading fruit. The contracts remind us of how absolute a dichotomy there was between the jobs for men and women.

The AFL Versus the CIO

The ability to maintain any kind of democracy in the union was undercut by the national AFL, which continued to display a noticeable lack of either enthusiasm or respect for the young cannery union. What the cannery workers needed was an international charter and a measure of autonomy within the AFL. According to a scholar writing in the 1940s, "Both the leadership and the rank and file sensed what later was made plain — that control of the unions of cannery workers rested in the hands of AFL executives over whom these workers had little influence."[29] In 1940, a California delegate to the AFL national convention tried to deal with the problem by proposing to set up the National Council of Cannery Workers, thus giving the cannery unions an international charter and parity with other internationals within the AFL. He pointed out that during the previous three years, cannery unions cast in the federal charter format had paid approximately $225,000 in dues to the AFL and had gotten little in return.[30] The proposal never made it to the convention floor, however. The following year, there was a similar resolution (which met a similar fate) from another California delegate, who pointed out that food processing was the second largest industry in the state.[31] The reluctance of the national leadership to endorse such demands evidently stemmed from a desire not to offend the Teamsters, who had long had their eye on the canneries.

The first inkling that the Teamsters might actually gain control of the cannery workers came in the *Union Gazette* in March 1945. The paper announced that the Teamsters had been awarded jurisdiction over warehousemen employed in the canneries. Fairly soon thereafter, the paper reported that other cannery locals were voting to go into the Teamsters as a unit, so as to maintain the integrity of the local; in other words, all the workers, and not just the warehousemen, were going into the Teamsters. In May, the same month that the AFL granted the Teamsters jurisdiction over eighty thousand cannery workers on the West Coast, San Jose's Local 20852 voted 168 to 5 to follow this pattern and join the Teamsters as a unit.[32] That this number of voters represented a tiny fraction of cannery workers in the Valley seemed to be ignored by the AFL.

But the rival CIO union, by this time called the Food and Tobacco Workers of America (FTA) and not UCAPAWA, refused to allow this patent disregard of union democracy to go unchallenged. The FTA persuaded the regional NLRB office in San Francisco to conduct real elections, arguing that the cannery workers had been ordered into the Teamsters without being consulted. In October 1945, the CIO then won a plurality of the votes cast in a region-wide election. The AFL and the Teamsters did not give up the battle, however. In February 1946, the regional NLRB office was overruled by the Board in Washington, which decided in a split decision to hold a new election in the canneries, owing to alleged irregularities in the October election.

While this drama was unfolding, the canners were in a quandary as to which was the legal bargaining unit for their employees. In March 1946, a representative of the Teamsters group announced that unless his union had a closed shop agreement with the employers group, California Processors and Growers, "nothing will be rolling." In other words, Teamster truck drivers would effectively shut down the canneries. (Clearly, this was the muscle that made the group attractive to those who voted for it.) California Processors and Growers decided to stick with previous AFL contracts until the dispute was settled, and then the AFL won the second jurisdictional election in late August 1946.[33]

J. Paul St. Sure, the attorney for California Processors and Growers, provided a detailed account of these events in an oral history interview conducted in 1957. St. Sure recalled that several Northern California cannery locals expressed opposition to being "gobbled up by the Teamsters." The employers' group was not necessarily thrilled with the Teamsters either, he said in the following decade, but when they learned that the CIO was planning to enter the fray and ally with the anti-Teamster contingent, employers quickly cast their lot with the Teamsters. To pressure the NLRB into conducting the second set of elections, the Teamsters charged to the House of Representatives subcommittee that dealt with appropriations for the NLRB that the Board was unduly influenced by radicals.[34] The Board then caved under the pressure and ordered another election. The ensuing events are best told in St. Sure's words.

> Well, they had the second election after a good deal of maneuvering around. All during the season, from February or March of 1946 until the second election was ended in August 1946, we had a season of rather complete chaos. We had strikes in individual plants. We had reopening of plants under Teamster direction, where they brought people in to man the plants; and they ran people through the FTA-CIO picket lines. The Teamsters put in the field a very interesting group of muscle men headed by Dutch Woxberg, who rode the highways protecting the loyal members of the Teamsters union and seeing to it that their trucks went through. There was some violence. There were a number of situations in which the canners directly planned with the Teamsters for the reopening of plants where the workers had walked out.[35]

Even after the second election, there were NLRB hearings that dealt with charges of unfair labor practices that had been lodged against the canners. During one of the hearings in San Francisco, the hearing officer had to leave abruptly to go to Washington to defend himself against the charge of being a subversive. St. Sure explained: "We, by this time, were in a position where we were charging that the FTA-CIO program was a Communist-dominated program."[36] He also remembered that the canners paid for an elaborate public relations campaign to make these allegations plausible.

The long-term consequences of these developments were harsh for women workers and for the character of the local labor movement, which had accepted so unsavory a deal (though how much choice its members had is open to question, given decisions that were being made by the national AFL). After the second election, the annual election of officers ceased, and the cannery local became much less responsive to the rank and file.[37] Moreover, the rules for determining seniority during the Teamster era favored year-round male workers at the expense of seasonal women workers.[38] These local developments also coincided with the passage of the Taft-Hartley Act at the national level in 1947. Bitterly opposed by organized labor and enacted over Harry Truman's veto, the law hampered labor's ability to organize and contributed to the weakening of labor's position in the Santa Clara Valley.[39] It would not be until new legislation was on the books, Title VII of the 1964 Civil Rights Act with its remedies for sex and race discrimination, that women cannery workers could effectively fight back.

Many decades later, it is possible to understand the shabby treatment meted out to the cannery union by the AFL, not only in terms of the conservative backlash of the immediate postwar years, but also in terms of the gender issues that were involved. Mainstream labor simply did not mobilize on behalf of women workers in the same way that leaders deemed appropriate for male workers then — and this would not change for many years. Scholars who have studied the history of women workers in the 1930s and 1940s have repeatedly documented this pattern. In her examinations of the labor history of Minneapolis during the Great Depression, Elizabeth Faue contends that women workers, who participated meaningfully in labor's mobilization there throughout the 1930s, were absent from "labor's language and iconography" as well as being institutionally marginalized. Indeed, for most analysts their class identity was determined by male struggle and activity.[40] Nancy Gabin, who researched the women in the United Auto Workers during and immediately after World War II, found that even this CIO union was far from being genuinely committed to protecting the interests of its female members. She discovered that UAW locals "actively colluded with management to deny women postwar employment by entering into agreements that arbitrarily defined the sexual division of labor."[41] In this context, it is not surprising that the AFL leadership saw so little reason to look out for the interests of seasonal women workers in California's canneries.

This set of developments, which would have been unfortunate under the best of circumstances, was all the more unfortunate because it so closely followed the ethnic transformation of the workforce. Because union democracy withered so soon after Mexican American women arrived in the canneries — and because the labor movement in those years offered women few real leadership opportunities — the Chicanas who became the heart of the workforce were doubly removed from influencing a union dominated by European American men.

Changes in the Fruit Industry

There were other important developments taking place in the canning industry in those years. In the first place, increasing mechanization of the canneries led to a decline in and then the disappearance of the piece-rate system. A report written for the CIO in 1946 enumerated some of the technological changes then taking place: a better peach pitter, a better cherry pitter, automatic fillers for cans of peaches and apricots, and improvements in the canning of tomatoes.[42] As of 1937, about 85 percent of California's women cannery workers had been paid by the piece. Ten years later, contracts abolished that system, and workers began to be paid according to time.[43]

The other major fruit industry development had occurred in 1939, when it began to be possible for a cannery worker to collect unemployment insurance during the off-season.[44] This meant that the cannery jobs — unionized, protected by a seniority system — became even more attractive to potential employees, despite the failure of union democracy.

Another war-based change to the Valley's ethnic fabric and to the ethnic patterns in the fruit industry came about because of Japanese internment. Like their counterparts in other parts of the West, the war brought painful change to the Valley's Japanese Americans, many of whom were successfully farming immediately prior to the war. The 1940 census revealed that 1,152 Japanese Americans were employed in the county, with 882 in agriculture. In May 1942, they were all evacuated as per the order of the federal government. Most would not return for years. According to Timothy J. Lukes and Gary Okihiro, leading students of the Japanese in the Valley: "The Farm Security

Administration reported on April 17 that all but 190 of the 580 Japanese farms registered with that agency in the county had been taken over by non-Japanese operators."[45] Some Japanese were able to rent their properties to friends and reclaim them after the war. Nonetheless, the disruption to the lives of the internees was substantial, because members of other ethnic groups, such as Filipinos, moved into San Jose's Nihonmachi — Japantown — and Italians and Portuguese filled the positions in truck farming previously occupied by the Japanese.[46]

The War Years and Local Politics

One of the most consequential changes during the war years lay in the realm of local politics: There was a virtual coup d'état in the city council. It is not often that a watershed moment in a region's metamorphosis is as identifiable as was the election of the Progress Committee candidates to the San Jose City Council in 1944. On the eve of that election, the city was employing the same manager, Clarence Goodwin, that it had had since 1920. Frugal and careful, Goodwin had learned to accommodate himself to the local status quo, which included a small-time boss who specialized in events at the municipal level, in order to enjoy such a long tenure in office.

A new generation of civic leaders was satisfied neither with Goodwin's lack of vision about the area's potential nor with his cozy relationship with Charlie Bigley, the putative boss. Because some incumbents on the council had left to fight in the war, this particular election afforded a rare opportunity to elect a new majority all at once, and a group of young men organized successfully toward that end. Once in charge, they immediately fired Goodwin and began to implement their transformative ideas. They also fired the police chief, the fire chief, and the city engineer. A particularly noteworthy aspect of the Progress Committee's triumph is that one of its stalwarts was a lawyer named Al Ruffo, who was elected to the council in 1944 and who would later go on to serve as mayor of San Jose. Ruffo constitutes a figure whose initial electoral success is a symbol of the full integration of Italians into local affairs by midcentury. He continued to be an important player for many decades.

The political change occurred at the same time that an extraordinary growth spurt, which quickly accelerated into a flood, started in the Valley. By looking at the newsletters put out by the Santa Clara County Office of

Education, it is possible to trace the influx of newcomers. In June 1951, the superintendent noted that between 1947 and 1951 the acreage in prunes and apricots had declined 18.6 percent, or from 77,020 to 62,693. During that same period, the county schools' average daily attendance had risen by 21.1 percent. Clearly, these two statistics are related. In December 1955, the superintendent reported that the elementary school population had doubled in the preceding five years, and in November 1957, he stated that 124 new schools had opened in the county between 1950 and 1957.[47]

Dutch Hamann Takes Charge

When the city council appointed Anthony P. "Dutch" Hamann to be the city manager in 1950 (the third since Goodwin), he was an unlikely candidate to be a revolutionary figure. He was a businessman who had never before filled any government position. Forty years old when he received the city assignment, he had been a teacher and then the district manager for Chevrolet. Like Al Ruffo, he had gone to Santa Clara University—indeed, he had succeeded Ruffo as student body president in the early 1930s. So he had good connections, he was a superb salesman, he had the energy to travel to New York on a regular basis to pitch San Jose bonds to easterners, and he had strong ideas about what was good for a city and what was not. Nor was he shy about putting those ideas forward and making claims upon the entire region. The San Jose Master Plan of 1958, for example, predicted that "[i]f the present rate of growth continues, the San Jose Metropolitan Area will become one of the four or five most important areas of the West Coast. . . . Because of its prominence in the system, San Jose has accepted responsibility for the planning of the entire area."[48] As it happened, many other jurisdictions, in particular both the city of Santa Clara and the county itself, took exception to these claims, and they would do battle with San Jose over what they saw as the city's imperial ambitions during the Hamann years.

Dutch Hamann's reputation had its ups and downs. At first, he was seen as a miracle worker in San Jose, owing to the city's explosive growth during his tenure in office. As San Joseans grew fatigued from the stresses and strains occasioned by the growth, however, his political star faded, and many indicted him for the forceful annexation tactics whereby the city grew eightfold in physical size during his nineteen years in office. (His annexation team became known as the "Panzer Division.") Decades later, it is possible to offer a more balanced assessment that stresses that, above all, Hamann was a man with a metropolitan vision for San Jose and the ability to conceptualize the steps that would be required to achieve this status. According to George Starbird:

> [Hamann] said, if you wanted to grow and be able to pay the bill, you had to annex surrounding areas to the City. To do that, you couldn't sit on your hands. Pretty soon you would become like Bakersfield and St. Louis, an enclave circled by other small incorporated cities or special service districts that would tie you up forever. If you got bottled up, your tax rate would put you out of the running for new industries; they would go to Sunnyvale or Santa Clara, your assessed valuation would remain frozen. It was as bad as being hemmed in by geographical barriers, samples of which were many in all size cities. It was really just that simple.[49]

The substantial extent to which San Jose is an ethnically and culturally diverse metropolis today owes much to Hamann's vision. There have been, however and not surprisingly, costs along the way.

Another individual who arrived in San Jose at about the same time as Hamann's appointment and who had a similar vision and a similar impact on the city was Joe Ridder, whose family bought the *San Jose Mercury* in 1952. Thirty-two years old at that time, he believed as fervently in the gospel of growth as did Dutch Hamann. The claim that he said "prune trees don't buy newspapers" may be apocryphal, but the prodevelopment sentiment was surely there. Together the two men made quite a combination. What one envisioned and tried to implement, the other could — and did — campaign for in his newspaper. The regional growth would have happened without them. It had already started before them, as mentioned earlier. But we can safely conclude that because of them, the growth was speedier and more of it was funneled into the jurisdiction of San Jose per se.

Many old-timers in San Jose now think that the 4th Army, which was stationed locally during the war, played a large role in promoting the initial population growth, a deduction that seems reasonable in that the newcomers had started to arrive even before the region's economic development had gone very far. Charles Davidson, a man who came to San Jose in 1952 as a recent graduate in engineering from Oklahoma A. and M. and stayed to build some five hundred subdivisions, put it this way:

> Who's responsible for all this development? [He meant in toto and not just the portion he is personally responsible for.] Let's assume we're discussing a musical play. All the individual names that a person could come up with to explain the main action were no more than walk-on and walk-off actors. The only star was the chorus. . . . The change happened after the war. The service people had been out here, and they saw how great the Bay was, and then they just flocked here when the war ended. . . . All the ingredients for a dynamic economy were in place. I could see that right away.[50]

The newcomers were flooding into the Santa Clara Valley, and Hamann was determined that San Jose would position itself as favorably as possible to benefit from this. During his tenure, the changes can only be described as staggering. In the first place, the San Jose Chamber of Commerce spent about $1 million to attract new industry to the area, an investment that paid off and that is the subject of Chapter 4. By 1970 (one year after Hamann left office), the city had grown from 95,280 in 1950 to 445,779 in population and from 16.98 square miles to 136.7 square miles in physical size, thanks to all of the annexations (more than 1,400 between 1950 and 1970).

A city that was growing this big this fast had to build infrastructure on a massive scale, and then it had to pay for that infrastructure. Local citizens had to be convinced to vote for bond issues, of course, but these citizens and their votes were necessary without being sufficient — that is to say, state and federal money had to come into play as well, and the Valley needed help from those who knew their way around the corridors of power in Sacramento and Washington. In other words, the political will had to be mobilized on many fronts to achieve the overarching goals, and then complicated issues had to be negotiated with respect to the particulars. It also took considerable dexterity to convince residents in inhabited areas, as well as landowners of uninhabited areas, to annex to the city.

The Infrastructure

The biggest asset Hamann and his team possessed in their attempts to annex on a vast scale was the sewer system. This was an area in which San Jose was well ahead of other jurisdictions because of an outfall to the bay constructed in the 1880s to accommodate waste from canneries. According to Philip Trounstine and Terry Christensen in their book about power in San Jose: "San Jose's greatest weapon in the annexation wars was its control of the sewer system. What water was to Los Angeles, sewage was to San Jose.... San Jose used this sewage monopoly in its battles with adjacent cities and with recalcitrant landowners."[51] For example, if there was a parcel of undeveloped land that seemed ripe for new homes, San Jose could offer a developer, in addition to such enticements as lower lot sizes and less stringent construction requirements, the sewer lines he needed. The city was especially eager to annex land in outlying areas, land that was cheaper than parcels closer in, to avoid being hemmed in. So there was congruence between what Hamann was trying to achieve in terms of ever-expanding city limits and what developers wanted, which was the cheapest land possible to maximize their profits. The result was a plethora of strip annexations, which led to San Jose's map looking like a slice of Swiss cheese for many years.

If sewers provided the biggest asset in the headlong dash to expand, then schools were the biggest stumbling block. Before 1953, California law required that the boundaries of a unified school district, such as San Jose Unified, be coterminous with the city limits. Were the city to annex the territory of a hitherto rural school district for a potential housing tract, that district would disappear as a separate entity — or see an important part of its tax base "stripped" away. Not surprisingly, school administrators were not happy about this prospect and fought to defend their turf. To deal with this problem, San Jose assembly member Bruce Allen introduced and shepherded through the state legislature AB1, which made it possible for school districts to remain intact, even as their territory was being incorporated into the budding metropolis. As soon as AB1 passed, the school districts' opposition to annexation ceased, and the flood of annexations began in earnest.[52]

Thus, the price of achieving the territory of a metropolis was the institutionalization of fragmentation in the schools, which was antithetical to the potential benefits of being part of a metropolis for low-income people. In the late twentieth century, there were a staggering twenty-four separate school districts within San Jose's city limits. When the residents of the barrio in East San Jose began to be incorporated into the city and to receive the accompanying municipal services in the 1950s and 1960s — a process that was still in

Map 3. The city limits of San Jose in 1950 and in 2000, at which point both the city's population and its physical size had grown some tenfold since 1950

complete as of 2003 — they had to deal with the problems occasioned by sending their children to underfunded schools. The schools were under-funded because they had a relatively puny tax base in an area famed for gen-erating prosperity.

It must be acknowledged that there is a long history of Americans being devoted to the concept of the neighborhood school and of suburban resistance to being part of a metropolitan school system.[53] Moreover, some of the districts fighting for their lives in San Jose in the 1950s had roots going back to the nineteenth century. That said, it must be emphasized that the crazy quilt of school districts has had a most unfortunate impact, especially in East San Jose. In the first place, there are the financial considerations. As of the mid-1960s, there was a stunning disparity in the assessed valuation in back of each child among the districts that now lie wholly or in part within the city of San Jose. The poorest district was Alum Rock (on the east side), with $5,131 per child. The richest was Orchard, with $56,937.[54] Such disparities have continued to plague the area to this day, despite intermittent state pressure to bring about reform. That the industrial development in San Jose has tended to cluster along certain corridors has exacerbated this problem.

Because of the unfairness created by the fragmentation, San Jose school districts have been embroiled in unremitting conflict for the past two and a half decades. To read the San Jose Public Library's clipping files on schools is to encounter powerful evidence of de facto segregation (by district and not just by school), poorly educated students, and unhappy parents — with a predictably high number of disputes, legal and otherwise. In the mid-1970s, the Santa Clara County Board of Supervisors and the city councils of San Jose and Palo Alto commissioned a report entitled "Housing Patterns, Zoning Laws, and Segregated Schools in Santa Clara County." Dick Randall, a developer, explained to the investigators that he and his colleagues preferred to build tracts aimed at a narrow slice of the housing market and that a wide spread of prices in a subdivision would be detrimental to potential buyers. He claimed that this practice was respectful of the feelings of low-income families whose "children would probably have difficulty adjusting to the affluence evidenced by the higher income families."[55] In other words, developers — and realtors — found it useful to create very homogeneous tracts and, when combined with the multiplicity of school districts, this pattern led to profound unfairness in San Jose's schools.

Schools were the biggest barrier to expansion, but they were far from being the only one. Nor were they the only sector of local life in which a cost was paid for expansion. A special edition of the *Mercury* announced on January 19, 1958, that all the progress in the area exacted no cost: "The face of the land continued to change markedly during 1957 as Santa Clara County proceeded to overlay urbanization on the traditional base of agriculture. The trees, blossoms, and crops are still here, but so are more homes, more and better roads, more water conservation, sewerage, and drainage projects." San Jose's Master Plan of that year also reflected much optimism, among other reasons because the first wave of postwar migrants tended to be very well educated. But the growth did have a cost on the declining downtown San Jose. The Master Plan sounded a cautionary note about the condition of the city's Central Business District, which the plan piously but ineffectually pronounced, "should receive every consideration and stimulation."[56] In fact, because shopping centers were springing up like mushrooms in outlying areas, the Central Business District was a wasteland for many years, and Kenneth Jackson, in his *Crabgrass Frontier*, was able to refer to San Jose as the "nation's largest suburb."[57]

The land itself bore the brunt of the growth. Many tried to preserve at least some of the agricultural land and to slow the pace of San Jose's annexation. None fought more forcefully than Santa Clara County Planning Director Karl Belser and his allies. In 1950, Santa Clara County had adopted a new charter that created a "strong executive" and afforded the opportunity for more vigorous leadership from this level of government. The charter did not become fully operational until 1955, however, which constituted a handicap for Belser in his fight to preserve the land, because much of the damage was done by that year. Another and even larger handicap lay in the character and circumstances of the local growers' community. We have seen how little they were able to stand together during the Great Depression. Many of them had begun to uproot fruit trees even before the blandishments of city officials or developers gave them a yet stronger incentive to do so. Indeed, the incentives were quite powerful blandishments under Dutch Hamann. His team would go door-to-door, trying to locate a grower willing to sell, and then they would offer zoning that would enhance the value of the grower's land.[58] Finally, most growers were small operators whose income from fruit had always been marginal and whose investment — emotional and otherwise — was concomitantly less. It would have taken a concerted effort by a critical mass of growers to stem the tide, and this was not forthcoming. The foes of development in the Valley did manage to get the state legislature to pass a Greenbelt Law in 1955, but absent the support of a substantial number of agriculturalists, they did not succeed in their efforts to preserve much of the land for orchards.[59] One county official recalled: "You could always tell when an orchard was getting ripe for subdivision, because the prune trees would be bulldozed out and strawberries would go in. That's a quick one-season crop while you wait for a buyer with the right price."[60]

In 1958, two geographers assessed the toll on the land in this way:

> Asphalt has covered much of the best soil. Only crops producing highest returns have been able to survive. Soaring land values threaten to crowd out even those crops which grow better here than anywhere else. Soil conversion statistics indicate that 257 acres of land have been used in this county to accommodate each 1,000 of population increase.[61]

A bitter Karl Belser wrote of the suburban sprawl he had been unable to prevent: "Perhaps the only use we will ever find for the hydrogen bomb will be to erase this great mistake from the face of the earth."[62]

There was something both comic and disorienting about the pace of growth in the Santa Clara Valley. An article in the *New Yorker* in 1963 captured both qualities. The author noted that one of the most difficult jobs in San Jose was that of taxi driver, because the layout of streets changed so frequently. Indeed, the Regal Map Company, founded in 1949 to deal with the consequences of growth, adopted an unusual strategy: "To keep pace with the constantly changing face of San Jose, the company makes daily alterations in a huge, detailed map of the area." Describing San Jose's Winchester Mystery House, built by Sarah Winchester over many years as an endless construction project, the author went on to quote a local resident about the resonance between the city itself and one of its most famous structures: "We're going to keep right on building our city, expanding, pushing ahead, tearing down, putting up, regardless. Nothing can stop us!"[63]

Who Ruled in San Jose?

The years in which San Jose was evolving into a metropolis under the leadership of Dutch Hamann, aided and abetted by Joe Ridder of the *San Jose Mercury*, were also years of intense struggle in other arenas. Among the liveliest battles were those going on over water, that precious, because scarce, resource throughout the West. The resolution of water issues affords a good opportunity to discern "the power lines" in the Valley.

What Dutch Hamann was to annexation—both the architect of and the sparkplug for change—Herbert C. Jones was to water. Jones, an attorney educated at Stanford, was elected to the State Senate as a Progressive Republican from Santa Clara County in 1913. That was a fateful year in California water history. Both Los Angeles and San Francisco were providing themselves with imported water from the Owens Valley and the Hetch Hetchy Valley, respectively. Although San Jose did not have the same urgent need for imported water as did the two giants, an invention in 1913 made it easier to pump groundwater out of wells, the chief way that Santa Clara Valley growers irrigated their orchards. Before long, these pumps caused a discernible drop in the water table. Those who cared about the future of the Valley's crops realized that something would have to be done about this problem. These people turned to Herbert Jones, who was their point person in the legislature until he retired in 1933—at which time he became the counsel for a newly formed water district.[64] He was counsel until 1954, when his distant relative, legal partner, and protégé Albert Henley replaced him. The latter served until he retired in 1990. Thus the lives of these two men encapsulate most of the region's twentieth-century water history.

A succinct overview of that history leading up to the postwar era is as follows. In 1921, an engineering report indicated that the falling water table accompanied by subsidence of the land constituted a serious problem—especially for growers. The report contended that the solution was the construction of dams designed to percolate water back into the aquifer. During the mid-1920s, Valley voters turned down a plan to do this on two occasions. (In his oral history at the Bancroft Library, Jones points out that percolation was, at that time, an untested theory.) In 1929, Jones shepherded through the legislature a carefully thought out bill that set up a new type of water district and that omitted any provision for bonds, so as not to scare off voters in his home county.[65] Following the passage of the Jones Act, voters approved the setting up of the Santa Clara Valley Water Conservation District. There were a number of further developments during the 1930s—a new law in 1931 gave the SCVWCD bonding capacity, for example, and voters at first turned down and then voted for water bond issues. There was also the dawn of a new era of state responsibility for water. By the end of the decade, the new district had built six dams, with more on the drawing board.[66]

That's roughly how matters stood when the hordes of newcomers began to arrive in the Valley after 1945. The issue of how to provide water for growth was complicated by the fact that San Jose, the largest jurisdiction, was served by a private water company and that there was a profusion of different retailers in the county to go along with the wholesaling SCVWCD — whose jurisdiction was not coterminous with the county in any event (another source of complication). More and more, it was clear that water for the Valley would need to be imported, but by which jurisdiction, from whom, by which route, at whose expense, and to serve whose interests? There ensued years of infighting, bureaucratic maneuvering, and general turbulence, but in the end, many disparate interests were protected. As of 1996, 42 percent of the Valley's water came from local reservoirs, 23 percent from the federal Central Valley Project (delivery started in 1987), 19 percent from the State Water Project (delivery started in 1965), and 16 percent was purchased from San Francisco's Hetch Hetchy aqueduct. These figures alone suggest the complexity of putting all this together.

The crux of the struggle for water was between advocates of state and advocates of federal water. State water would be more quickly available and would arrive via a more northerly route, both advantageous for developers. Federal water, on the other hand, would arrive via Pacheco Pass to the south of San Jose and would take longer to obtain, but it would be especially helpful for the agricultural areas in the south county, where it might be used for percolation.[67] The eventual resolution, which took many years to hammer out, protected both sets of interests. There is now a special district, the Santa Clara Valley Water District, whose jurisdiction is coterminous with the boundaries of the county. This district sells water to all the municipalities within the county at a fixed price, irrespective of the water's origin.[68]

It is instructive to compare this metropolitan solution for the delivery of water with what happened in respect to schools. In the case of water, powerful local interests were dug in on opposite sides, thereby forcing a metropolitan resolution that could accommodate multiple interests. In the case of schools, however, most of the powerful local interests endorsed or could live with the fragmentation that ensued from the AB1 bill, which divorced school districts from political boundaries. Those most adversely affected by the fragmentation and the attendant inequalities in tax base of the twenty-four districts that came to lie wholly or in part within San Jose's city limits — that is, the poor — were not powerful.

East San Jose Barrio

But these years, years in which inequality was institutionalized in education and in which the cannery union was being swallowed up by the Teamsters, were also years that saw the dawn of truly effective political organizing in the East San Jose barrio, thus launching the process of incorporating people of color into the political mainstream. And this organizing would ultimately bring results of consequence, not only in San Jose itself but also in other parts of California. To understand how this could happen, we need first to revisit that small group of liberal intellectuals who had played an important role in the labor strife of the 1930s.

At midcentury, two of the most prominent and most valuable members of this community were Frank and Josephine Duveneck of Los Altos Hills, a small town tucked away in the foothills between Palo Alto and San Jose. During the course of their long lives (she died in 1978 at age 87, and he in 1985 at 98), the two put their energy into countless causes — from founding the country's first youth hostel in 1937, to launching a chapter of the Sierra Club, to helping Japanese Americans relocate after their release from internment, to founding a camp for inner city youngsters during the 1960s, to working with the American Friends Service Committee for many decades. In addition, before their move to Los Altos Hills, Josephine served on the Palo Alto City Council for four years in the 1920s.

In her memoir, Josephine Duveneck explains the creation of one of the most important groups with which she and Frank were affiliated. Activists in the American Friends Service Committee had become concerned about race relations during World War II, as they witnessed the many people of color arriving in California. Out of this concern, and the concern of other members of the faith community, grew councils for civic unity in a number of California cities. These councils would work on housing and social justice issues for the newcomers. Eventually, an umbrella group, the California Federation for Civic Unity, was formed to coordinate activities for the state.[69]

Into this network came Fred Ross, who had been associated with Saul Alinsky's Industrial Areas Foundation in Chicago. After Chicago, Ross had gone to Los Angeles following the Zoot Suit Riots of 1943 to organize the Mexican American community on behalf of the Alinsky group. His efforts, in conjunction with those of Angeleno Tony Rios, led to a vibrant Community

Service Organization in Los Angeles, one that soon became independent from its Chicago sponsor, and to the election of Edward Roybal to the Los Angeles City Council in 1949, the first Mexican American elected to that body since 1881.

Josephine Duveneck recalled that the Friends' Community Relations Committee had worked with the CFCU to obtain a small grant to bring Fred Ross to the Valley. They wanted Ross to organize in East San Jose, following the Los Angeles success. The most immediate catalyst to action was the 1952 flood in the East San Jose barrio. The subsequent public health problems caused by overflowing cesspools prompted a Mexican American public health nurse to spearhead a group of people to deal with the problems. Thanks to the nascent organizing of this small group, three thousand new voters were registered in the neighborhood, and the barrio began to get more attention from the authorities.[70]

During this period, Ross had a fateful encounter with Cesar Chavez, one of the towering figures in twentieth-century California. At the time, Chavez was living with his family in the East San Jose barrio. The night after their first meeting in June 1952, Ross wrote in his diary: "I think I've found the guy I'm looking for."[71] For his part, Chavez was at first reluctant to talk to Ross, because he had learned to be suspicious of Anglo social scientists with their nosy questions about life in the barrio. But when he understood what Ross had in mind, a political and civil rights organization for Mexicans and Mexican Americans, he was favorably impressed. By that time, Chavez had already been introduced to the history of farm labor organizing in California and to the philosophy of nonviolence by Father Donald McDonnell, a priest who was trying to build a parish in the barrio.[72]

There was another remarkable person organizing in East San Jose in those years, Ernesto Galarza. Born in Mexico and raised in Sacramento, Galarza had gone on to obtain a doctorate in history from Columbia University. In 1947, he decided to make his permanent home in San Jose, because he believed it to be a strategic location for reaching migrant Mexican Americans. Eager to extend the benefits of unionization to farm workers, he tried to bring them into the fold by working within the framework of the short-lived National Farm Workers Union. Galarza even tried to organize a civil rights movement for Mexicans within the AFL, although without success. His most significant ally in the Valley was Josephine Duveneck.[73]

The Community Service Organization chapter that emerged from the infusion of all this energy would play a very substantial role in East San Jose for decades. As early as 1955, for example, the group had persuaded the city of San Jose to install twenty-five streetlights in recently incorporated sections of the Mayfair district.[74] CSO activists accompanied members on visits to city and county offices, they assisted with income taxes and family immigration problems, and they helped newcomers locate work. Chavez himself left the CSO in 1962 to found the union that eventually became the United Farm Workers. Galarza, too, devoted himself to a larger stage than San Jose per se — he tried, without success, to organize farm labor in the Central Valley for a number of years.

That a new middle class was taking shape among Mexican Americans in postwar San Jose enhanced the possibilities of political organizing. By this time there were dozens of small businesses, several lawyers, and at least one realtor within the Mexican American community. The CSO was able to draw upon this new middle class, as it did, for example, in the long-term leadership of Herman Gallegos, who worked for San Jose's Department of Youth Services.[75]

There is one extant membership list for the San Jose CSO. From 1956, it contains 274 names, of which 189 appear to be female.[76] The scholar of this organization, Stephen Pitti, has found that not only did women belong and perform the labor-intensive work, but they also ran for office throughout the decade. On the other hand, these activist women, many of whom were cannery workers, seem not to have participated in the Teamsters cannery local.[77] No doubt, this was not because they were apolitical, but because meaningful participation was impossible for them at that time.

The answer to the question of who ruled in San Jose at midcentury must receive an unequivocal response: white, male developers and their allies — with some power still being exercised on behalf of agricultural interests, especially in the instance of water for the Valley. Yet Mexican Americans, including many women, were organizing to defend their interests. And by the 1960s, there was another female constituency coming into the picture: Middle-class women constituted a disproportionate share of those who were beginning to oppose the area's rapid growth.

In 1962, voters elected the first woman, and the first antigrowth activist, to the San Jose City Council, the deeply conservative Virginia Shaffer. By

1969, the antigrowth sentiment, fueled primarily by homeowners' concern about being taxed to support the growth, was strong enough to force Dutch Hamann to resign. In the 1970s, the antigrowth movement would become even stronger and much less conservative, and it would help propel Janet Gray Hayes into office as the nation's first woman mayor of a city larger than 500,000 in population, thus launching the Valley's reputation as "the feminist capital of the nation."

The Fruit Industry on the Eve of Silicon Valley

As of midcentury, in the midst of the extraordinary growth and change, it is striking to find that there seems to have been a widespread belief that the fruit industry would survive unscathed. An article in the *Saturday Evening Post* of April 13, 1946, for example, trumpets the idea that the Valley was a new type of industrial site: It was a place in which not only could orchards and industrial plants coexist, but also workers themselves could move between the two types of work. The caption for a picture of men emerging from their jobs at Joshua Hendy Iron Works proclaims: "The double life pays off here. When the employees of this engine plant in Sunnyvale, California, are not working in the shop, they are harvesting prunes, apricots, or pears on their adjoining farms."[78] In fact, the article stated that IBM had just decided to locate a plant in San Jose, attracted by the fact that there was a rural quality to the Valley with "a rosebush in every yard."

> In the past two years, twenty-eight other companies have selected Santa Clara County, for which San Jose is the seat and business Mecca, for new plants. Not all of them went around scanning for a rosebush in every yard, but all were looking for what the rosebush in every yard stands for — a chance to decentralize production in a rural atmosphere where workers own their homes or live on farms in the surrounding countryside.[79]

Although the rural atmosphere would not last into the high Silicon Valley period, one other goal in moving to the country would be realized very well. Plant owners hoped that the move would avoid labor trouble by creating factories in the country. The fact that the high-tech industry contains almost no unions is proof that this goal was realized.

Postwar Fruit Industry

There were other changes in the postwar rural scene in addition to those set in motion by the explosive growth. In the first place, the Japanese began to return to their farms in early 1945. Many landowners came back to find that their fields were full of weeds or even, in some cases, that their homes and barns had been ransacked. But most landowners were able to get back on their feet without too much difficulty. The status of those who had been tenants, however, was more problematic.[80] Nonetheless, by January 1946, the War Relocation Authority reported a total of seven thousand persons of Japanese ancestry in the county. Many in the Santa Clara Valley were initially reduced to the status of migrant laborers, but they were very substantially aided in their attempts to rebuild their lives by the combined efforts of prosperous members of the Japanese American community and the San Jose Council for Civic Unity, about which we have already learned.[81]

Another change lay in the presence of braceros. So important still was agriculture to the Valley in the 1950s that agricultural economists at Berkeley selected the county to conduct a case study of the value of the bracero program statewide. The authors found that braceros were present in each month of the year in 1954. Learning that these workers constituted only 5 percent of the Valley's seasonal labor force, they nonetheless concluded that the program did reduce the uncertainty of the labor supply.[82]

The presence of the vulnerable braceros, in turn, led to the creation of the Educational Project for Seasonal Farm Families, funded largely, it would appear from the fragmentary evidence, by the religious community. Beginning in 1956 and lasting until at least 1960, the project held summer classes for the children of migrant families, taught by a credentialed teacher operating out of a Council of Churches bus. In addition, there were adult literacy classes, one of which was conducted at the farm labor camp on the corner of Highway 9 and Homestead Road, a site that is today near the heart of Silicon Valley, inasmuch as it is very close to the main campus of Apple Computer.[83]

Particularly noteworthy about this program is the fact that its director asserted fervently in a report that if the youngsters in migrant families were below grade level in achievement, it was because of their disrupted education and not their relative lack of intelligence. What they needed were bilingual teachers, she contended. The director's attitude constituted a significant departure from previously noted opinions about the capacities of Italian immigrant youngsters some forty years earlier, and it bears witness to the impact of World War II on racial/ethnic attitudes.[84]

But in the very years in which those concerned about braceros chose to study Santa Clara County and those concerned about social justice set up educational programs for migrant workers, the balance tipped toward having an economic mainstay for the Valley other than fruit growing and processing. In 1956, for the first time since the development of the "Valley of Heart's Delight," industrial wages (other than cannery) equaled cannery.[85] In the years to come, the nonagricultural scale would weigh ever heavier.

In the 1940s and 1950s, under the joint impact of World War II and the cold war, San Jose was born as a metropolis that would eventually become an important part of the economic dynamo known as Silicon Valley. This happened because certain visionary leaders fought for the growth, because people flocked to the region after the war ended, because the war had provided the catalyst for a defense industry to take shape in the Valley, because so much technological expertise centered at Stanford (see Chapter 4), and because a number of businessmen saw the advantage of locating industrial plants in a garden spot. One wonders whether those who assumed that they could avoid labor troubles by moving to the Valley had any notion of the strife during the Great Depression under the impact of the march inland. Surely the San Jose Chamber of Commerce would not have felt it necessary to provide a history lesson. We can speculate that, if the subject came up at all, the cannery union could have been dismissed as mostly composed of women and, therefore, not very formidable.[86]

Dutch Hamann and his allies were, collectively, the midwife for the birth of the metropolis, but none of them fully grasped what it would entail, nor how much prosperity it would help generate — at the cost of the glorious landscape. (Their opponent Karl Belser, it must be said, understood how the landscape would change, but he thought that the housing tracts would quickly metamorphose into slums.) The progrowth forces displayed little sentimentality about preserving agriculture and food processing as the chief sustenance of the community, because the two industries had proven too unreliable during the 1930s. But those same forces seemed to have believed that the landscape itself could be preserved to reflect the glories of the Valley of Heart's Delight. Ironically enough, the older Valley has been so important to one of the chief catalysts of change, IBM, that as late as 1998 the firm owned an orchard across from its main plant in south San Jose where visiting dignitaries could be introduced to the splendors of local horticulture. Run by two brothers — who explain that it was kept more pristine than a real, working, for-profit fruit ranch would be — it was a kind of Potemkin orchard for the benefit of out-of-towners.[87]

Hard on the landscape but a potent force for regional prosperity, the emerging metropolis fell short of delivering its full promise. Even those who were most farseeing about the advantages of creating a community capable of being inclusive were unable to formulate their metropolitan imaginings to include the needs of schoolchildren or people of color. Yet in some ways, the expansive boundaries these leaders created for San Jose have borne fruit for Latinos, the area's largest minority group, if not for the schools attended by their children. In 1998, San Jose voters elected Ron Gonzales as mayor. The city, with a downtown that has received massive investment after decades of neglect, contains a beautiful plaza at its core — between the Tech Museum of Innovation and the Fairmont Hotel — named for Cesar Chavez. Nearby is a truly impressive monument to Ernesto Galarza. None of this would have happened without the earlier expansion that created a metropolis.

In sum, there were many gains as a consequence of this period of rapid growth. But the community that had spawned and nurtured an unlikely union of seasonal women workers, with house meetings in Goosetown and public rallies in St. James Park, had been swallowed up in the rush toward gigantism. Those who would later attempt to organize among high-tech workers would lack the compact and personalized spaces — except in the barrio — that had fostered cannery organizing. And, as we have seen, the cannery union itself had been seriously weakened as an instrument for defending the interests of women workers.

The most effective organizing among women in the high-tech era would largely come either in ethnic organization in the barrio or among the middle-class women who eventually produced "the Feminist Capital of the Nation." This organizing would be of great consequence in helping its participants lead better lives and in humanizing aspects of life in the Valley, but it would leave many working-class women, especially working-class immigrant women, vulnerable in the workplace.

Toward Silicon Valley

For several decades, the fruit industry coexisted with the dawning high-tech industry, which was, in its initial stages, fueled primarily by the defense plants that came to the area in the 1940s and 1950s. Nikita Khrushchev's visit to San Jose in the late 1950s was a symbol of that coexistence: Not only did he meet IBM CEO Thomas Watson, Jr., but he also received a gift box of Santa Clara Valley prunes. This balanced existence did not last long, however.

This chapter describes how the balance tipped decisively from fruit to chips, as well as how high tech came to focus more on goods for an industrial or a consumer market than on products for the military. The chapter also discusses the impact of these transitions on working-class women, who formed the preponderance of production workers at the bottom of the fruit job hierarchy and then of the high-tech market. Furthermore, this chapter deals with the latter-day consequences of the ease with which the local labor movement accepted the unsavory deal in which the AFL turned cannery workers over to the Teamsters. In concert with other developments that sapped the vitality of local labor, this event left high-tech production work-ers in an especially vulnerable position. Yet paradoxically, just as the fruit in-dustry was shrinking and the labor movement was showing its weakness vis-à-vis the semiconductor industry, dissident cannery workers succeeded — using Title VII of the 1964 Civil Rights Act — in forcing cannery union re-form. In short, it was a period of remarkable change.

Before the Chip: The Origins of Electronics in the Valley

As with so much that characterizes twentieth-century Northern California, the origins of electronics in the Valley can be traced back to the gold rush. That world-historical event created a powerful need for technological know-how in general and for machining in particular. Indeed, Joshua Hendy Iron Works had scored its first big success in manufacturing machinery for hy-draulic mining. One scholar referred to the Bay Area of the late nineteenth century as "an oasis of scientific technology" in which there was an early col-laboration between the electric power industry and university engineers.[1] Thus, to understand the development of high tech in the Valley, we must go back to a time before Stanford's legendary promoter of electronics growth, Frederick Terman, before William Hewlett and David Packard, and even be-fore Dutch Hamann.

In the late nineteenth century, scientific breakthroughs with radio waves were pointing the way to new applications, some of which would later prove to be of commercial and even military value. Innovation in both realms took place in the Bay Area, including the world's first ship-to-shore radio trans-mission, first commercial radio station, and first television tube.[2] The most important single breakthrough came in the years before World War I. In his Palo Alto laboratory, Lee DeForest invented the vacuum tube, a means by which electrons could be controlled in an oscillating, feedback circuit. During the war, the firm DeForest had been working for, Federal Telegraph (a firm capitalized in part by Stanford's first president, David Starr Jordan), was able to develop the first effective worldwide radio communication sys-tem for the U.S. Navy.[3] In 1919 a number of eastern firms, including General Electric, the American Marconi Company, and Westinghouse, cre-ated the Radio Corporation of America to develop the new technology, with the idea that RCA could serve as a patent pool.[4] Because DeForest had been working for Federal at the time he created his tube, however, Federal could not manufacture vacuum tubes without paying royalties to RCA — clearly an enormous advantage for the development of Bay Area electronics.[5]

In the years after World War I, a number of other electronics firms joined Federal in the Bay Area, although Federal itself left for New Jersey in 1932. (Another link with the gold rush era lies in the fact that William Crocker of the famed San Francisco financial family had helped Federal obtain capital for tube manufacture shortly before its move.) When Federal departed for the East, twenty-three-year-old Charles Litton, who had just graduated from Stanford, took over the Bay Area operation and founded what would eventually become Litton Industries.[6]

There were other important electronics firms, such as Heintz and Kaufman Company and Eimac, which manufactured shortwave radio systems for aircraft and sophisticated tubes, respectively. In those early days, there was a permeable boundary between the science and the craft of what the firms were fabricating. Some of the most valuable employees, for example, were highly skilled glassblowers who made the tubes. Gifted machinists were also in high demand. Not surprisingly, because women had historically never had access to training in these skills — since they had been discouraged from careers in science — they were not then part of the workforce, so far as can be discovered, except in a clerical capacity.

The 1930s brought the development of the television tube in Philo Farnsworth's San Francisco laboratory. Farnsworth was able to draw upon local talent for his research effort, including a Stanford graduate by the name of Russell Varian, who figures substantially in the pages to come. Engineering professor Frederick Terman often visited the lab, another indication of the importance of the Stanford connection in so much of the high-tech story. Lest it be thought that only university-trained individuals were responsible for innovation, however, it should be noted that Farnsworth himself was a self-taught inventor from Idaho.

Finally, we must note the unusual camaraderie that developed among these founding fathers of electronics in the Bay Area. A highly regarded book by AnnaLee Saxenian about the more modern period, which compares Silicon Valley and Route 128 in Boston, stresses the relatively cooperative spirit among competing firms in the former. This spirit had also been there in the earlier period — before the chip: Eager to avoid domination by RCA, the West Coast electronics firms cooperated to avoid being gobbled up, and the habit was born.[7] It should be emphasized, however, that the habit originated as a hardheaded business strategy in response to California's quasi-colonial status vis-à-vis the big players on the East Coast, and not as a matter of "mellow vibes" in the land of sunshine.

The Stanford Connection

To say that Stanford University was important to the birth of high tech in the area is both a cliché of writing about Silicon Valley and also profoundly true. But if we remember that Stanford itself, as well as its engineering program, came into being and flourished directly out of gold rush–created wealth and gold rush–created technological imperatives, we can place the truism in a meaningful context.

As was mentioned in Chapter 3, certain university leaders began to move in the direction of sponsored research in the 1930s, partly because of the financial exigencies created by the economic downturn. Prominent among those who wanted to see a rapprochement between private industry and the university were Frederick Terman and former president and Stanford alumnus in engineering Herbert Hoover. The former had witnessed the way in which industrial fellowships had enabled Cal Tech and MIT to develop their engineering programs, and in the late 1930s, Terman "became an adroit and indefatigable developer of industrial contracts . . . seeking fellowships, research support, and access to useful information but with mixed success."[8] Moreover, he was eager for this to happen because he and some of his colleagues had become convinced that the region had been too tied to agriculture and that it was necessary to diversify the economy to achieve parity with the East.[9] Then came an invention, in 1938, that precipitated many changes, including an unprecedented policy that gave the university proprietary rights in a patent to be developed by private industry: Russell and Sigurd Varian created a new and very valuable microwave tube, the klystron, and Sperry Gyroscope Company contracted to develop it.

The Varian brothers were brilliant, unconventional men who had their own, however unlikely, Stanford connection. Born in 1898, Russell had grad-

Figure 11. Sigurd Varian (above) and Russell Varian with the klystron tube in the 1940s. Photograph by Ansel Adams. Courtesy of Varian Medical Systems, Inc.

uated from Stanford in 1925 with a degree in physics. He had worked with the Humble Oil Company in Houston, as well as with Philo Farnsworth, and had already acquired a number of patents. Despite his achievements, Stanford rejected Russell in 1934 for the Ph.D. program in physics.[10] Sigurd was a pilot who, in the wake of devastating bombing raids in Spain and China, had been urging his brother to invent something that used microwaves to make it easier to detect a potential aerial attack. In the mid-1930s, the brothers were working out of the family home in Halcyon, California, some 220 miles south of Palo Alto, but found themselves frustrated by the limitations of the lab they had cobbled together.

The Varian brothers traveled to Stanford to seek help from physics professor (and old friend) William Hansen. Hansen introduced the Varians to the head of the physics department, David Webster, and both university physicists — themselves pilots — soon appreciated that the brothers might be onto something. The university gave the brothers lab space, but no salary, and agreed to contribute $100 toward supplies. The agreement was that any returns would be divided equally between the brothers and Stanford, with Hansen eventually taking a share, too. Thus was launched a venture that would eventually earn Stanford "millions in royalties plus the fringe benefits of pioneering microwave research."[11] Russell soon conceived the principle of "bunching" electrons in order to control their stream. After the team had a design to implement this principle, Sig started building the tube. Following a number of refinements in the design, Sperry Gyroscope Company signed a contract with Stanford and the Varians to patent the klystron and then to develop it. And, thus, a new era was born.

Almost simultaneously with the creation of the klystron came the creation of the single most important pioneering firm in the Valley's high-tech firmament — the Hewlett-Packard Corporation — again with material involvement from Stanford. William Hewlett and David Packard were both graduates of the university, and both had worked with Terman. By 1937, Packard had gone to work for General Electric in New York, but he missed the Bay Area. Thus he was amenable to persuasion when Terman lobbied for his return to Palo Alto to set up an electronics business with Hewlett. Terman then arranged for the new company to receive a modest start-up loan from Crocker Bank, and the two men launched Hewlett-Packard in a Palo Alto garage, with audio-oscillators as their first product.

The firm they established on a shoestring — the Packards had to live on Lucile Packard's salary at first — has gone on to be not only highly profitable but also remarkable by most corporate standards in its loyalty to its employees — though determined that workers remain outside the bounds of organized labor. In fact, Packard was prescient enough about the future of electronics and eager enough to maintain a nonunion workforce that he provided leadership for the founding of the staunchly anti-union Western Electronics Manufacturers Association in 1943, a trade organization that has evolved into a powerful player in the Valley under its current name (since the 1970s) of the American Electronics Association.

Thus, even before World War II and before the invention of the transistor, a remarkable flowering of electronics was occurring in and around Palo Alto, with Stanford faculty, especially Frederick Terman, often playing the role of midwife. The urgent need for sophisticated electronic equipment after the war broke out would, in the long run, intensify this tendency, but first a number of the key players went East to perform their war work, among them Terman and the Varians.

The Militarization of the Valley of Heart's Delight

Almost from the beginning of the agreement between Stanford and Sperry there were conflicts. The first eighteen months of the klystron work took place in a Stanford physics lab, to which Sperry personnel had also been assigned and for which Sperry was footing the bill. It was a situation made-to-order for problems:

> Long and heated negotiations between the physicists and Sperry's president and director of research eventually produced a truce between the company and the physicists, but it was short-lived. In late 1939, Sperry directed Stanford's physicists to forego research on the development of the klystron and instead to think up patentable variations on the klystron to strengthen the company's patent position.[12]

Soon the mobilization for war muted these conflicts, as there was an overriding need for all-out effort to develop the klystron's military applications.

At this juncture, the entire Stanford klystron group, including the Varians and William Hansen, departed for Sperry's new laboratory in Garden City, New York, where they worked on the tube's application in Doppler radar. But the Californians came to dislike Sperry's management style, and Russell began to dream of starting his own company, which he would run on a different set of principles.[13]

In the meantime, Terman became head of Harvard's Radiation Research Laboratory in January 1942. His wartime sojourn in Massachusetts reinforced his conviction that the future would see a huge expansion in electronics, fueled by military spending, and that Stanford should position itself to take advantage of this. After the war, he returned to Stanford as dean of engineering. Thus, he was even better able to build the alliances he had long sought. By mid-1947, the engineering school was already receiving more money from military contracts than from the university itself.[14]

But in these years of explosive postwar growth in the Valley, it was not just the initiatives of Terman and his protégés that led to a militarily based local economy. Sunnyvale's Joshua Hendy Iron Works had become one of the Valley's largest employers during the war years. When the war ended and the need for engines for Liberty ships vanished, the firm had no further purpose for being, even though it was the largest machine shop in the West. In 1947, Westinghouse acquired Hendy, at first focusing on building generators and transformers to be used in new subdivisions. But the emphasis soon shifted. In the words of a history of the Westinghouse Marine Division—as it became known:

> The secret to the division's success has been military contracts. When it was purchased, the plant had to scratch out profits by selling small-scale electrical equipment in the commercial and public utility worlds. No more. The systems that the Marine Division now sells are large in scale, technologically sophisticated, and vital to our national defense. . . . The contracts that the division works on are often worth hundreds of millions of dollars and last five years or more.[15]

The small-scale electrical equipment that the company had started with had two disadvantages for those at the Sunnyvale facility. In the first place, though manufactured there, the products had been developed in the East;

hence they did not give the California personnel a chance for much creativity or autonomy. In the second place, such equipment did not fully utilize the vast scale of the installations that had been developed for the building of two-story Liberty ship engines. Products developed in Sunnyvale for the military, however, would address both of these problems.

To get a good picture of what the Westinghouse Marine Division took on, we need look no further than a mid-1950s project. The division built a wind tunnel so that the Air Force could test the aerodynamic properties of jets and missiles. For the Tullahoma wind tunnel, "Sunnyvale built what is known as the 'world's largest machine.' Five compressors were lined up in series along a shaft the length of a football field. . . . The entire installation was so long that in setting the bearings on the shaft, the installers couldn't use a level because the earth's curvature would have introduced an error."[16]

The Struggle Over Westinghouse

Though never employing as many people as Hendy had at the height of the war effort nor as Lockheed Missiles and Space Division — soon to be the Valley's largest private employer — would during the height of the space race, this division, with its approximately three thousand employees by 1957, would nonetheless constitute an important part of the local economy. And its hourly employees' affiliation with a shifting cast of unions — the International Association of Machinists (IAM), United Electrical Workers (UE), and International Brotherhood of Electrical Workers (IBEW) among them — created a pool of relatively well-paid male workers and a few women. Lola Vaughan, for example, the former Hendy "Rosie the Riveter," continued to work for Westinghouse, but in a clerical capacity, until her retirement in 1984.

The saga of what happened with respect to organized labor at Westinghouse's Sunnyvale plant is, like the saga of the Teamsters' absorption of the cannery workers, a cautionary tale about the weakening of the American labor movement in the postwar years. During the war, the IAM (an AFL affiliate) had been the bargaining unit at Hendy. A few months after the war ended, the union struck to maintain the same take-home pay as they had had during the war.[17] When Westinghouse took over in 1947, the firm tried mightily to foster a company union, the Independent Westinghouse Workers' Union, but the National Labor Relations Board ordered an election, and the "independent" union went down to defeat, replaced by the IBEW, the IAM, and the Teamsters, which shared the jurisdiction.[18] A few months later, an arbitrator found in favor of the IAM in a dispute in which the machinists claimed that the firm was forcing employees to join the IBEW, which had originated as a relatively conservative crafts union for electricians in the construction trades.[19] In 1951, UE Local 1008 replaced the IBEW, winning an election that gave it the right to represent several hundred workers at Westinghouse, a right it subsequently lost in 1956 when defeat at the union ballot box cost it a place at the Sunnyvale plant.

Events in the Santa Clara Valley echoed struggles among these unions on the national level. Coming out of the war, the UE had been the third largest union in the CIO, with 700,000 members, about 40 percent of whom were female. As it happened, the union was also quite left-wing, containing a number of Communists.[20] The passage of the Taft-Hartley Act in 1947 put these leaders in an untenable position, because the act required the officers of all unions seeking the services of the NLRB to sign an affidavit that they were not Communists. UE leaders refused to sign, announcing that the union could protect itself from raids by other unions with the militancy of its rank and file without appealing to the NLRB. This course, however, did not appeal to the main body of the CIO leadership, which was becoming more hostile to its left-wing colleagues as the cold war heated up. In 1949–50, the CIO and the UE parted ways, and the CIO chartered a new international for electrical workers, the International Union of Electrical Workers (IUE). The UE hemorrhaged members in the late 1940s.[21] Issues of the *Union Gazette* from the 1940s show the extent to which mainstream labor treated the UE like a rogue. Despite its presence in the Westinghouse plant, for example, the UE failed to garner any mention at all in the labor newspaper. Moreover, other unions did not respect its picket lines. By the 1960s, UE Local 1008 had virtually disappeared as a force at Westinghouse. It had been weakened both by events at the national level that sapped the vitality of its parent organization and by very substantial red-baiting in the Valley itself.[22]

The tragedy for women workers in this situation — those at Westinghouse and those who would follow in the related semiconductor industry — was that the UE was one of the very few unions in the country at that time with any genuine interest in the welfare of its women members.[23] Though not necessarily enlightened in its treatment of women by present standards, it was vastly ahead of most organized labor in that it had held conferences of working women and it had taken on the issue of pay equity for its women members.[24] When the UE lost its vital presence in the Valley, women workers lost their best chance of having labor commit resources to organize them. The cannery union, as constituted under the Teamsters, had lost its grassroots energy, and the defense industry, as it developed, would be organized by much more standpat labor unions than the UE, although they did a good job of protecting their own.

The Arrival of Lockheed

The defense industry presence in the Valley would become much stronger with the arrival of Lockheed Missiles and Space. In November 1955, attracted by the proximity to Stanford University, Lockheed Aircraft purchased 275 acres of land in Sunnyvale and leased 22 additional acres in Palo Alto, choosing the Valley as the location of the new missile division that had been created two years earlier.[25] During the groundbreaking ceremonies, Lockheed's president announced that because business was taking off at so healthy a pace, the plant would be three times bigger than originally thought. Table 4.1 shows the amount of money that the military sector brought to the area.

As early as 1959, there were nearly nineteen thousand employees.[26] The Sunnyvale plant would employ about twenty-five thousand people at its peak, and it would generate a way of life for its employees and their families. This way of life was captured especially well by a Lockheed employee's son, David Beers, in his book *Blue Sky Dream*. Beers evokes memories of suburban prosperity and of sun-filled summers that were somehow darkened as he came to understand that his scientist-father was engaged in military-contract work for Lockheed so secret that the senior Beers could divulge almost nothing about it to his family.[27] Lured to the Valley in 1957 by a brochure extolling life in "the Valley of Heart's Delight," the father worked for Lockheed until the firm's post–cold war retrenchment in the early 1990s.

The elder Beers was a professional, so it is not surprising that he was able to provide the good life for his family. But even today, Lockheed's hourly workers have been able to partake in the California Dream, because they belong to the International Association of Machinists. They enjoy the benefits of union wages and job protection. Arline Smith, for example, was a divorced mother with two children when she went to work for the firm in 1960.

TABLE 4.1
Leading Military Contractors in Santa Clara County, 1977,
and Gross Output of the Electronics Complex, 1976

Company (Location)	Military Product	Prime Contracts (millions of dollars)
Lockheed (Sunnyvale)	missiles, satellites	918.6
Ford Aerospace (Sunnyvale)	radar, computers	118.8
Westinghouse (Sunnyvale)	missile propulsion	94.7
United Technologies (Sunnyvale)	missile propulsion	85.8
GTE Sylvania (Mountain View)	electronic warfare	71.8
ITEK (Sunnyvale)	electronic countermeasures	52.2
ESL, Inc. (Sunnyvale)	electronic countermeasures	46.2
Hewlett-Packard (Palo Alto, Santa Clara)	instruments, computers	37.2
Varian (Palo Alto)	electron tubes	34.0
Watkins-Johnson (Palo Alto)	electronic countermeasures	17.5
Teledyne (Palo Alto)	microwave equipment	6.3
California Microwave (Sunnyvale)	microwave equipment	6.2
TOTAL		1,489.3

Sectors of County Electronics Complex	Gross Product (millions of dollars)
1. Transport Equipment (i.e., aerospace)	2,042.5
2. Nonelectric machinery (i.e., computers)	1,516.8
3. Electrical Equipment (i.e., components and communications equipment)	498.9
4. Instruments (i.e., controls)	292.5
TOTAL	4,350.7

SOURCE: John F. Keller, *The Production Worker in Electronics: Industrialization and Labor Development in California's Santa Clara County*, Ph.D. Dissertation, University of Michigan, 1981, p. 77.

Employed first as a secretary in Palo Alto, she switched to working for maintenance as a dispatcher on trouble calls, because "it paid a lot more money." Subsequently transferring to perform the same work in Sunnyvale, she became active in her IAM local, where she served as a steward for ten years and where she won elections among a preponderantly male group of coworkers. She now says unequivocally, "Lockheed was one of the best-paying places there was, because of the union." After taking management classes for two years, she opted to stay as an hourly worker, rather than salaried, because she felt that there was more stability of employment among the ranks of the hourly. She retired comfortably in 1988, secure because she owned her own home in Sunnyvale.[28]

Elements of Smith's story were replicated in thousands of other female lives. The proportion of Lockheed's workforce that was female hovered at around 20 to 25 percent, with a low of 17.5 percent in 1972.[29] An examination of back issues of the employee newsletter, *The Lockheed Star,* during these years reveals many pictures of and stories about women performing skilled blue-collar jobs, such as that of an electrical mechanic — although it is unclear how many women held such jobs, as opposed to clerical work (which was, itself, under union contract).[30] There were even a few pictures of women scientists and engineers.

Firms devoted to working on military projects, with the benefits of cost-plus contracts, had a different corporate ethos than what would later be generated by firms in the semiconductor industry and their progeny. The evidence suggests, for example, that among military contractors, such as Lockheed, employees were far likelier to spend their careers with one employer than has been the case in high tech.[31] Moreover, high-tech firms have created a way of doing business — a mantra of "faster, cheaper, better" — that has often entailed outsourcing work to third world countries. Not so with Lockheed in the days created by cold war budgets. However repugnant a bloated military budget may be, the fact is that Fordism — here defined as the idea of paying all workers in a firm enough money so that, when generalized throughout the society, it is possible to sustain prosperity on the basis of consumer demand — never had it so good as with the firms making products for Uncle Sam. When military contractors dominated the local economy, in short, there were thousands of blue-collar jobs for both men and women that permitted a comfortable lifestyle. This possibility was enhanced by the fact that housing was much more affordable in the 1950s and 1960s than it would later become.[32]

David Beers compares high-tech firms with aerospace: "My family clung to the code of the military contractor . . . sober reliability."[33] This is in high contrast to the go-go mentality of those in high-tech jobs. The high-tech employer's tolerance for personal eccentricity if an employee is important enough and productive enough to warrant this level of consideration also differed from the more conservative aerospace industry. The special quality of "life in the fast lane" of high tech is a subject that will receive much attention in the pages to come.

One important way that defense differed from fruit industry employment, it must be emphasized, is that the former could, by law, employ only U.S. citizens. Therefore new immigrants could work in the unionized fruit industry but not in the unionized defense industry. And when the former began to dwindle in size, so too did the opportunity for union-wage jobs for new arrivals.

Before the 1950s had ended, and while the area was still the world center of fruit processing, Lockheed, Westinghouse, and the pioneering electronics firms had been joined by many other major corporations, drawn by the magnet of contracting for the government or subcontracting for aerospace.[34] Indeed, as of 1967, 60 percent of all electronics orders nationally were placed by the Pentagon or the National Aeronautics and Space Administration, with California's aerospace industry being the single largest receiver of the components.[35] IBM built a large plant in south San Jose that opened in 1958 and that would eventually employ 9,500 people.[36] GE built a nuclear division in San Jose. Sylvania located in Mountain View, as did Ford Philco. What's more, in addition to the unions at Lockheed and Westinghouse, many of these firms — although not IBM — had unionized workforces. That characteristic of the electronics industry would change, however, when semiconductors became the predominant product.[37]

Varian Associates as a Case Study of High Tech

Because Varian Associates was the first tenant of Stanford Industrial Park, because Russell Varian was a truly unusual human being who left a written record of many of his ideas, and because the archival materials bearing on the firm's history are both rich and accessible, Varian will furnish a case study of one firm's evolution from a focus on military to one on nonmilitary markets.[38] The firm's well-documented history also provides the opportunity to trace, in detail, its evolution from a small start-up to a billion-dollar business, with sales offices and manufacturing facilities in a number of foreign countries. Finally, the firm's records reveal telling insights about the presuppositions with respect to workers at the bottom of the job hierarchy, most importantly that the firm would not be unionized if leaders could help it.

After the war ended, Russell Varian returned to the Bay Area as a research associate in physics at Stanford. Upon his return, he stayed with Frank and Josephine Duveneck at Hidden Villa Ranch in Los Altos Hills, where, in his leisure hours, he threw himself into activities dear to the hearts of the Duvenecks as well to his own — the ACLU, the American Friends Service Committee, and the Sierra Club, to name a few. A socialist and an idealist, he dreamed of communal living arrangements for the employees in the firm he was hoping to found. In fact, he did not own his own home until he was fifty and had married for the second time. (He had met his second wife Dorothy on a hike, and they were married at Hidden Villa in 1947.[39])

It took a few years before all the key individuals were in the right position to found the new firm. Sig had stayed on at Sperry to oversee things there, though the Varian group had given up on a long-term relationship with Sperry after the company responded negatively to the idea of its setting up a lab in California. By 1948, Sig was back in the Bay Area, as was another of the major players, Edward Ginzton. Ginzton was both an accomplished scientist — trained in electrical engineering by Frederick Terman — and a man with a head for business. Therefore, he was essential to the brothers' plans. In 1948, however, as the father of a young family, Gintzon had taken a position in Stanford's physics department and would at first be able to serve in an advisory capacity only.

The brothers chose the name Varian Associates for their firm to suggest the kind of collegial environment they would try to create — though Russell's dream of cohousing never happened. The eight men and two women who constituted the original team in April 1948 included, among others, the two brothers, Ginzton, Dorothy Varian — Russell called her the associates' "entire overhead" — and Fred Salisbury, who was their master glassblower and machinist. At that point, their operation consisted of tube production for the military, with their first modest order of $22,000 being thrown their way by Charles Litton. They opened for business in a shabby rented building in San Carlos, about ten miles north of Palo Alto in San Mateo County. In 1966, the firm achieved its first FORTUNE 500 listing. By the time Varian celebrated its twentieth anniversary in 1968, the military end-use sales were less than 40 percent of its business — "we are major factors in tubes, instruments, vacuum equipment, digital technology, linear accelerators, industrial processing machinery, and much more" — and it had twenty-four divisions and subsidiaries operating worldwide.[40]

In early issues of the firm's newsletter, Russell articulated his goals for the type of workplace he envisioned. While working for Sperry, he and Sig had learned what not to do: "We learned that research could not be successfully run on production principles. . . . We also learned that decisions should not be made at a level in the organization above the level where the technical factors affecting the decision were understood."[41] He also felt strongly that employees had the right to know the significance of what they were doing, which meant there had to be teamwork between a scientist and his technical support. A picture from the September 1956 issue of the newsletter shows 150 employees (including a number of women) attending a bull session, which was one of the ways in which this principle was implemented. The goal was to create the optimal atmosphere for research.

Idealist though he was, Russell Varian also knew that firms need to make money. In articulating the firm's objectives, he stated that Varian would "establish and maintain facilities which will insure: a) Proper environment for research and development and b) Low-cost manufacturing of goods." Moreover, "Varian Associates wishes to become a low-cost competitive producer."[42] In fact, the tension between these two goals continues to plague the firm, with the new CEO in 1990, Tracy O'Rourke, explaining that he had been brought in because certain members of the board "felt that Varian Associates no longer could be run . . . 'somewhere between a business and a university.'"[43]

Trying to address potential conflict between the need for a creative atmosphere for science and the need to make money, Russell differentiated between "higher caliber" jobs, for which the atmosphere was critical, and those of a repetitive nature in which it was more important that a worker's output be constant.[44] For the latter, the atmosphere was less important; although to do Varian Associates justice, the firm seems to have made good faith attempts to create a decent environment for its hourly workers. Nonetheless this distinction, drawn so clearly by an idealistic dreamer decades ago, has persisted over time and has taken hold throughout the industry. Unfortunately, it has only become more pernicious over the years. It is why the high-tech industry can have the public reputation of having created one of the most freewheeling and even funky work environments known to American capitalism—often true for professionals—while using components that may sometimes be manufactured under brutally exploitative conditions at home or abroad, a fact less well known to most Americans.

What Varian Associates did *not* have to protect the integrity of a repetitive worker's job was a union. But there were a variety of other means, in addition to bull sessions, that attempted to address the situation. In the first place, the firm created a Management Advisory Board to discuss such issues as working conditions and benefits on behalf of workers. Issues of the newsletter reported the deliberations of the board and gave profiles of those serving on it. In late 1958, board member Mel Harrison, for example, an African American man, was working as an incoming inspection foreman with the Tube Manufacturing Division, and board member Becky Short, a white woman with an engineering degree, was working as an instrument field engineering export order supervisor.[45] It is hard to tell the difference between this board and a company union—which must have been what the federal government thought when it objected to the board, after which the board "quietly disappeared."[46]

The informality of companies in the early days, including in the relationships among personnel, was another means of enhancing the work environment. When Nora Farrell, the fourth woman to be hired (in November 1949) retired in 1972, for example, she evoked memories of a most unusual workplace at the time she was engaged. Being a housewife had not equipped her to work on microwave tubes, she conceded, but like other employees in those days, she became a jack-of-all-trades anyhow: "I ran the furnaces, stretched wire, made brazing rings, did all kinds of assembly work." Russ or Sig would walk out on the floor of the San Carlos facility and say, "Let's do it this way," she recalled.[47] Moreover, there were frequent picnics and parties, at which the top brass would dress up in silly costumes. But as the firm became larger and more bureaucratic, the informality and easy camaraderie necessarily dwindled. By 1965, the newsletter had become much less folksy,

reflecting the diminution of the early informality, although the firm continued to have personnel policies that encouraged its employees to feel respected.[48] Frank Jeans, an employee who had been hired in 1951, wrote to
what was by then the company magazine. In his letter, he reiterated key elements of Russell's philosophy that he found to be relevant in his 1978 job as
administrator of technical information for the Microwave Tube Division: No
job is unimportant; the division of labor should not entail isolation; there can
be a window for seeing an operation as a whole; Varian employees constitute
a community.[49]

From the earliest beginnings of the klystron, as we have seen, there had
been a special relationship between the Varians and Stanford University.
Three Stanford physicists sat on Varian's board of directors in the early
years, and many other professors held stock in the firm. The military sponsored research at the university on microwave tubes, with the faculty who
were involved then serving as consultants for Varian. Stanford graduates who
had worked on this research while enrolled at the university were subsequently able to get jobs at Varian upon completion of their degrees.[50] Thus,
as plans for Stanford Industrial Park took shape in the early-1950s, it was
only natural that Varian would be the first occupant.

Another component of Varian's relocation to Palo Alto was a change in
the federal tax code that facilitated expansion in small companies whose work
was vital to national defense. With this sort of encouragement, the company
hired a "world-class European architect" to design the campuslike facility
that would pioneer a new type of industrial architecture in the Park.[51] After
the move in 1953, an already close relationship between Varian and Stanford
became even closer.

To read the newsletters from these years is to marvel at the sheer creative
exuberance that Varian's employees manifested. They developed so many new
products that over the course of several decades only the much larger General
Electric won more awards for innovative products from *Industrial Research*
magazine.[52] There was a plethora of patents — 1,820 between 1949 and 1985.
There were also some developments that were kept as trade secrets. Thus, the
collaboration between industrial and university research bore much fruit in
inventions. In addition, these were inventions in such areas as nuclear mag-
netic resonance, which would permit Varian to move toward medical technology and away from overreliance on the military market, a cause especially

dear to Ed Ginzton's heart.[53] This abundance of new-product development also meant that after the transistor began to replace the tube in most applications, Varian was in the position to move in new directions, such as the manufacture of equipment to fabricate the semiconductors themselves.

Companies like Varian also diversified through acquisitions and overseas expansion. The first foreign operation was launched in Ontario in 1954, when the firm established Varian Canada, Ltd., as the only klystron-manufacturing company in Canada. In 1959, Varian acquired two smaller firms to consolidate its position as the world's leading manufacturer of microwave tubes. That same year, Russell Varian died of a heart attack, Ed Ginzton resigned from Stanford and took over as chairman of the board, and Ginzton's leadership provided the impetus for more diversification, more overseas expansion, and more acquisition. (Within two years, Sig, too, would be dead, killed in a plane crash in Mexico.)

What the loss of the firm's principal founder meant is difficult to state with precision. For years before the fatal heart attack, poor health had increasingly forced Russell Varian into the role of senior statesman. But he had continued to write his columns for the newsletter, articulating his views on a wide range of subjects. While he was alive, he was a guarantor of certain values. Simply put, he was sui generis — though Ed Ginzton himself was no slouch in the social conscience department. In 1963, the Sierra Club published a portfolio of photographs in honor of Russell Varian, taken by his friend Ansel Adams.[54]

With all the creativity, energy, intelligence, and business acumen the firm could muster, with all the acquisitions and expansion, there has been one persistent problem — the bottom line. Although Varian pioneered much significant technology and many of its products represent the industry standard, it has had a difficult time returning an adequate profit to its investors.[55] One aspect of the problem was summed up in a history published to commemorate the fiftieth anniversary of the firm's founding: "Over the years, losing money on a technically alluring product with too little commercial appeal would be a familiar experience for science-driven Varian."[56] Then again, the history of high tech is filled with stories of firms losing market share to those who are more ruthless competitors, if not necessarily manufacturers of better products. Because one of the characteristics of a ruthless competitor has usually been the ability to cut production costs to the bone, including by outsourcing, the logic of Varian staying in the game has been to follow the industry into offshore production in low-wage economies.

At first, the overseas operations involved plants set up in places such as Turin, Italy, where workers were likely to be treated as well as in the United States — if not better. But in 1970, Varian acquired Pulse Engineering, which manufactured transformers, among other products, with the bulk of its production taking place "just south of the U.S.-Mexico border." In other words, Pulse was running a *maquiladora*, established "to meet rising production costs which were posing problems for Pulse's U.S. operations at the time."[57] A bilingual article in a later issue of Varian's magazine explained that seven-eighths of the plant's six hundred employees were female — "women have better finger dexterity" — but that it was not a typical maquiladora, because there were opportunities for the employees to grow.[58]

It is clear that the men in charge of Varian in these years, above all Ginzton, believed in their civic responsibility. Ginzton was one of the founders of the Stanford Mid-Peninsula Urban Coalition, which was established to deal with such issues as fair housing. Varian Associates founded the Palo Alto Capital Company, the nation's second Minority Enterprise Small Business Investment Company.[59]

Varian is a firm that was launched with wonderful intentions, many of which continued to be manifest for decades and to be embodied in corporate policy (within the context of the union-free environment that evolved in the Valley's high tech). The company's resort to offshore, low-wage production, therefore, is especially telling about the imperatives of staying competitive.

With respect to its treatment of its women workers in the Valley, Varian looks much better than was typical of the industry, especially in the early days. It is impressive that housewife Nora Farrell got a job in 1949 and wound up as a jack-of-all-trades in tube manufacture. An October 1956 newsletter reported on the "Varianettes," a group that was open to all women employees. The group had seven sections, each with about twelve members. Thus we know that the firm had more than a handful of women working for it. In fact, an explicit statement of its policy in 1958, before any affirmative action mandate existed, stated that employees would be selected "without reference to age, sex, race, or creed."[60]

Although Varian has its share of relatively low-level production jobs, it has more crafts-type jobs than what is typical of the high-tech industry as a

TABLE 4.2

Occupational Distributions in Varian's Domestic
Workforce and in the Semiconductor Industry
in Santa Clara County, 1985

Occupations	Varian	Semiconductor Industry
Professional	18%	28.2%
Managerial	12%	7.3%
Clerical	15%	15.0%
Service	4%	3.5%
Production workers		46.0%
Operatives	25%	
Technicians	16%	
Crafts workers	10%	
	100%	100%

SOURCE: *Varian Associates Magazine*, March/April 1985;
Ramon Sevilla, "Employment Practices and Industrial
Restructuring: a Case Study of the Semiconductor Industry
in Silicon Valley, 1955–1991," Ph.D. Dissertation, UCLA,
1992, p. 274.

whole. Women have been hired for those jobs from early on, as the story of
Nora Farrell attests. Comparative data from 1985 are suggestive (see Table
4.2). The data are not fully comparable, inasmuch as Varian disaggregated
the "production" category. Nonetheless the data do indicate that, as the firm
that evolved into the "tool and die maker" for the semiconductor industry,
Varian has provided a workplace in which a craft tradition has been able to
survive — and in which, we have reason to believe, women have been able to
participate as well as men. Another woman profiled in the magazine, Maxine
Scheutzow, worked at Eimac as a senior tube technician, and she aspired to
become a master tube technician. In a 1973 article devoted to the survival of
crafts skills in a variety of hourly jobs, she was singled out for attention. She
ordered parts — or made them — assembled the tubes, did spot-welding, and
performed up to fourteen tests to insure proper performance.[61]

The employment of women in skilled blue-collar jobs can be contrasted with what had happened at Hendy Iron Works during World War II, when the jobs themselves were de-skilled before women and inexperienced men took them during the wartime crunch. It can also be contrasted with what would unfold in semiconductors, where "female" assembly jobs would, for the most part, be dead-end, poorly paid jobs.

Finally, it should be noted that many of these workers chose to live in San Jose. From the beginning, San Jose has been a bedroom community for aerospace and high tech, because its housing stock has tended to be less expensive than in points north. As a consequence, despite the fact that the initial technological developments centered to the north, the impact of high tech has always been felt throughout the Valley, including in San Jose. A 1962 questionnaire given to Stanford Industrial Park employees, including Varian's, brought 2,499 responses. Of those queried, 7 percent lived outside of the region between San Carlos to the north and San Jose to the south. As for the remaining 2,320 questionnaires, more than 56 percent of the respondents lived to the south. Inasmuch as Dutch Hamann's Panzer Divisions were out garnering annexations at just this juncture, more and more of these respondents over time would be living within the city limits of San Jose, whether they had originally chosen to live there or not.[62]

How Silicon Valley Got Its Name: The Birth of the Semiconductor Industry

To talk about the maturation of high tech in the place that was soon to receive the nickname of "Silicon Valley" is to talk about the substance silicon itself. The use of silicon stemmed from the 1947 invention of the transistor by William Shockley and two others at Bell Laboratories in New York. This was followed a few years later by Texas Instruments' substitution of silicon for germanium, which had been used as a semiconductor in the first transistors made at Bell, a choice subsequently endorsed by the nascent industry. In 1955, Shockley decided to set up his own firm, the Shockley Transistor Corporation, in his hometown of Palo Alto. He was able to fabricate semiconductors because a consent decree from the justice department had placed some of the technology developed by Bell Laboratories in the public domain.[63] Shockley, a famously difficult person, would soon see eight of his top people — "the traitorous eight" — leave to found their own enterprise, Fairchild. It was spin-offs from Fairchild that created Silicon Valley.[64]

To understand the production jobs, as well as the work environment, that evolved, it is necessary to grasp certain fundamentals of the semiconductor technology. It all starts with the need to get electrons to behave appropriately for a given application. To do that, the scientist or engineer must create switches, the tinier the better. Certain elements — copper oxide, germanium, silicon — have fewer free electrons than do metals but more than insulators, such as ceramics or plastics; hence these elements are "semiconductors," something that was discovered in the 1930s. The transistor developed a decade and a half later is "a three electrode device, in which a small current introduced into one electrode can control a large current between the other two electrodes, enabling the signal in the control electrode to change the silicon from insulator to conductor."[65] And a switch is born.

An integrated circuit contains several transistors, plus resistors, capacitors, and diodes, on one small portion of a silicon wafer, the portion being the "chip." Research teams at Fairchild and at Texas Instruments independently developed the integrated circuit between 1959 and 1961. The integrated circuit is fundamental to much of the technology that has been developed since, because it transmits vastly complex electrical signals in a miniaturized component. Vacuum tubes had been much bulkier, much less reliable — filaments burn out, for example — and much bigger consumers of electric power.

How, then, is a chip fabricated? Silicon has been the element of choice over the decades, partly because it is very abundant. The silicon destined for integrated circuits is made from silicon dioxide (quartz, the main component of beach sand), which is painstakingly purified and then modified with tiny amounts of a dopant to adjust its electrical properties. At this point, a single crystal lattice is grown and turned into an ingot, from which wafers are sliced with a diamond saw — ready to become chips. (Wafer fabs, as the manufacturing plants have become known, are enormously expensive to build — about $1 billion as of 2000 — because every step of the above process must be carried out in such a way as to preserve the utmost purity of the chip. The tiniest impurities will ruin a yield. Moreover, at no point is an error reversible, so mistakes are very costly, and the work environment and physical surroundings in "clean rooms" must conduce toward error-free performance.) The next step, placing the integrated circuit onto the chip, is performed by photolithography and is now automated.

What follows in the production process is what has caused so many health problems for workers, although difficulties do exist at other stages. Various hazardous materials can and have been used to etch the chip at this point and to implant more dopants. In the early days, before much was known about the occupational safety issues in the semiconductor industry, there was a rather freewheeling employment of acids, solvents, and other toxic chemicals and gases. Over the years and in response to worker activism or the threat of lawsuits, the big companies have improved their safety records in this regard. But among smaller firms, the problem is still raging — and nowhere has it entirely disappeared, as we shall learn.

Writing in 1985, a student of the industry had this to say:

> Toxic chemicals and gases are used at every step of the semiconductor manufacturing process. When silicon crystals are formed, workers add arsenic, phosphorus, and boron to liquid silicon in order to enhance its electrical conductivity. After the crystals are cut into razor-thin wafers, the wafers are cleaned in sulfuric and nitric acid and a variety of solvents, coated in "photoresist" (a light-sensitive material dissolved in solvent), and etched in hydrofluoric acid. Some of the most dangerous poison gases in industry today — arsine, phosphine, and diborane — are used as "dopants". . . . Finally, epoxies and metals are used in the bonding, soldering, and electroplating process.[66]

The final steps in the production of a component are much less fraught — though still somewhat hazardous — and much less costly. Chips receive tiny wires, bonded to them under a microscope, and then they are assembled into a component, tested, and packaged. This is the work that has so often been outsourced to third world countries, although the wafer fabs themselves, when built offshore, have typically been built in countries with well-educated workforces and stable political systems, since no company would build a billion-dollar facility in an iffy location. Fabs have also been built in areas of *this* country in which the cost of living is lower than in the Bay Area, such as rural Oregon or Albuquerque.

Intel

At this point in the story it is necessary to talk about Intel, since it was at this Fairchild spin-off that the next breakthrough — the microprocessor, or "computer on a chip"—was developed in 1971. Robert Noyce and Gordon Moore were two of the traitorous eight who had gone to Fairchild, had become dissatisfied there, and had left to found Intel in 1968, bringing in fellow scientist Andrew Grove to form the third member of the leadership group. In 1971, Intel was a relatively small firm with no military contracts (to avoid Pentagon-mandated paperwork). A Japanese calculator company requested that Intel develop a specialized component. Intel employees came up with a four-chip set that had (1) a central processing unit, (2) a memory chip for working data, (3) a read-only memory chip with the program written specifically for the calculator, and (4) a device to deal with input and output.[67] This set was a rudimentary microprocessor, and it would prove fundamental to the development of the personal computer, to say nothing of its myriad other uses. It would also be fundamental to the flip-flop in relative importance of the military market versus the consumer market for electronic components. Today, the museum at Intel's Santa Clara headquarters proudly and insistently proclaims: "We are a memory company."

Thus by 1971, the year a local journalist came up with "Silicon Valley," all the elements were in place for the subsequent explosion of entrepreneurship and inventiveness. Not only had the integrated circuit been invented, but also its more sophisticated cousin, the microprocessor, had come into play. Firms such as Varian, which were capable of manufacturing equipment for the burgeoning semiconductor industry, were in place. There was also a large pool of technically adept people, owing to the Stanford/Berkeley effect, to the presence of aerospace, and to the region's long-standing tradition of innovation in electronics.

To talk only about the outstanding success stories of such companies as Hewlett-Packard, Varian, and Intel would be to obscure how difficult and how challenging it was—and is—to launch a successful high-tech enterprise. George MacLeod, a man who was in on the ground floor of Silicon Valley but retired to grow wine grapes in Sonoma County some twenty-five years ago, shares his illuminating reminiscences. MacLeod, a 1943 Stanford graduate who then did graduate work in petroleum geology after World War II, was part of a small start-up formed to grow silicon crystals in the late 1950s. Monsanto Company, which was headquartered in St. Louis, explored buying the start-up, opted not to, but hired MacLeod to sell silicon in the territory west of the Mississippi. MacLeod made his way up the corporate ladder while selling silicon to and working with the pioneers of the semiconductor industry. In 1968, Monsanto gave him the responsibility of launching a new division to make light-emitting diodes (LEDs), now ubiquitous in various types of electronic displays, but at that time in the initial stages of development. What happened next is best told in his own words.

> I wasn't sure we could make it work, but our only chance was out here in California. I came to Cupertino with fifteen engineers to start something from scratch, and we got the operation going. I hired women as technicians and production personnel, by the way, and that really startled them in St. Louis. Before long we had two or three hundred employees in California and plants in Jakarta, Tijuana, and Malaysia.
>
> Pretty soon we're a big success in most ways. My engineers and my salesmen are telling me all the things that are going to happen with LEDs, and I'm trying to convince the corporate Monsanto people in St. Louis to have patience.
>
> These technologies take a lot longer to become profitable than anybody thinks. Even if it's the greatest thing since sliced bread, people have still got their bread knives, incandescent bulbs in this case. . . . There's a basic emotional mismatch between managers who are used to overseeing a mature product line, and those of us who are managing in a field where innovation is so constant. . . . I had a wonderful four-year run, and then they decided I was the problem.
>
> It isn't always preordained what's going to work, and you grind up managers like crazy in the process.[68]

Having been ground up, MacLeod decided to cultivate his garden, literally. He now has the satisfaction of seeing how ubiquitous light-emitting diodes are — and how profitable they are to the companies that manufacture them. All the rosy predictions of his engineers have come true.

A Triumph for Reform/The Twilight of Fruit

The Santa Clara Valley's fruit industry came out of World War II riding a wave of prosperity after the hard times of the 1930s. The best example of this is the way the working capital of the two largest firms (Calpak and Libby), their net sales, and their profits had all soared (with the net sales and profits growing by 281 percent and 398 percent, respectively) during the war years.[69] Although these figures do not represent the industry average, they do indicate how healthy the food-processing future must have looked in 1945. An immediate consequence of this growth was the further mechanization of the industry, inasmuch as firms could afford the capital investment. The good times lasted for some years: As late as 1960, there were still 215 food-processing operations in the county.[70]

The situation was mixed for the women cannery workers. On the one hand, they were frozen out of genuine influence in the Teamster-run cannery local. On the other, "By 1976 workers enjoyed cost-of-living adjustments, eleven paid holidays, and pension, medical, dental, drug, and vision plans."[71] But the benefits were much greater for the "male" jobs, which tended to be year-round. As of 1967, under the impetus of Title VII of the Civil Rights Act, jobs were no longer classified as "male" and "female" under the collective bargaining agreement, but rather as "regular" and "seasonal," with the former receiving greater benefits. Because men were the ones who disproportionately held the "regular" jobs, the "reform" had little practical value for women.[72] "No woman had as fair a shot at a good job as any man," according to an attorney involved in subsequent discrimination cases.[73]

Thanks to Patricia Zavella, an anthropologist who conducted research among Chicana cannery workers in the 1970s, we have good information about this period. Her subjects were understandably angry about the unequal treatment meted out to them by their union. Nonetheless, they had usually been able to build good lives. They were home-owners, for example — often in East San Jose — and many were saving to send their children to college, though they themselves had been lucky to finish high school.[74] Their jobs were relatively secure, and in the off-season they were able to collect unemployment benefits, which enhanced their ability to contribute to the household economy. In short, fruit industry jobs for women often helped furnish the families with stable lives — as had been the case for earlier cannery worker families of Italian immigrant background. At the same time, however, the jobs themselves tended to be "hot, heavy, dirty, hazardous, and debilitating," because of the machinery the women worked with.[75]

Concurrently with Zavella's interviews, the Chicano/a activism of the late

1960s and early 1970s, most particularly that of the United Farm Workers under the leadership of Cesar Chavez and Dolores Huerta, was energizing rank-and-file cannery workers, especially since the UFW was itself doing battle with the Teamsters over jurisdictional rights to organize farm labor. Inspired by the UFW and directly helped by the union in establishing a legal project, a dissident group, the Cannery Workers Committee (CWC), organized to combat the old guard in the San Jose cannery local.[76] (There were also other dissident caucuses organized throughout the region.) The dissidents charged the Teamsters with racial, ethnic, and sex discrimination. In 1975, with help from the Mexican American Legal Defense Fund, the dissident group brought suit against California Processors, Inc. (formerly California Processors and Growers) and the Teamsters California State Council of Cannery and Food-Processing Unions. At this juncture, the San Jose local had twelve thousand members, more than half of whom were Spanish-surnamed and 60 percent of whom were women. Yet the leadership was male and Italian-surnamed. The old guard had been able to hold onto its position year after year, because its members had scheduled elections in the off-season when men such as themselves were the most predominant in the workforce. That same year, recognizing the unfairness of the situation, Teamster president Frank Fitzsimmons ordered that the region's cannery elections be held in the peak season.

The following year, the plaintiffs won their discrimination suit (*Maria Alaniz, et al.*), with the court ordering that an affirmative action program be established within the canneries and that the invidious distinctions between regular and seasonal workers in the contracts be reduced. The most important provision was that "[w]omen and minorities were granted seniority, or bumping rights, dating back to their employment as seasonal workers rather than their admission to the full-time work force, the past practice."[77] Moreover, women were guaranteed a certain number of positions in the high-bracket jobs that had historically been male. Finally, in the elections of 1978, the CWC won six of the ten positions it sought.[78]

But the forces of union democracy were winning just as the local fruit industry was going into a precipitous decline. Indeed, by 1973 the county's orchard lands had decreased from the 1940 figure of 101,666 acres to 25,511 acres.[79] A number of other factors were also coming into play to sap the industry's vitality as well. In the first place, the national market for canned goods was diminishing as a result of the growing practice of importing fresh fruit from other countries. In the second place, Valley canners had long pumped their wastes into the bay. The environmentally conscious 1970s brought more stringent regulation of this long-established custom, which dramatically increased the canners' sewage and disposal costs. Before long, they began to relocate or close altogether.[80] By 1987, there were only eight canneries left in the county that had once contained the greatest concentration anywhere in the world.[81] In addition, the largest orchard the world had ever seen was a pale shadow of its former self. What's more, a study of the subsequent job history of a selected group of laid-off women cannery workers found that even though most found new work, it was generally at a much lower wage than the cannery work, whose entry-level wage was $7.92 in 1984.[82]

A 1984 story in the *San Jose Mercury News* proclaimed, "A multimillion-dollar high technology center is rising out of the ruins of canneries located only minutes from downtown San Jose." Five years earlier, the future had looked grim for this collection of vacant fruit facilities, the article explained, but now a $40 million project was to be built there, so the future would be bright.[83] Given that housing developments were being built on orchard land, it is surely fitting that high-tech facilities were to be built on cannery land.

The Feminization of the Semiconductor Workforce

As employment possibilities for relatively unschooled women in fruit shrank, there was something to take up the slack — and then some, though with poorer possibilities for compensation. Semiconductor production, especially assembly, began to employ vast numbers of women: The transition from tubes to transistors entailed a de-skilling and a concomitant feminization of the workforce. In the words of one student of the industry: "The most significant change in the composition of the production workforce in electronics since the 1950s has been the rise in the percentage of women employees. Census data shows [sic] that between 1950 and 1970 the ratio of men to women in production became reversed from roughly 3:1 to 2:3 (in 1960) to 1:2." And where the jobs were relatively unskilled, there was "an almost total absence of men."[84] The semiconductor jobs for unschooled women in the Valley would eventually run into the tens of thousands, thus creating a sit-

uation whereby the high-tech industry would "provide more low-status occupations to women as a group, than do non-high-tech industries."[85]

A detailed discussion of who these female workers were and what befell
attempts to organize a union among them is reserved for the next chapters.
For now, it is important to note the cramped opportunities and poor standard of living that the jobs provided for those who held them in the "adolescence" of the semiconductor industry. For example, in the period between
1974 and 1978, the starting salaries of semiconductor engineers rose 33 percent, while the entry-level wage of an assembly worker rose only 7 percent,
or from $2.80 an hour to $3.00.[86] To put this wage in perspective, these were
years in which the price of a nice tract home in Sunnyvale or San Jose was
beginning to approach $100,000, while in more expensive markets, such as
Palo Alto or the foothill communities, a home would have cost much more.
Even home ownership in the barrio would have been difficult to achieve on
this wage. Thus it is not surprising to learn that in 1974, a woman doing assembly work at the lowest wage, who was also a head of household, was able
to qualify for state Aid for Families with Dependent Children.[87] Students of
the industry have contended that the compensation for Silicon Valley electronics assembly workers has been unusually low by the standards of U.S.
manufacturing wages as a whole. Indeed, the wages have been among the
country's lowest.[88] What is clear is that the assembly wages were much lower
than the union wages that had been afforded by cannery work.

These were also years of extraordinary gender segregation in high tech
(see Table 4.3). Patricia Lamborn, a union official in Oakland, recalled a story
that encapsulates this phenomenon. Having taken an assembly job in the
1970s as part of an attempt to organize a union, she was struck by the fact that
her fellow assembly workers — all women — wore blue smocks, while the
technicians — all men — wore brown. To everyone's amazement, one of the
assembly workers was finally promoted to technician. Lamborn asked her
how she liked her new job. "It's fine, except for one thing," the woman
replied. "The jacket buttons the way a man's does." It had not occurred to
those in purchasing that there might ever be a female technician, so there was
no gender-appropriate garb when the promotion finally took place.[89]

Pat Sacco Woods, an engineer with Signetics, confirms Lamborn's recollection of pervasive sexism. She landed her first job with Signetics in 1977 as
a lowly scheduler, though she had a college degree in English. She fought

TABLE 4.3

High-Tech Employment by Sex: Production
and Services, Santa Clara County, 1980*

		Male	Female
TOTAL		61%	39%
Managers	(13%)	86	14
Professionals	(27%)	83	17
Technicians	(14%)	75	25
Sales workers	(2%)	68	32
Clerical	(15%)	20	80
Craft workers	(7%)	62	38
Operatives	(20%)	32	68
Laborers	(1%)	43	57
Service workers	(2%)	85	15

*Based on *1980 EE01 Summary Report of Selected Establish-
ments from the Technical Services Division, OSP, Equal Employment Opportunity Commission.* This table includes survey data
on SIC codes 357, 366, 367, 376 (guided missiles), 381, 382,
383, 737 (computer services), and 739 (business services).
Although the EE01 business services category in Silicon
Valley consists primarily of research and development labs,
it also includes a number of non-high-tech firms.

SOURCE: Lenny Siegel and Herb Borock, *Background Report
on Silicon Valley,* prepared for the U.S. Commission on Civil
Rights, September 1982, p. 45.

long and hard to be allowed to train as technician. When the company
started a training course, she was not encouraged to apply, and she subsequently recalled that it was only because of federal equal opportunity mandates that she finally won the right. "Eighty-eight people applied, and my
score was second!" Though she has come to love the work, she has found the
environment to be consistently hostile to female achievement.[90]

Thus, just as new public policy along with new activism were permitting
dissident women cannery workers to mount a successful challenge to rigid
gender segregation in what was, essentially, a declining industry, a new in-

dustry was taking shape in which equally rigid gender segregation was to flourish. The extent to which workers have been able to mitigate the gender segregation in high tech furnishes an important topic for further discussion in the chapters to come.

The Silicon Valley Ethos

It is not surprising that there was an élan, not to say hubris, attached to being among the creators of Silicon Valley; what they accomplished was truly remarkable, including the co-invention of the integrated circuit, the invention of the microprocessor, and the development of the personal computer at Apple, along with the commercial exploitation of these various inventions. Between 1959 and 1976, forty-five semiconductor firms were established in the country, forty of which were in the Santa Clara Valley.[91] During roughly the same period, nearly 210,000 new jobs were added to the local economy.[92] And the burst of technological energy was still going strong thirty years later. This has proven to be one of the most dynamic regional subcultures to have developed in the history of the United States.

By 1970, not only did the unique economic features of the world's high-tech Mecca emerge — the presence of a growing community of venture capitalists, for example — but so too did the special ethos that would characterize it. According to a 1985 article in the *Mercury*, Silicon Valley's denizens were "By Work Obsessed."[93] Though engineers and programmers might show up for work dressed casually, there was nothing casual about their attitude toward their jobs. Anthropologists from San Jose State University have conducted an ambitious study of the ethos as it has evolved in the 1990s and have detailed some of the current particulars: Certain companies supply catered food for employees at dinnertime, because not only do people not want to take the time to go out to a restaurant, let alone go home, they also begrudge the time to go to an in-house cafeteria, which involves the risk of losing precious moments in idle conversation; beauticians wear beepers so that they can respond as quickly as possible to their hyperbusy clients; and so on.[94] By all accounts, the thrill of being involved in developing so much innovative technology has been a narcotic of sorts. Once you're hooked, the rest of life fades into inconsequence.

Not only was there a Valley-wide spirit based on devotion to work, often at the expense of the rest of life, but there were also separate corporate subcultures at each of the major companies.[95] For example, as it is well known, Hewlett-Packard has "the H-P Way."[96] Hewlett-Packard has tried to foster loyalty in its professional employees by treating them well: granting them flexible schedules, sponsoring recreational activities, and the like. Even more fundamental to the H-P Way has been the practice of "management by walking around," which means that even the top executives have made it a practice to involve themselves in the activities and decisions of those at less-elevated levels of the corporate hierarchy, with the aim of democratizing the work environment. In his memoir, David Packard discusses Hewlett-Packard's commitment to keeping parts bins and storerooms open so as to encourage people to tinker fruitfully at home.[97]

Other firms, such as Varian, have also experimented with various means of breaking down artificial barriers among employees so as to foster both loyalty and creativity. George MacLeod recalls the Friday afternoon "show-and-tell" sessions at his Monsanto division in Cupertino, wherein all the workers were given the opportunity to quiz their bosses. "Corporate headquarters in St. Louis was deeply suspicious of us. They accused me of blurring the line between exempt [from wages and hours rules] and nonexempt workers."[98]

The H-P Way has become the stuff of local legend, and so too, has the corporate subculture of National Semiconductor, one of the many Fairchild spin-offs — but in quite a different way. National Semi employees have been known as "the animals of Silicon Valley," and the firm has been famed for its "aggressive, macho corporate style." One observer of the Valley called National Semi a "lousy" place to work, with its huge assembly building being the "closest thing in the Valley to a sweatshop." What's more, he maintains, the pressure-cooker atmosphere has led to much drug use.[99] Capitalizing on its reputation, the firm went so far as to create an "animal of the month club." In a *Mercury* feature on this club, a woman manager said that the style encouraged fist-pounding at meetings: "The culture that I'm in is very tough. The biggest sin is to show any emotion."[100]

Yet another corporate subculture has been that at Intel, where the atmosphere has been more formal than at some of the other firms. An article in the February 1993 issue of *Inteleads*, for example, proudly announced that Intel had made it into the second edition of *The 100 Best Companies to Work for in America*. Since the authors' first visit, there had been changes at Intel, the article went on to explain: The rigorous nature of the performance review had been softened, the late list that tracked employees who entered the building after 8:00 A.M. was gone, and showers had been installed for those wanting to work out. Showers have long been standard equipment at many other Valley firms, so the fact that it took until the 1990s to build them at Intel is a good indication of the fact that the latter has afforded a less relaxed workplace than most. Another idiosyncratic feature of the firm has been the attitude toward research. Although Intel spends many millions on research, it has no separate R and D laboratory. In the words of cofounder Gordon Moore:

> Intel operates on the [Robert] Noyce principle of minimum information: One guesses what the answer to a problem is and goes as far as one can in a heuristic way. If this does not solve the problem, one goes back and learns enough to try something else. Thus, rather than mount research efforts aimed at truly understanding problems and producing publishable technological solutions, Intel tries to get by with as little information as possible. . . . Intel's R & D capture rate is much higher than Fairchild's ever was.[101]

This philosophy can be contrasted with that of Varian Associates, where for many years an employee's acquisition of a patent was highly prized for its own sake, though not all of the patents resulted in a product, let alone in a money-making product.

Finally, a few firms have treated their assembly workers better than the norm. In 1980, for example, a reporter from the *San Francisco Chronicle* spent a day assembling circuit boards for Tandem in Cupertino. With about eight hundred employees, most of whom were women, the firm had built a company pool and a volleyball court. The workers had flextime, and they were allowed to chat on the job. On Friday afternoons, there was free beer and wine after work. The reporter's fellow employees assured him that Tandem was a better employer than other companies they had worked at.[102]

In her book about Silicon Valley, *Brave New Families*, sociologist Judith Stacey discusses some of the toll taken by Valley workaholism. In the divorce-happy 1970s, the Valley's divorce rate greatly exceeded the national average. Further, drug use by parents often destabilized the home environment in which children were being raised.[103] In other words, for all the Valley's thrilling achievements, there has been a human cost. But the biggest cost has been paid by the assembly workers: exposed to toxic chemicals, poorly compensated, forced to compete for housing in what would become one of the most expensive markets in the world. That the industry took shape at a time in which the local labor movement had little interest in organizing — California Teamsters cooperated with growers in an attempt to defeat the United Farm Workers; the IAM had crossed picket lines at Sunnyvale's Westinghouse; the UE had been vanquished there — meant that the workers had little or no help from the one component of the community that might have been expected to offer them support. By the time labor activists began to focus on the burgeoning semiconductor industry, the character of its workforce had evolved in such a way as to make it especially difficult to organize. To that story we now turn.

New Immigrants and Silicon Valley: Struggles, Successes, and Transformations

In 1965, the United States liberalized its immigration laws, thereby inaugurating a new era in the history of American immigration, not only to its shores, in general, but also to California, in particular. During the late twentieth century, tens of thousands of these immigrants went to the Santa Clara Valley, with San Jose's population going from 7.6 percent foreign-born to 36.8 percent foreign-born between 1970 and 2000.

As semiconductor production began to take off circa 1970, the Valley's high-tech industry recruited and employed women to fill the burgeoning number of assembly jobs. Owing to the new law, high-tech assemblers would be preponderantly immigrant women, similar to the fruit industry workers at the dawn of the twentieth century. In fact, post-1965 immigrants would constitute a new working class in the Valley, one that would face an especially tough time getting established not just because of problems in the workplace, but also because of the soaring cost of real estate soon after their arrival.

Yet it must also be understood that some of the newcomers have done very well indeed. Those who have arrived with a good education or with other resources have been able to secure professional jobs, and a handful of them have become legendary entrepreneurs, such as Jerry Yang of Yahoo and Sabeer Bhatia of Hotmail. Just as immigrant growers in the early twentieth century received credit from A. P. Giannini and his Bank of Italy, so too have immigrants many decades later been able to benefit from what we now call venture capitalists among their co-ethnics. There are even immigrant women who have enjoyed outstanding success as professionals, though not necessarily as high-tech entrepreneurs.[1] An exception to that generalization is Indian immigrant Vani Kola, founder and CEO of RightWorks Software, who in March 2000 sold half of her company for $657 million. That she was the thirty-six-year-old mother of two young children makes her story even more noteworthy.[2]

San Jose and its environs had always had an ethnically diverse population; after 1965, this characteristic became far more pronounced, and the physical manifestations of the diversity became ever more visible. When the new light-rail system opened for business in the 1990s, to cite just one example, the signage was trilingual: English, Spanish, and Vietnamese. But that is merely the tip of the iceberg. The arrival of people from so many parts of the world transformed the Valley. In 1999, the Santa Clara County Board of Supervisors commissioned a study of the needs of new immigrants, with focus groups not only in Chinese, Spanish, and Vietnamese, but also in Bosnian, Farsi, Russian, Somali, and Tagalog, among others.[3]

The questions this chapter deals with are these: How have the new arrivals coped? How have they affected the Valley? How has the nature of the local working class evolved over the years since their arrival?

The Immigration Act of 1965

A good way to begin thinking about the Valley's transformation in the late twentieth century is to focus on one Cupertino neighborhood adjacent to the intersection of Homestead Road and Wolfe Road. This area embodies many of the changes that took place.

Before the arrival of high tech and the large influx of immigrants post-1965, this land contained orchards and a packing house to prepare the fruit;

nearby residents were overwhelmingly European Americans. In 1962, seventeen families joined together to develop a 200-acre parcel of this land for industrial and commercial purposes.[4] They called the area Vallco Park. In 1965, Varian Associates announced plans for a 470-acre light industrial park in the vicinity, of which Varian would be the major tenant, an indication that Vallco Park was growing in scope. Before long, Hewlett-Packard had a facility there, too. In the 1970s, two shopping centers opened on the land, Vallco Fashion Park and Vallco Village. The latter was a typical suburban crossroads center containing a supermarket and small shops, but the former was unusual in that it contained a local history display mixed in with the department stores and assorted retail businesses. The developer, who had once grown fruit on the land, wanted to honor the orchard past, so there were various farming implements in cases, as well as substantial text discussing the evolution of the Valley of Heart's Delight. Circa 1990, outsiders bought Vallco Fashion Park and removed all the local history elements to maximize the square footage devoted to shops. Hence in the rush to develop, not only were the orchards and packing sheds gone, but so too was an exhibit commemorating the past. The "specialness" of this particular mall vanished. It was no longer a sought-out destination, because it became indistinguishable from any other mall.

Yet there is still a destination shopping center in the area. Vallco Village was bought by Peter Pau, a Hong Kong developer. Pau renamed it Cupertino Village, and as of 2000, the village contained only stores that cater to the nearby Asian-American population, though many other residents enjoy them, too. Cupertino also elected a Chinese American mayor, who oversaw a population that was nearly 25 percent Asian American. Asian American students comprised 44 percent of the population of the Cupertino Union School District, which includes not only Cupertino, but also parts of Sunnyvale, San Jose, Los Altos, Saratoga, and Santa Clara. Like its counterpart, Monterey Park, in southern California, Cupertino now bears literal signs of being a suburban Chinatown. From the outside, the supermarket in Cupertino Village looks like any other supermarket, for example, but the signage is bilingual. Moreover, an examination of what is on the shelves gives one the sense of being in Hong Kong. If someone who had been away from the Valley since 1960 returned, he or she would find not only light industry and shopping centers in place of what had once been the orchards but also a population that has dramatically changed in character. There are many more people of color, and these people of color are much less confined to various ethnic enclaves.[5]

We begin the discussion of the new immigration with a snapshot of the Valley's population in 1970, before the impact of the 1965 law was felt. By this time, the descendants of the southern Europeans who had emigrated to the Valley in the early twentieth century were well established in the community and were, for the most part, middle-class. The few thousand Asian Americans who were there in the county during the immediate postwar years had grown to 43,000 by 1970 (out of a total county population of 1,065,313).[6] As for Latinos, their numbers had been growing since World War II, with 186,525 in the county as of 1970. (There had been only about 35,000 in 1950.) In the city of San Jose lived 97,373 "persons of Spanish language or Spanish surname," 88 percent of whom were native-born, with 60 percent having been born in California. The number of African Americans was (and remains) relatively modest as a percentage of the whole — less than 5 percent of the county's population, though there has been growth here as well, if not on so dramatic a scale.

Moving forward two decades, the Latino population of 2000 was 24 percent of the county's total population and 30.2 percent of San Jose's. Of these, the overwhelming majority were of Mexican descent. What's more, by the 1980s, 35 percent of the students in San Jose Unified School District were Latino. After two decades of heightened immigration, the proportion of foreign-born among the county's Latinos had risen to 30.9 percent. And the county's Asian American population went from 43,000 in 1970 to 430,095 in 2000.[7] By anyone's standards, this represents impressive growth. How did it happen?

It can be said that the Immigration Act of 1965 was necessary but not sufficient as an explanation for the change. Silicon Valley, with its tens of thousands of new jobs, exerted a pull. And thanks to the legislation, it was possible for tens of thousands of those previously unable to immigrate to come to the United States to fill the need for workers.

The 1965 law, enacted in a Congress as liberal as any since the days of the New Deal, represents one of the truly significant legacies of Lyndon Johnson's presidency. But even before its passage, immigration and naturalization policy had begun to change from the 1920s-era status quo. The

McCarran-Walter Act of 1952 reaffirmed the concept of quotas based on national origin, as in the Immigration Act of 1924, *but* it abolished the total exclusion of immigrants from Asian nations, and it eliminated the category of "aliens ineligible for citizenship," whereby those from Asia could not become naturalized citizens. Finally, the McCarran-Walter Act established a system of preferences for visa assignment based on desirable professional expertise, which was the origin of the H-1B visa so much in the news during the early twenty-first century.[8]

All the evidence indicates that the architects of the 1965 law did not foresee the extent of the change that they would be making possible when they set out to revise McCarran-Walter. Ever since the passage of the McCarran-Walter Act, grassroots organizations had been working to revise its provisions.[9] Moreover, a number of leaders, including John F. Kennedy and Lyndon Johnson, had been calling for the elimination of immigration based on national quotas, arguing that this system was an embarrassing anachronism. The new law established much less discriminatory grounds for entrance. Significantly, it demoted job skill in favor of family preference as a reason for permitting entry, the provision that would be so consequential in bringing newcomers here.[10] Yet job skills have continued to play a role. In 1990, Congress passed a revised immigration statute that nearly tripled — from 54,000 to 140,000 — the number of H-1B visas granted on the basis of professional skills. Most Valley high-tech leaders are outspoken advocates of even more liberal policies with respect to the entry of foreign-born scientists and engineers under the H-1B visa.[11]

Although the 1965 law and various later revisions in the 1970s capped the total number of people allowed in (even for people coming from countries in the Western Hemisphere), family unification provided a reason to up the total of those coming in legally — as would the entry of political refugees.[12] Because Asian Americans were less than 1 percent of the American population in 1960, no one anticipated the way family networks would take shape to produce an Asian chain migration. Nor did anyone predict the arrival of tens of thousands of political refugees from Southeast Asia. Latinos, too, benefited from the family preference provision of the Act. Another factor that played a role in bringing immigrants from Mexico to the Valley was the bracero program. During its years of operation (from 1942 to 1965), the program brought hundreds of thousands of Mexican sojourners to agricultural areas of California. Those who came to San Jose and its environs would have found a barrio with growing vitality and, therefore, would have felt at home in East San Jose. Many former braceros came back to San Jose, whether legally or illegally, to make permanent homes.

Thus during the same years, roughly speaking, in which forty new semi-conductor firms were launched in the Valley and 210,000 jobs added, the size of the Asian American and Latino populations exploded. Most of the new-comers arrived in serious need of a job and in a poor position to bargain for advantageous wages or working conditions.

Newcomers to Silicon Valley

We can examine the newcomers to the Valley through the lens of gender and national origin. All immigrants had to make multiple adjustments to their new home, but women, in particular, were faced with a special set of cir-cumstances that would shape their attitudes toward their new homes. Happily, there is now a growing scholarly literature that focuses on immi-grant women's unique experiences, hence much more is understood about them than even ten or fifteen years ago.

In the first place, for many women, the ability to acquire more modern domestic implements than what they had known in their homelands has been a real blessing. Appliances such as washing machines, which genera-tions of American women other than the poorest of the poor have come to take for granted, can seem like a revelation to a newcomer; they can make her feel validated about a decision to immigrate.[13] A man, on the other hand, may be focused on what he has lost, and thus may have a more negative at-titude toward the change than does his wife.

In the second place, married women who immigrate as part of a family group, especially if they become wage-earners for the first time when arriv-ing in the United States, may find that they have more influence in the household than what they had in the old country. Having said that, it must also be acknowledged that this is one of the most hotly debated issues among scholars. One literature emphasizes "not the liberating consequences of mi-gration for women but the disadvantaged status held by many immigrant women within the majority society. Terms such as *multiple jeopardy* and *triple oppression* increasingly dominate discussion."[14] Another group of scholars focuses on the opportunities for women to have more intrafamily influence. Moreover, one literature sees family solidarity as a resource for immigrant women; another sees it as a source of oppression. What all scholars agree on is this: Migration is a profoundly gendered experience, a phenomenon that had been all but ignored even in the first wave of feminist scholarship. Scholars also agree that whatever the intrafamily dynamics may be, the high-tech jobs so often filled by the newcomer women have left them wide open for exploitation.

A scholar of female migration, Donna Gabaccia, provides the following schema to classify immigrant women:

1. Women who come as political refugees — they may be part of a family, but not necessarily.
2. Women who come with their husbands.
3. Women who come to be reunited with husbands who had migrated earlier.
4. Women who come without a nuclear family to be wage-earners themselves.[15]

All of these categories have been represented among San Jose's new immigrants, but the first three have been numerically most significant. There is also another category in the Valley at the dawn of the twenty-first century: women in the Chinese immigrant community whose husbands travel constantly in pursuit of global business interests, thus necessitating that a wife raise the family almost on her own.[16]

Unfortunately, we do not yet have the kind of fine-grained analysis for any of the Valley's recent immigrants that would permit confident generalizations about most family issues, though Vietnamese and Mexican American women in other locales have been studied by anthropologists. What we know most is information about their experiences in the workplace.

Then there is the issue of national origin. Most of the immigration has been from Asia and Latin America, but there is one group of European immigrants, the Portuguese (especially from the Azores), that has had a significant presence in high-tech production work. After the elimination of the quota system based on national origin in 1965, the Portuguese immigration for the country as a whole rose from about three thousand a year in the early

1960s to nearly twelve thousand a year in the succeeding decade.[17] The San Jose/Santa Clara area is one of the best-established Portuguese communities in the country, with nearly thirty-eight thousand living in the county in 1990. As of 1999, about ninety thousand Portuguese Americans lived in the Bay Area, out of about one million in California. This gave the state the largest concentration of Portuguese immigrants anywhere in the world.[18] In the Valley, there is a Portuguese American Chamber of Commerce, a Portuguese American exhibition at the San Jose Historical Museum, and a vibrant community around San Jose's Five Wounds Catholic Church.

Nonetheless, these immigrants, like many other new immigrants, have been vulnerable to exploitation. Dee McCrorey, a high-tech trainer in the Valley for many years, tells about an experience she had while employed with a start-up, a situation in which a company often tries to cut corners as vigorously as possible. McCrorey was working with a crew that was entirely composed of Portuguese immigrant women, none of whom spoke English. As it happens, she herself had studied Portuguese and was able to communicate with them. She noticed that they did not regularly change the gloves they wore to protect themselves from toxic chemicals, a procedure that should be a daily routine. Inquiring of one woman why she kept wearing the same gloves day after day, she was told that the boss had promised a bonus to those who could keep their gloves for six months.[19] Needless to say, this violated every bit of knowledge — not to say common sense — that has been garnered about how to protect the safety and health of workers. The fact that it happened during the 1990s, at a time when the knowledge about hazards in the industry was readily available, is even more shocking.

This episode illustrates several important points. The first is the fact that even those coming to an ethnic community as well established as that of the local Portuguese Americans could face shabby treatment in the workplace. Secondly, the work group was composed of one immigrant group. Many scholars have documented the pattern of ethnic concentration among the Valley's high-tech workers. Says the urbanist Ramon Sevilla:

> The ethnic concentration of production workers in companies arose then as a combination of initial supply conditions (which provided a low cost and docile pool of labor) and from the perceived benefits of employing these workers. The initial core of workers in turn resulted in "chain hiring" (through referrals) along ethnic and kinship lines.[20]

Employers have found such ethnic concentration to be useful, not only in terms of procuring workers in the first instance, but also because the more senior members of a group usually function as guarantors of the good behavior of more recent hires. This would be especially important should a firm be defending itself against an attempt to organize a union.[21]

The three groups that have been numerically most significant as production workers in the Valley's high-tech industry have been Latinas (by no means uniformly immigrant in origin), Vietnamese, and Filipinas — although the first-named are less numerous than they were in the early stages of the industry. Most long-term observers of the industry believe that employers have tried to hire workers who would have no reason to feel attached either to organized labor or to militant social movements. There apparently came a point at which Latinas moved into this invidious category, to their detriment in being hired in electronics. We can infer that this probably coincided with growing support among Mexican American women in the 1970s for the United Farm Workers and the Cannery Workers Committee. Hence workers drawn from the ranks of Mexican American women were less appealing to employers. Occupation health physician Dr. Joseph LaDou has been a close student of the industry for thirty years, and has a vivid memory of the nature of his practice suddenly shifting about that time, and he saw far fewer Latinas and far more Asian Americans.[22]

Thanks to Patricia Zavella's 1970s research on cannery workers, we know that Mexican American women in this industry were able to build stable lives. Those in high tech, on the other hand, have had a tougher time. At no time have the Valley's Latino residents been well served by the public school system, as we have seen, and this has dampened their chances of securing electronics employment beyond the least skilled. Indeed, as of 1999, only 56 percent of the Valley's Latinos graduated from high school.[23] Further, as new immigrants come in, they typically arrive with only an eighth-grade education.[24] The largest component of the Valley's population other than European Americans, Latinos have clearly benefited the least in the transition from fruit to electronics as the mainstay of the local economy. Indeed, one scholar who studied a group of Mexican immigrant women in the late 1980s in an unnamed Bay Area community found that domestic work was an especially significant source of employment for them, rather than jobs in the nearby high-tech industry.[25] Other work-life trajectories for this population might be restaurant work to hotel work to hospital work, each job requiring slightly more English and of-

fering slightly better wages.[26] Latinas are represented in the high-tech industry, but not in proportion to their significance in the population. Nor do they
fill many of the jobs that possess a chance for advancement.

John Keller, a scholar who studied the semiconductor industry in the 1970s
and who worked at Fairchild himself, conducted interviews with his coworkers. These interviews provided valuable information about various ethnic
groups then working for that pioneering company, including Latinas at a time
when there were still a reasonable number of them working in the industry.
There were seventeen Latinos/as in Keller's sample, nine from California and
three from other southwestern states. Of the remaining five, two were from
Mexico, two from Cuba, and one from Honduras. The American-born
women in his sample were typically from farmworker families and were typically performing assembly jobs. At the time that Keller was working on his
study, other researchers were learning that even though the sex ratio among
Mexican immigrants was more or less even, there was a preponderance of
women (67 percent) from Central and South America. This was echoed by a
figure of 62 percent female for the first-generation Latinos, other than
Mexican, in the county.[27] That is to say, of the immigrants from south of the
border, only those from Mexico arrived in relatively even numbers of men
and women. We can thus infer that many Central Americans came as single
women explicitly to be wage earners. In more recent years, a number of
Mexican women have immigrated by themselves, but they have done so to re-
unite with their husbands who had preceded them to the United States.[28]

As for Asians, thousands have come to the Valley from China, Hong
Kong, and Taiwan. As of 2000, there were 115,781 Chinese Americans living in Santa Clara County. The recent arrivals constitute a group that is better educated than the average U.S. citizen, let alone the pool of their fellow
immigrants: "[I]n Santa Clara County, 1990 census data indicate that 20 percent of the Chinese immigrants from China, 28 percent from Hong Kong,
and 38 percent from Taiwan have degrees from graduate schools as compared to the 7 percent of the general U.S. population."[29] Clearly, this educational level explains why so many have done so well in high tech. A recent
development is the pattern whereby men, who are used to being part of the
power elite in Taiwan, go back to that island when they bump into a glass
ceiling here. They usually then leave their families in the Valley so that the
children can get an American education. Worth noting is the fact that some

observers believe that Taiwanese women find it easier to adapt to the United States than do their mates: "Because of their subordinate role in the family, Chinese women have a rebelliousness that suits the American temperament," says one Taiwanese American woman.[30]

Another group that is significantly represented in the Valley consists of those from India. As of 1990, there were 28,520 Indians in the region's work-force, 98 percent of whom were immigrants.[31] This group's importance to high tech continues to grow, as do its numbers in the general population. As of 2000, many well-educated immigrant wives of high-powered Indian men found themselves consigned to unemployment due to the requirements of U.S. immigration law governing those who come in as spouses of people with H-1B visas. In consequence, these women have formed support groups: "Lacking work visas, the Indian spouses of high-tech employees in Silicon Valley band together for support in adapting to more dependent roles."[32] At home in India they may have been doctors, lawyers, and computer scientists. In the Valley, many function as 1950s housewives.

The Vietnamese and Filipino Communities

Other Asian Americans, especially Vietnamese and Filipinos, now comprise the largest single component of assembly workers. Over the course of the twenty-five or so years since the fall of Saigon, the Santa Clara Valley has become one of the country's most important receivers of Vietnamese immigrants, with the third largest concentration of Indochinese refugees (behind Los Angeles and Orange Counties) living there. As of 1993, there were an estimated 66,029 Vietnamese living in Santa Clara County.[33] This is a group about whom it is difficult to generalize. On the one hand, as political refugees, they have received special assistance and special access to a number of programs. On the other hand, as displaced people, they have had to struggle to reconstitute family lives in a very different environment from the one in their home country. Many have the benefit of an education from home that is not always available to immigrants from poor countries, but they also have to deal with the pain of not being able to secure employment in the same fields they occupied in their homeland without massive additional training.[34] One scholar has referred to their circumstances as "a high-demand, low-control situation that fully tests the refugee's emotional resilience and coping resources and produces severe psychological distress even among the best prepared and even under the most receptive of circumstances."[35] Some have succumbed to the pressure, and the Valley has seen Vietnamese gangs, Vietnamese on welfare, and Vietnamese preying on their co-ethnics in crimes of breaking and entering.[36]

These hardships notwithstanding, by the mid-1980s there were beginning to be success stories among the Valley's Vietnamese: twenty-six medical doctors, seventeen dentists, five lawyers, fifteen full-time real estate agents, sixteen accountants, twenty-four insurance agents, more than two hundred engineers, and nearly three hundred restaurant and small-businesses owners. By 1980, the entrepreneurial activities on the periphery of downtown had become so dense that Vietnamese immigrants have been widely credited with making a material contribution to the rebirth of San Jose's downtown.[37] As of 2000, many Vietnamese immigrants also owned shops that they ran out of homes in East San Jose, a strategy that enhances the possibility of entrepreneurial activity for them and for other immigrants.[38] (The zoning regulations in that area are more relaxed than in other parts of the city.) Moreover, a December 1994 in the *San Jose Mercury-News'* Sunday supplement was devoted to the Valley's Vietnamese Americans. It included success stories about college professors, policemen, a bond salesman, and the editor of a gay-interest publication. In short, the diversity of occupation and the success stories for Vietnamese Americans continue to multiply.

Although there are a surprising number of success stories for the Vietnamese, given the trauma that precipitated their arrival in the United States, most have wound up with low-level jobs in high tech. As of the mid-1980s, it was estimated that the industry had more than two thousand electronics technicians, more than three thousand support services workers, and more than five thousand production workers of Vietnamese descent. Here again one finds the phenomenon of ethnic enclaves. In 1984, for example, there were four thousand Vietnamese Americans employed at Hewlett-Packard.[39]

The Valley's Vietnamese tend to be on the conservative side, as manifested in their political affiliation after they achieve citizenship.[40] One can infer that this conservative character has made them especially attractive to semiconductor employers. All the union organizers interviewed stressed that high-tech personnel policies and practices have been refined to an art form so as to produce a workforce that is least likely to succumb to the blandishments of an organizer. Hence it is unlikely that the political cast of this community escaped notice in Human Resources offices, which has no doubt contributed to their attractiveness as employees.

Members of the Vietnamese community have not only demonstrated tenacity in trying to get a toehold on the ladder of success in the Valley; they have also employed noteworthy strategies. One woman told a San Jose State University anthropologist that she was able to buy a house in the Valley's high-flying real estate market, because relatives all over the world helped her out.[41] Conversations with people in a variety of upscale suburban Valley neighborhoods have produced stories about nearby homes occupied by several Vietnamese families at once as a means of pooling resources. Actually, the squeezing in of two or more families into a space built for one has been a time-honored immigrant coping mechanism, going back to before the tenement. What's new in this situation is a pricey suburban dream home as the venue.[42]

Like the Latinos, the Filipinos represent a group with a long history in the Valley whose numbers have grown substantially in the postwar world. As of 1970, there were 6,314 Filipino Americans in the county, of whom about half were foreign-born. In 2000, there were 76,060. Like other Asian immigrants, Filipinas have been favored employees in high tech. They have been especially prominent in the workforces of National Semiconductor and Advanced Micro Devices. Indeed, as of 1984, the two thousand Filipinos/as employed at the former accounted for about 25 percent of National Semi's total workforce in the Valley.[43]

A 1977 study done in Mountain View gives particulars of the Filipino American population at that juncture. In the first place, more than 80 percent of the city's Filipinos had moved there since 1970. Strikingly, 77 percent were immigrants to the United States, but more than half were citizens — in other words, this is a group that sought and achieved citizenship at a remarkable rate. Eighty-nine percent were Roman Catholic, and about 40 percent worked as assemblers in high tech.[44]

One informant for this study explained that Filipino Americans, many of whom come from extremely poor rural areas, are handicapped by the strong imperative to send money to needy relatives still living in the Philippines. This hampers their ability to maximize their education in the United States.[45] This is a pattern common among many groups of immigrants, but it seems to be the most prevalent among Filipino Americans.

In contrast to the stereotype of Latinas as potential "troublemakers," there is abundant evidence of invidious stereotypes going in the other direction in respect to Asian American women. In the words of one woman worker:

> At my company, most of the assemblers are Asian American women. Since the company thinks that we are least likely to cause any problems, they favor us for these do-nothing assembly jobs. However, being silent and invisible has its problems. At my company, even though we are the largest group of workers, we have the least say. Whenever the managers want any worker input, they go to Asian men to get the Asians' input and to white women to get the women's input. In this way, we are never consulted and always ignored.[46]

Another woman, a Filipina, stated: "[Being Asian American] really helps when you look for a job. Just because you are Asian American, the managers automatically think that you will be a very diligent worker and that you will not cause any trouble."[47]

Managers have voiced feelings that confirm the reality of these women's perceptions. One administrator told the social scientist Karen Hossfeld: "Asian women are more subservient than American females. If I refer to them as 'girls,' it's because to me they act like girls: They only speak when they are spoken to, do exactly as they are told, and so forth. So I play into it—I treat them firmly, like a father figure."[48] Another manager said, "The blacks had their Black Power and the Mexicans with the Chavez thing. The Asians just work hard and don't rock the boat or go against the business or government or anything."[49]

Thus, a quirk of history produced an abundant workforce at just the right historical moment for high-tech employers in search of diligent and compliant employees. As one manager told Hossfeld, the employee qualifications most in demand for production work were "small, foreign, and female."[50]

The High-Tech Jobs They Have Filled

Some of the Asian American newcomers have become high-tech entrepreneurs, especially in recent years, just as a handful of earlier immigrants had done in the fruit industry. There is evidence that one reason for the high-tech entrepreneurship has been a glass ceiling for Asian American professionals, based on a presumed (by some non-Asians) inability for them to be managers. If Asian Americans want to move up in the industry, then starting their own firms affords the surest opportunity.[51]

In the go-go entrepreneurial climate of the late 1990s, some Asian immigrants became very successful indeed, such as Yang and Bhatia. The latter spoke at a Stanford University conference entitled "Silicon Valley as a Center of Innovation" in June 1999. He described the way he and his colleagues secured capital, established an innovative company, and were subsequently bought out by Microsoft within less than three years. One gauge of the Hotmail success lies in the fact that the firm paid stock options to one of its initial employees, a young man who had just graduated from high school and worked three months in the summer. He subsequently cashed the options in for $250,000!

As the success of Yang and Bhatia indicates, the favored countries of origin for Asian entrepreneurs have been Taiwan, China, and India. As of 1998, Chinese and Indian engineers were running one-quarter of Silicon Valley's high-tech businesses. What's more, in that year, their companies collectively accounted for more than $16.8 billion in sales and more than 58,000 jobs.[52] The trend through 2000 was toward increasing numbers of Chinese and Indian entrepreneurs: 13 percent of startups between 1980 and 1984, but 29 percent between 1995 and 1998. A smaller number of Vietnamese immigrants have become entrepreneurs, in part because these refugees received a powerful message from their parents about the necessity to play it safe.[53] Indications are, however, that this is about to change: Second-generation Vietnamese immigrants have begun to construct "angel" networks to put together capital for their co-ethnics to launch start-ups.[54]

A number of Asian immigrants are working as professionals in the high-tech industry. For example, a recent study found that immigrants (about two-thirds of whom were Asian) account for one-third of the Valley's scientific and engineering workforce.[55] In concert with the entrepreneurs, these immigrant successes have created a dense network of social and work-related organizations that link capital and expertise among the countries of origin and Silicon Valley. Indeed, Chinese Americans have coined the term "astronaut" to characterize those among them who are so high-flying that they constantly travel between Asia and Silicon Valley.[56] The preponderance of the professionals in this instance are Chinese or Indian (as of this writing there is an Indian Business and Professional Women's group), but there are also formal or informal networks among the region's engineers from Iran, Korea, Japan, France, the Philippines, Israel, and Singapore.[57] As of 1997, there was also an *Asociacion de Profesionistas Mexicanos en Silicon Valley.*[58]

In general, immigrants from regions other than Asia have not enjoyed as much professional success. Within the high-tech realm, there is widespread inequity based on race, with deleterious effects on immigrants other than those from Asia. In 1999, Jesse Jackson announced an initiative to bring more people of color into decision-making roles at Silicon Valley firms. Toward that end, the Rainbow Coalition purchased stock in fifty firms. Prior to that, of the 384 directors on the boards of these firms, only one was a Latino — and five were African American.[59]

In April 1999, the *San Jose Mercury News* published voluminous data on the ethnic composition of the high-tech workforce. The data were drawn from 1997 statistics gathered by the Equal Employment Opportunity Commission. Although we cannot know for sure how many in each category were immigrants, the data do suggest the extent to which the high-tech industry is segregated, especially in the area of blue-collar jobs for contract companies. These companies often employ temporary workers who are especially vulnerable to exploitative conditions, as we will discuss later. In that area, Asian Americans comprise three-quarters of the workforce (see Table 5.1).

The concentration of immigrants in low-wage jobs, despite the conspicuous success of some, is reflected in figures on home ownership. As of April 1999, 68 percent of whites owned homes, 36 percent of Latinos, 55 percent of Asians, and 42 percent of blacks. These figures constitute a great contrast to the early twentieth century, when the percentage of home owners was actually larger in the immigrant community than it was among the general population (see Chapter 1).

That immigrant families have fallen behind in the ability to own a home no doubt owes much to the women's consignment to assembly work, poorly paid jobs that have overwhelmingly been filled by immigrant women and/or women of color. Even though much of the least-skilled work has been outsourced abroad and even though much of the wafer fabrication has been located abroad or in regions of the United States that have a lower cost of living than Silicon Valley has, there remains an ongoing need for assembly

TABLE 5.1

High-Tech Diversity in 1997

| | Population, Santa Clara Co. | White-Collar Jobs | Blue-Collar Jobs | |
			Original Manuf.	Contract Companies
White	51%	60%	15%	7%
Hispanic	24%	7%	23%	14%
Asian	22%	31%	59%	77%
Black	4%	3%	4%	2%
	101%	101%	101%	100%

NOTE: Where percentages do not add up to 100, this is because of rounding.

SOURCE: *San Jose Mercury News*, April 16, 1999. Copyright © 1999 San Jose Mercury News. All rights reserved. Reproduced with permission.

workers in the Valley. In fact, as of 2000, a sociologist studying the Valley estimated that there were still forty to fifty thousand production workers in high tech in the region.[60]

Women as Assembly Workers

Those who work in wafer fabs, especially in clean rooms, have extraordinarily demanding jobs. At first, no one fully understood how readily the wafers could be contaminated or how this would affect the yield of usable chips. Workers at that time wore smocks and hair coverings rather than the elaborate costumes, or "bunny suits," that are currently standard. Today, suiting up for work is a job in itself. As of 2000, women are forbidden to wear makeup, even though they are completely covered by suit, hood, face mask (with goggles), and booties. After suiting up, workers walk through an air shower that blows stray particles of dust off of them. They must be similarly precise about all procedures once they are in the clean room itself. Indeed, because human beings are a source of contamination, this type of work is increasingly being performed by robots. Another reason that the fabs have been stressful places to work is that the technology has changed so rapidly

Figure 12. Intel workers wearing "bunny suits." Courtesy of Intel Corporation.

that "[e]very few weeks there would be a new procedure to watch for, every few months a new piece of equipment to learn how to operate."[61] Any way one looks at it, these are punishing jobs.

There are jobs in wafer fabrication that are not for low-skilled workers, but these jobs, such as technicians and engineers, have disproportionately gone to men. Women are not confined to the clean rooms, however. There are many types of less-demanding assembly work that have almost invariably gone to women. At one time, for example, workers inserted the circuits into printed boards and then tested and calibrated the eventual products, a type of work known as "board-stuffing." Although much of this work has since been outsourced and/or eliminated by automation, there is enough product development going on that there are still thousands of women assemblers who check the work performed by robots or rework it. In addition, much of the assembly work is now being undertaken by subcontractors, many of whom employ temporary workers. As of 1999, about one-fifth of the Valley's manufacturing was done by little-known companies that contracted with such giants as Hewlett-Packard or Cisco Systems, and the projections are that this percentage is likely to increase.

The Effects of the H1-B Visa

Parallel to the growth in contingent production workers is the growth in the use of immigrant professionals, who are allowed into this country on a provisional basis (the H-1B visa) and thus have fewer rights in the workplace than American citizens have. Indeed, one of the most controversial issues relating to immigrants and high tech has been the debate over how many H1-B visas Congress should authorize each year. Employers have been eager to maximize their numbers. Critics of the program, however, allege that employers use the professionals who come in via an H-1B visa as workers who will toil longer hours for lower salaries. For immigrants who use an H1-B visa as a first step in applying for a green card, there is a strong incentive not to make waves at the workplace. While the green card application is pending, the employee cannot readily change employers. There is a widespread belief that this situation has led to a form of indentured servitude because the immigrant worker had to accede to a supervisor's demands if he or she wanted to keep the application process flowing smoothly. In September 2000, the Immigration and Naturalization Service and the Department of Labor launched an investigation into possible fraud and other abuses connected with the program.[62] In October 2000, Congress raised the number of these visas from 115,000 to 195,000 annually, but it also provided that an immigrant can move from one employer to the next at the moment when the next employer petitions for him or her.[63]

To explain why the work conditions for immigrant workers have deteriorated in recent years — a subject to which much more attention is devoted in Chapter 7 — we must examine the failure of attempts to unionize as Silicon Valley took shape and as the large numbers of immigrants began to arrive.

Early Attempts to Organize a High-Tech Union

In 1972, Amy Newell and John Case, two highly educated young people, moved to the Santa Clara Valley from Buffalo, New York. Once here, they secured high-tech employment in low-level jobs and began trying to organize a union on behalf of the United Electrical Workers. So far as the record discloses, this represents one of the first concerted attempts to unionize the Valley's semiconductor industry.[64]

In the 1950s, the UE had lost its presence in Sunnyvale's Westinghouse plant when it lost an election there. As of the early 1970s, the most vital UE presence in the Bay Area was Oakland's Local 1412, to which Newell and Case belonged on an at-large basis. They also had close ties to the national UE on the East Coast because of Newell's family background.

Amy Newell was born to parents who were both key UE activists. Her father, Charles Newell, became the first UE business agent at a big Westinghouse plant in 1935 as part of the union's founding moment. Her mother, Ruth Allen Newell, organized a Sylvania plant for the UE, and it was the couple's union work that brought them together and led to their marriage. As a result of the bitter internal struggles in the UE in the 1950s, however, the Newells left organized labor and moved to Watsonville, California (slightly south of the Santa Clara Valley), with their daughter — though they kept ties of friendship with many UE leaders, particularly Jim Matles, the national secretary-treasurer. Growing up in California, Amy Newell attended Stanford University, graduated in 1969, and then departed for points east for graduate work. Coming home to visit her parents in 1972 as a doctoral student at SUNY, Buffalo, she noticed a big change since her last visit home. "There was this huge nonunion industry with an overwhelmingly female workforce."[65] She sensed an opportunity, went back to Buffalo, urged her boyfriend (Case) to join her, and the two were living in the Valley as of December 1972, having permanently abandoned their graduate studies.

Although neither Newell nor Case had any technical background, they did not have any trouble landing jobs. Newell went to work in a photomasking department at a semiconductor firm, Siliconix, where the task was to reduce a drawing to what could be placed on a chip. (This wJork is now digitized.) With no training and no prior high-tech experience, she attempted to talk up a union without losing her own job in the process. She recalls the workforce as having been "polyglot," though her own department was relatively white and English speaking. Case secured a job with a small firm, Tomco Electronics, as a solderer in an assembly operation and dedicated himself to the same objective. The UE gave them the name of the international's representative on the West Coast and made a modest investment in their efforts, but sent no full-time organizer until a later period. By the time the full-time organizer arrived, Newell had decided to move back East to join the UE staff, where she would eventually rise to become national secretary-treasurer. Case stayed in the Valley until 1976, when he, too, departed for UE staff work in the East. They had won a few skirmishes in the high-tech industry in securing union elections at a few small plants. At no time, however, did their efforts ever result in an election at one of the big plants.

Asked in 1999 to evaluate whether there was anything they could have done differently at the time that might have resulted in more success, they each provided thoughtful answers. Said Newell:

> There was plenty of unrest. . . . But there were four or five hundred in the bargaining unit, and it was difficult to meet enough of them to make a difference. We did house visitation, I started a volleyball league so as to meet women on other shifts. . . . I even rotated among all three shifts myself so as to meet more people. Pay, favoritism, lack of upward mobility — those were the issues. But there was so much turnover among employees, which is what the companies wanted. We called it the "electronic circuit." When a woman thought of bettering herself, she would dream of work at IBM or Hewlett-Packard, the Cadillac plants, rather than of what a union might be able to do for her.
>
> By the time I left, we had people working at Fairchild, National Semiconductor; we had a core of people . . . but I was getting antsy. Maybe the UE wasn't the right union to organize high tech.[66]

In her correspondence with UE headquarters at the time, she said in a letter, dated September 5, 1974:

> [W]e have succeeded in bringing forward at Siliconix a solid core of in-plant leaders and in signing up just under a hundred members, and . . . this is a substantial base from which the union drive can be continued and developed. If the UE were to decide on a concerted effort at Sili-

conix with open leadership, I would be willing — indeed anxious — to remain there through such a period. I myself believe that this would be the best course; but there is considerable opinion that much more quiet work need be done.

The letter provides a key to why the UE was probably not the right union to take on Silicon Valley. The union's glory days were past. It had not recovered from the toll taken by red-baiting and internecine struggle and therefore had to be parsimonious with limited resources. Only a very strong international, in fact, could have taken on so formidable a task as organizing high tech. It should be pointed out that none of the contemporary correspondence mentions any help or resources for Newell and Case from the Valley's own labor movement or its constituent elements, such as the cannery local or the International Association of Machinists, which then had a big local at Lockheed.

Asked about these issues, John Case points out that the national UE was then paying for more field organizers than the national IAM; in other words, though small, the former had a genuine commitment to broadening the reach of organized labor. "Why do I think that the IAM reacted as it did? Some have talked about prejudice against women, against immigrants. I think that the most important thing was that it was just too hard. . . . They weren't sure how to do it; even Jim Matles [of the UE] was skeptical about organizing electronics. There were formidable structural obstacles." In Case's view, the obstacles included both rapidly changing production processes and market forces that created rising wages. Most formidable were the anti-union tactics then being perfected: "The expensive attorneys would come in and raise hell [if the company got wind of a potential organizing drive]. They terrorized people; they were blatant. All this stuff was illegal, but immigrant workers are very unsure of their rights." He explained that his and Newell's only real successes were in relatively small crystal-growing plants. "If you relied on the National Labor Relations Board, you were crazy. We had a drive where everybody who had identified him or herself with the union got fired, and the Board didn't help us."

Though we have no comparably detailed local sources from the management side to document the efforts to keep out unions, there is abundant evidence nationally that employers were developing highly effective techniques for this purpose. An article in the November 12, 1979, issue of *Business Week*, for example, described the immense growth in union-busting law firms and consultant groups during the 1970s. The preceding month, there had been Congressional hearings at which union witnesses had testified to practices that were "clear-cut violations of labor law." Two years earlier, in fact, the National Association of Manufacturers had formed a Council on a Union-Free Environment to advance these goals.[67] More locally, we do know that the organization that evolved into the American Electronics Association oversaw "mutual aid agreements" in the Valley to keep out unions among its membership, and that it offered a yearly seminar on "How to Keep the Unions Out of Your Plant."[68] We also know that in the 1980s another union organizing attempt by the UE fell afoul of the firings of virtually every organizer by firms such as Intel, National Semiconductor, and Advanced Micro Devices, a subject to be more fully discussed in Chapter 7.[69]

Says AnnaLee Saxenian about these issues: "The general failure to organize Silicon Valley's technology firms was due in part to effective prevention by management and in part to weak enforcement of federal labor laws. Equally important was the failure of industrial unions to develop innovative approaches."[70] What she does not include on her list is the fact that tens of thousands of vulnerable new immigrants, ignorant of their rights under American labor law, were arriving in the Valley at the optimum moment for high-tech employers in search of a workforce with no ties to the American labor movement.[71]

Barriers to Unionization

Another factor that should be mentioned as we try to account for the failure of the early unionization efforts is the change in the nature of the working-class community since the days of the march inland. In the 1930s, working-class people had lived near one another in San Jose, especially in Goosetown, thus facilitating the job of those making house visitations. Working-class people had also repeatedly congregated in St. James Park for rallies. By the 1970s, not only had the culture changed (above all with the advent of television) so that people, other than students, were much less likely to attend protest rallies than they had been in the 1930s, but also the vast suburban sprawl of the postwar years had substantially dispersed the housing of working-class people, with the exception of those living in the barrio of East San Jose.

Further, firms adapted the strategy of outsourcing and/or relocating very soon after the birth of the semiconductor industry, both to save money and to avoid "labor trouble." This sent a message that could not have been lost on workers. As early as 1972, for example, Intel had launched an assembly operation in Penang, Malaysia. By 1975, "Penang accounted for more than half of Intel's entire worldwide assembly capacity."[72] Firms outsourced their assembly to third world countries and built wafer fabs in U.S. cities that had a lower cost of living than Silicon Valley had. John Case recalls that when he and his colleagues won a certification election at Tomco Electronics in the 1970s, "the whole place shut down."[73] The record also discloses that in 1992, after a six-week strike by a predominantly Mexican American workforce at Versatronex in Sunnyvale, the firm announced the permanent closing of the plant on Christmas Eve.[74] Knowing that an employer's threat to move elsewhere might well be implemented surely had a chilling effect on workers.

Finally, a certain number of workers no doubt have entered the U.S. illegally, which has contributed to their quiescence. In the spring of 1984, the Immigration and Naturalization Service staged a number of raids on local high-tech plants, following a favorable U.S. Supreme Court ruling that permitted this to take place. One report at the time claimed that 25 percent of the Silicon Valley workforce was deportable, and the INS Commissioner for the Western Region promised to raid two Silicon Valley firms a week.[75] In response, the San Jose City Council voted 9 to 2 to denounce the raids and directed the city attorney to look into legal means of preventing further raids.[76] The council also voted to direct the chief of police not to aid in the raids. After a war of words between local politicians and INS officials, the raids died down. Interestingly enough, when the Immigration Reform and Control Act of 1986 permitted undocumented people to apply for amnesty under certain conditions, there were 41,687 such applications from San Jose, according to the INS.[77]

Organizing That Produced Results

Though the efforts to bring high-tech workers within the ranks of organized labor came to naught, there *were* gains for immigrants and/or people of color, especially Mexican Americans. We have heretofore discussed, for example, the successful outcome of the class action suit against the canners and the Teamsters in the 1970s. In Chapter 7, we examine the successes of the

Justice for Janitors campaign. There were also victories for feminists, the subject of Chapter 6. Finally, there was one attempt to restrain the power of high tech that *has* borne fruit.

With respect to successes for Mexican Americans, we earlier learned that the residents of the barrio in East San Jose began to be politicized in the 1950s, under the auspices of the Community Service Organization. Growing numbers in the population eventually led to representation on local governing bodies. In 1971, Al Garza became the first Mexican American appointed to serve on the San Jose City Council. In 1978, district elections replaced at-large elections (of great consequence for women politicians as well as for those of color), and two years later, Blanca Alvarado won election to the city council as the twentieth century's first elected Latino council member. As of 2000, Alvarado was on the Santa Clara County Board of Supervisors, a five-person body, and Ron Gonzales, former mayor of Sunnyvale and former County Supervisor, was mayor of San Jose. In 2000, Latinos comprised 10 percent of the composition of the county's school boards, less than their 24 percent of the population, but closer to their 13 percent of the registered voters.[78] Not surprisingly, they have been especially well represented in districts on the east side of San Jose, such as Alum Rock.

How did the change come about? In the late 1980s, the Latino Issues Forum emerged as a potent coalition of service and professional organizations that also included the Hispanic Elected Officials of Santa Clara County and the Stanford Center for Chicano Research.[79] (It should be noted that the ardent Chicano nationalism of the 1960s has tended to give way to a pan-Hispanic identity, or "Latinismo," that has fostered coalition-building.[80]) The LIF successfully worked to bring district, rather than at-large, elections to certain jurisdictions within the county. The group also formed an alliance with San Jose Mayor Susan Hammer, the immediate predecessor to Ron Gonzales.[81] As a consequence of their heightened visibility as well as their growing numbers, the Latino community won significant victories in the 1990s, including the placement of a statue of the Aztec god Quetzalcoatl in a downtown park — unpopular with the religious right — and the dedication of Cesar Chavez Plaza in the heart of downtown.[82] There is also a new Latino cultural center, the Mexican Heritage Plaza, in East San Jose. So dense were the cultural resources, in fact, that in 1999, *Hispanic* magazine chose San Jose as the most "livable" city in the United States for Latinos. "The thing that impressed me the most [about] San Jose is that the Latino community there seemed very empowered, very organized," said the author of the article.[83]

As for Asian Americans, they, too, have won some notable electoral victories, starting with the election of Norman Mineta as mayor of San Jose in 1971, the first Japanese American to be a big-city mayor in the continental United States. In 2000, the two most prominent Asian American politicians in the Valley, in addition to Mineta (the Secretary of Transportation during the Bush administration), were Assemblyman (and Congressman-elect) Mike Honda of San Jose and Cupertino Mayor Michael Chang. According to anthropologist Bernard Wong, there is great eagerness in the Chinese American community, in particular, to become politically active and to run for office, so that these immigrants will not be perceived as in any way marginal, which had been the fate of earlier generations of Chinese immigrants.[84] Nonetheless, it is also true that Asian Americans have not yet flexed the political muscle to which their numbers and resources entitle them.[85]

Asian Immigrant Women Advocates is not a union, because it does not engage in collective bargaining on behalf of workers, but it is an organization that affords workers some measure of protection from the worst exploitation. Based in Oakland with an office in San Jose, AIWA is funded by progressive foundations, including some sponsored by liberal religious denominations. The group informs women working in sweatshop-type conditions about their rights under state and federal law. It also helps women gain access to English-language instruction and child care.[86]

Immigrant and minority organizing in the political realm has benefited these communities, though it has done little to restrain the immense power of the high-tech firms. There was, however, one movement in the last decades of the twentieth century that did, in fact, bring high tech to change some of its practices, and this was the movement to protect the local environment from chemical ravages.

Ted Smith was a young lawyer who moved to San Jose in 1971, while finishing up at Stanford Law School. His ambition at the time was to concentrate his practice on cannery workers as the Valley's major industrial workforce, and he quickly threw himself into the legal effort to reform the Teamsters Union. But even as the victory was won, the canneries were closing down or moving away, so Smith's original plans had to change. By the late 1970s, he was married to another lawyer, Amanda Hawes, and the couple was becoming aware that the action for progressive lawyers was shifting to high tech. Hawes began to work with an occupational safety and health group for tech workers — a major focus of Chapter 6 — and Smith observed how difficult it was for her and her colleagues to get the public to care about workers' safety. Then fate intervened when a story broke in the *San Jose Mercury News* about the health problems in a south San Jose neighborhood adjacent to a Fairchild plant, apparently caused by chemicals leaking into the water supply. The world then began to learn about the dangers of the "clean" semiconductor industry. Says Smith, "When the chemicals got out of the plants and into the drinking water, I saw that as a chance to wake up the community that wasn't paying that much attention to the workers."[87]

In September 1980, workers had found chemical leaks in the soil near the South San Jose IBM plant, with a few more such discoveries being made near other plants in succeeding months. Then in December 1981, the news got worse. This time a leak from Fairchild of TCA, the solvent used to clean silicon chips, had produced traces of contamination in a well owned by the Great Oaks Water Company. A few weeks later, a housewife who lived in the neighborhood served by this water company and who had read the newspaper accounts wrote a letter to Great Oaks providing the names of eight women in the Los Paseos neighborhood, including herself, who had suffered miscarriages or had given birth to children who were stillborn or who had birth defects, all within a three-year period.

From these beginnings came a movement to regulate and control the industry. The movement eventually became a major national story that resulted in the Environmental Protection Agency designating twenty-nine Superfund sites in Silicon Valley. It turned out that the problem of chemical leakage was widespread among even the Valley's blue-chip companies, in part because of the ten thousand old agricultural wells in the Valley (see earlier discussions of water), which served as perfect conduits for toxins to penetrate into the aquifer.[88]

"We knew we needed a coalition of labor people, environmentalists, neighborhood people, public health people," Smith explained in 1999. "I thought that the labor people would be hard to recruit and the environmentalists easy, but it turned out just the opposite because this was such a non-union industry [and the labor people were looking for ways to embarrass it]. . . . The environmental community was centered in Palo Alto, and many of them were the high-tech managers. They hung back. There was a strong class skewing."

Smith became the founder of the Silicon Valley Toxics Coalition; he was also the person as much responsible as any other human being for the launching of the coalition. Since its founding, the group has enjoyed many successes, but Smith thinks it is impossible to "get ahead of the curve" on regulation. This is because the industry innovates so constantly that the production processes, including the selection of chemicals, are constantly changing. But the Coalition proves the larger point — the industry is not above and beyond any sort of successful organizing to control some of its practices.[89]

In early 2000, there was an initiative by the national labor movement that may have an effect on Silicon Valley. In February 2000, the AFL-CIO officially altered its stance and embraced the cause of immigrants. Included in its new policy was a call for amnesty for undocumented workers, a dramatic turnaround in national policy. Something about the synergy that this changed stance may foster was suggested by a large public meeting in East San Jose on April 29, 2000. Attended by some five hundred people, it was billed as an "AFL-CIO Hearing on Immigrant Rights," and the program was sponsored by, in addition to the Central Labor Council, the Asian Law Alliance, the Diocese of San Jose, the Santa Clara County Summit on Immigrant Needs, and a number of individual unions. Present, too, were a representative from the National Association for the Advancement of Colored People and a number of elected officials, including Assemblyman Mike Honda. Many people in the audience waved the red banner of the United Farm Workers, and a large picture of Cesar Chavez on the wall (the meeting took place in a Mexican American youth center) provided a reminder of the farmworker tradition. Indeed, the audience frequently chanted the UFW slogan, "Si, se puede," or "Yes, it's possible."[90] This was especially powerful in response to the testimony of a gay Indian computer programmer, in the United States on an H-1B visa, about the multiple problems that he has encountered and his activism around these issues. The testimony of Katie Quan, a longtime organizer in the textile industry, made it particularly clear why labor changed its mind. She asserted that the courts have repeatedly ruled that violations of immigration law trump a worker's right to protection under the NLRB.[91] This, in turn, provides employers of undocumented workers with a strong hand to use against their workforce.

Time will tell whether the promise of the new policy will be realized — and to what extent.

Those Who Struggle

Because so many thousands of immigrants continue to arrive with few resources and poor job skills, there has been a steady infusion of the needy and the, perhaps, desperate into the Valley. In an earlier period, Indochinese refugees, some of whom had been "boat people," constituted a truly traumatized group. A study of their mental health, conducted in 1984, revealed the dimensions of their problems. Of the 378 Cambodians (the poorest group) in the sample of 1,684, for example, about 95 percent had seen relatives disappear into the "custody" of the Khmer Rouge, never to be heard from again. Arriving with an average of six years of education, these refugees frequently required public assistance — 77.5 percent of the sample, in fact, with 84.7 percent unemployed. Almost 60 percent of them rated their health as "fair to very bad." They lived in cramped apartments in downtown San Jose.[92] By 2000, many of the Cambodians had escaped from their original desperate circumstances by opening small businesses, such as doughnut shops.[93] That 66 percent of the sample had been going to school back in 1984 may be part of the explanation for that escape.

Concerned about the situation of the vulnerable newcomers, the Santa Clara County Board of Supervisors commissioned a study to probe the lives of the largest groups of immigrants, those from Mexico, Vietnam, China, the Philippines, and India, set against a control group of U.S.-born and with survey data gathered according to the principles of random sampling. The full data set, released to the public at a "Summit on Immigrant Needs and Contributions" on December 6, 2000, can only briefly be glimpsed here. What it documents is that the thousands and thousands of newcomers are subject to a multitude of special problems. They are 88 percent more likely not to be paid time and a half for the overtime they work, for example, and 365 percent more likely to be working for less than the minimum wage. They are four times more likely to be paid in cash (and, therefore, probably under the table) than are the U.S.-born. Above all, "the random sample of the top five immigrant groups in the county shows that four of the top five immigrant groups [all but those from India] experience household income significantly below their counterpart U.S.-born households." For their part, immigrant women make only 57 percent of the weekly wage of immigrant men, as opposed to the national figure that shows women making 73 percent of the male wage in 2000.[94]

A good way to get a feel for the neediest immigrants in 2000 is to examine the work of the East San Jose Community Law Center, a project sponsored by the Santa Clara University School of Law and supported by community and foundation money, as well as the 25 percent of funding that comes from Santa Clara University itself. Founded in 1994 and staffed by law school faculty and students, the Center gives free legal counsel to families, many immigrant, whose total income falls below $21,000 a year. The 1,600 clients in 1998 were 69 percent Latino, 13 percent Asian/Pacific Islander, 11 percent white, 6 percent African American, and 1 percent Native American. They were almost all employed, but their jobs as child care workers, gardeners, or electronics assemblers (31 percent of the clients worked in electronics) didn't pay enough to keep them out of poverty.

The Center focuses on four areas: immigration rights, workers' rights and workers' compensation, consumer fraud, and small business consulting. The sums involved in these cases are not large enough to be remunerative for the private bar, so people come to the Center as their only resort for obtaining justice. Margaret Stevenson, the director, explains that one of the chief client requests is for help with collecting back wages. They also see clients who have been hurt on the job, and are then subsequently fired, thus requiring medical services at the very moment when their income, such as it is, has vanished. Or staff may be called on to help an undocumented woman who is being terrorized by her legal-resident husband, as in the following case.

> Antonia, an undocumented woman, is married to a lawful permanent
> resident of the United States, and has a U.S. citizen child. Although
> Antonia's husband can petition the INS to legalize her status, he refuses
> to do so in order to continue intimidating and controlling her. Antonia's
> husband repeatedly attacked her, once punching her in the face for not
> cooking dinner. . . . [They separate, and she obtains a restraining order.]
> Antonia lives in fear of running into her husband, who has threatened to
> take their child away and have her deported.
>
> The Center filed a petition with the Immigration and Naturalization

Service under the Violence Against Women Act so that Antonia can obtain lawful status independent of her husband.[95]

A study conducted by the San Francisco feminist law firm Equal Rights Advocates and published in April 1999 confirms the vulnerability suggested by such stories. The study looked at the needs of the area's Mexican and Vietnamese immigrant women on welfare. In 1997, according to the study, there were 63,618 people in Santa Clara County who required public assistance, 21 percent of whom were immigrants. Of these, the two largest groups were those from Mexico and those from Vietnam. Drawing samples of seventy-five women from each group, researchers found that both groups suffered from poor English skills and lack of education. Indeed, the Mexican women had an average of 6.5 years of schooling, with 8.7 years for the Vietnamese. Approximately 10 percent of the participants were not even literate in their native language. When they *were* employed, the most frequently held job for the Vietnamese was electronics assembly, with the Mexicans working in food services, house cleaning, and child care. Particularly striking is the fact that "[t]wo women told ERA that they had received job training for electronics assembly and found temporary jobs in that industry. They work at home and are being paid by piece rate. Their pay adds up to less than California's minimum wage."[96] Hence, as in the case of the clients of the East San Jose Community Law Center, to work is not necessarily to avoid the problems of poverty, including, in the latter case, the need for public assistance.

In December 1999, ERA, in conjunction with the Asian Law Caucus, filed suit in San Jose's Federal Court to try to bring redress of such grievances. The case is *Kamsan Mao v Top Line Electronics, Inc. and Lite-On, Inc.* In its announcement of the suit in its spring 2000 newsletter, the law firm explained: "Like the garment industry, the electronics assembly industry depends upon the work of scores of poor, immigrant workers. In many cases, companies violate wage and hour laws, hiding beneath the cloak of subcontracts or purported independent contractor arrangements. We hope this lawsuit will send a clear message to the computer manufacturing companies that they cannot continue to profit on the backs of low-wage workers."

In an area with one of the highest costs of living in the country, especially in the realm of housing, how do people survive, especially in an era when public assistance is diminishing? Fortunately, there are a number of private and public agencies dedicated to helping immigrants make it, in addition to the Center discussed above. One impressive agency serving the very neediest is the Centro Obrero, sponsored by the Society of St. Vincent de Paul and working with day laborers. Only a few years old, the Centro had two locations as of 2000, one in East San Jose and one in Los Altos. There, recent arrivals could go for English classes and for help in locating a casual job with an employer who has registered with the agency and can thus be held accountable for paying his employees. All services are free.

In October 1999, two of the Centro's clients, Caleb and Jose — two of the estimated tens of thousands of undocumented workers in the Valley — talked about their lives, about what brought them to the United States, and about their dreams for the future.[97] Caleb explained that in his part of Mexico, Oaxaca, there is so much desperation owing to unemployment and poverty that people will resort to violence to put food on the table. Though he wanted to complete high school, circumstances were too grim for that to be a possibility. He decided to come to El Norte two years ago, arriving first in Los Banos in the Central Valley. There he worked in the fields but met no English-speakers. He decided to move to the Santa Clara Valley to improve himself, especially by learning English. He found a job in a restaurant preparing salads. As for housing, that was tough. Lacking papers, he couldn't sign a lease himself. According to Caleb, the way it works is that someone who has been here in the country long enough to be legal will make the arrangements, and then enough men will share the apartment to make up the rent. Yes, there are risks, he said, but those risks start the minute a person decides to cross the border, so it's just part of the price you pay. He sends his parents money regularly, because they are old, and he doesn't want them to work so hard in the fields. For recreation, he plays soccer or basketball with his friends.[98]

From Oaxaca, too, Jose left behind a wife and two children so as to try to improve his family's fortunes in the United States. In Mexico, he was a barber, but he cannot obtain a barber's license in the United States because of being undocumented. Therefore, he works as a gardener. He has also thrown himself into activities at the Centro. Like Caleb, he sends money home, but as a married man, he has greater obligations, including not only his immediate family but also his parents and a sister who is a student. He would like his children to grow up here, but he doesn't know how that would be possible. Originally planning to stay three years, he has scaled back to two — he's very homesick — with the goal of returning not merely with savings but with new gardening skills. When nostalgia and loneliness threaten to overwhelm him, he plays his guitar for solace.

Though we lack in-depth studies by social scientists of the long-term consequences of such disruption and deprivation for Santa Clara Valley immigrants, we know from studies conducted in other parts of the country that there can be a fearful toll in stress and anxiety. For example, in a study of Vietnamese immigrants in an eastern community, Nazli Kibria found a disjunction between the conventional wisdom about stable Asian families and the men and women she encountered in her field research, people struggling to reconstruct and redefine family life in unfamiliar circumstances.[99] She employs the concept of "family tightrope" to characterize the balancing act required of her women subjects. "They often spoke to me about the importance of preserving Vietnamese family traditions in the United States and of not assimilating into the familial behavior of people in the United States." This was because, among other things, the women valued male breadwinning and were suspicious of any forces that might erode the commitment to it. Then, too, mothers were afraid that their own authority might be undermined by American ways. So strong were these feelings that women were even ambivalent about the protection from domestic violence offered by the American legal system.[100]

In sum, there are thousands of recent arrivals in the Valley who must engage in a daily struggle against loneliness, poverty, and cruel treatment from employers. As family members and as members of various religious communities, they may have social services available to them, in addition to dwindling public resources, but it is clear from the report prepared for the Summit on Immigrant Needs that there is huge shortfall in such services, given the extent of the population requiring them. They may also be able to visit the East San Jose Community Law Center for free legal counsel. But as workers, they have few organizational resources, particularly in the realm of collective bargaining, a right that earlier immigrant workers were eventually able to claim.

One recourse may be to work to escape the world of exploitative labor via education, a possibility that *is* being utilized by immigrants as reflected in statistics provided by a local community college district. For the San Jose/ Evergreen Community College District, the figures for the fall 1997 term suggest a truly substantial usage by immigrants: "[A]t Evergreen the proportion of Asian students exceeds the proportion in the community 50% to 21%. African American students approximate the community, 6% to 5%. Hispanics are equivalent at 26% to 27%, and white students at 12% are far below the 47% found in the community." The figures for San Jose City College were quite similar. When coupled with the large enrollments for English as a second language classes at the colleges, these data suggest that thousands of immigrants are availing themselves of a low-cost escape route from poverty. It should also be pointed out that this district has a Transfer Admission Agreement with San Jose State University that permits its students to attend a four-year institution after completing certain courses. "It [the transfer agreement] is an invaluable aid to many of our first generation students whose parents have not attended college, helping them feel more secure about making this step."[101] Yet it must also be remembered that San Jose still has the stunning number of twenty-four school districts within its city limits and a concomitant highly unequal tax base among them. This pattern militates against immigrants' being able to gain mobility through education, since the areas in which they live are in the poorest school districts, a form of institutionalized injustice that has persisted for decades.

Another way to improve one's situation is to apply for citizenship. As of April 1999, so numerous had the applications been to the San Jose office of the Immigration and Naturalization Service that the office had a backlog of some sixty-five thousand cases. Doris Meissner, head of the INS, announced that the agency was adding staff to try to reduce the wait for an interview from two years to six months by the fall of 2000.[102] In 1994, California voters approved Proposition 187, with its harsh measures against undocumented immigrants (measures gutted by court decisions), thus constituting a clarion call to many, not just in San Jose, to apply for citizenship.

One Who Has Made It

Lien Phan was born in Hue, Vietnam, in 1949, the daughter of a policeman and a retail saleswoman and one of fourteen children. All of the children attended high school, and Lien went on to college, became a middle-school teacher, and was on the verge of obtaining her degree when Saigon fell. April 30, 1975, was a memorable day for her. Not only did the South Vietnamese

Figure 13. Lien Phan, a woman who made the transition from high-tech assembly worker to a management position. Courtesy of Lien Phan.

regime collapse then, but she also got married — to a man who had been in the South Vietnamese army. After the arrival of two children and many vicissitudes, the family escaped to Hong Kong in 1979 in a small boat. In March 1980, they left for Minneapolis, Minnesota, and a new life in the United States. They arrived with few resources and little English, but with an all-important educational background.

Looking back, Lien credits many different sources of help in the early period. They received support from the federal government for three months. Her husband got a grant to study electronics. Most important for her, however, was the personal tutoring in English that she received from her sponsor, who came once a week to work with her until her skills were adequate.

All her subsequent success, she believes, stems from this hands-on learning experience. In 1983, her husband graduated, and the couple decided to relocate to get away from the snow. With relatives in San Jose, they chose Silicon Valley.

Lien's story is a mix of both good fortune — the educational background, the kind sponsor — and a truly impressive work ethic. Once in the Valley, the family lived in a nineteen-unit apartment complex in downtown San Jose, which the owner asked her to manage when he observed how organized and careful she was. This enabled the family to save for the home they now own. With three children by this time, Lien got a job in Santa Clara as a waitress at a small restaurant that served American food (she could carry it off because of her English skills). She also enrolled in an electronics school. There she learned how to identify components, how to solder, how to wire, and so on. After six months of training, she got an assembly job with Santa Clara Systems, a small firm that produced hardware. Thus she began her rise. The boss liked her because she was willing to learn and was outgoing, she says. He wanted her to get more electronics training. She took on the assignment and completed it in nine months. "In my country, we all had to be good at math." She then became a leader, supervising twenty other women. After three years, her company merged with Novell, which produced software. Most were laid off, but Lien had acquired so much knowledge of the schematics that she had become a valuable employee, and she was asked to stay on. She is now in management, in quality assurance. "Assembly work was a boring job. I always knew I wanted a phone and a desk. My friends are mostly in engineering and accounting, but they're not management like me." As of the interview in January 1998, her oldest two children were university students, and the family seemed to an outsider to represent a perfect exemplar of the California Dream, realized.[103]

But not everyone has Lien Phan's luck and drive. In Chapter 7, we learn more about those left behind, many of whom are immigrants, and the problems they face. The most serious of these problems is the fact that they must deal with employers who are part of a sophisticated global economy, one that is more tightly integrated than at any previous time in human history. But before we take up the global economy and its impact on the Valley, we will explore the area's host of powerful and pioneering women.

The Valley as "Feminist Capital of the Nation"

In 2000 a woman, Amy Dean, headed the Santa Clara County Central Labor Council, and another woman, Carly Fiorina, headed Hewlett-Packard, the oldest and most prestigious firm to have developed in the Valley. When Fiorina was chosen for the position in the summer of 1999, she became the first woman to run a FORTUNE 30 firm. By the same token, when Dean assumed the helm of the Labor Council in 1994 at the age of thirty-one, she became the youngest such leader in any large council in the country, let alone the youngest woman leader.

These women were not the first in the area to take leadership roles. There was a historical precedent that goes back to the late nineteenth century. The work of women throughout the years eventually led to the area being dubbed the "feminist capital of the nation" in the 1970s, when Janet Gray Hayes became the country's first woman mayor of a city larger than 500,000. This reputation was consolidated in 1980 when women won majorities on both the San Jose City Council and the Santa Clara County Board of Supervisors.[1]

Paradoxically, even as an unprecedented number of women were being elected to office in the Valley, a culture was taking shape in the local high-tech arena that has been repeatedly described in terms of its macho qualities: work-obsessed, hard on family life, celebratory of the male nerd. How could such contradictory developments have occurred in the same place at the same time? What is it like to be a woman professional working in high tech in "the feminist capital"? Was it as difficult as working as a production worker?

This chapter deals with these issues as well as with the question: How can we account for the number of women officeholders — and other women in leadership positions — and what difference have they made to the lives of lower-profile women, especially working-class women?

Foremothers

The story of politically mobilized women in the Santa Clara Valley dates back more than a century ago. Interestingly, many of the most significant leaders of the state's suffrage movement in the late nineteenth century came from San Jose — and so did male feminists, though the term was not in use at the time. For example, in 1869, Senator William Knox of San Jose introduced a successful bill into the legislature whereby a woman would no longer be required to seek her husband's approval to write a will disposing of her separate property. Knox died the following year, and his widow, Sarah, went on to become one of the state's "preeminent women's rights activists," supported in that endeavor by the estate she had inherited.[2]

In 1869, the year of the founding of the state's first women's rights organization, Laura Watkins of San Jose attended a suffrage meeting in San Francisco and returned home imbued with a fighting spirit; the following year, she founded a suffrage society in San Jose. Along with Sarah Goodrich, wife of a prominent architect, Watkins kept open house for visiting suffrage luminaries, such as Susan B. Anthony. Others in the circle included a male attorney by the name of C. C. Stephens and the local Unitarian minister and his wife, the Reverend and Mrs. Charles Ames. Impressively, these San Joseans lobbied the state legislature on behalf of a bill to permit women to hold school board office.[3] As of 1880, San Jose had a branch of the Woman's

Christian Temperance Union, an organization without peer in its ability to galvanize women into political action in the late nineteenth century.[4] Finally, in 1894, women founded the San Jose Woman's Club, which was destined to play a significant role for years.[5]

No doubt the most remarkable San Jose woman of the period was Clara Shortridge Foltz, California's first woman attorney. Foltz, born in Indiana in 1849 and married at fifteen, came to California in 1874 with her husband and five children. Fairly soon thereafter, she divorced her husband and cast around for a means of supporting herself and her family. Living in San Jose, she found help from C. C. Stephens, who allowed her to read law with him. She was then admitted to the California bar in September 1878. Having achieved this status, she drafted an amendment to the state's Code of Civil Procedures, whereby the law was changed to read that the qualification for the bar was to be a "citizen or person" rather than a "white male citizen." This amendment passed the legislature, was signed by the governor, and became state law.[6]

The next major achievement for Valley women lay in conservation, which was an area of special concern for California women at the dawn of the twentieth century. At the founding of the California Federation of Women's Clubs (an affiliate of the national organization, the General Federation of Women's Clubs), women from some forty constituent clubs around the state, including one in San Jose, committed themselves to "forestry" as one of their bedrock issues. This antedated the birth of the national conservation movement during Theodore Roosevelt's administration, though it followed that of the Sierra Club in 1892.

With the state federation committing to this position, San Jose women were at the forefront of the founding of Big Basin, California's first state redwood park and one of the first state-owned parks in the United States. In May 1900, two leaders from the San Jose Woman's Club, along with influential men from the greater Bay Area, went on what would prove to be a historic camping trip in the Santa Cruz Mountains. During the trip, the campers decided to form a club called Sempervirens Club, which was named after the coast redwood, *Sequoia sempervirens*. The Sempervirens Club successfully petitioned the state legislature to purchase land in these mountains so that a tract of the giant trees could be preserved. One hundred years later, a portrait of Carrie Stevens Walter, a member of the club, hangs in the park supervisor's office, a reminder of the leadership role she played in the Sempervirens Club.[7]

In 1924, Edwina Benner of Sunnyvale joined this distinguished array of female leaders by being elected her city's mayor — the first woman mayor in California. Between 1920 and 1948, when she wasn't acting as mayor, she served on the city council. Professionally, she was an office manager for the Libby plant in Sunnyvale.[8]

Although it would be a mistake to make too much of these precedents, they are suggestive, because political scientists have learned that female leadership begets female leadership. Where there is such a tradition, later residents seemingly find it less strange to accept a woman candidate or officeholder.[9]

When discussing the foremothers for "the feminist capital of the nation," we must also take note of the courageous example of women in the labor movement. Though in the 1930s, there was only one woman in the leadership of the mainstream cannery union, there were a number of radical women in prominent positions.[10] We have taken note, for example, of the important role played by Communist Party members Dorothy Ray, Caroline Decker, and Elizabeth Nicholas during the depression decade. Moreover, it is clear that there would have been no cannery local had not the preponderantly female rank and file supported their leaders. The 1970s saw a new birth of female activism among cannery workers, with Mexican American women achieving key goals of gender and racial equity, though this proved to be a hollow victory inasmuch as the canneries left the area. Women's roles in the East San Jose's Community Service Organization, discussed in Chapter 3, should also be remembered.

Taken together, the female activists, politicians, and union members provide a historical backdrop that helps us understand the political developments of the 1970s and 1980s (discussed later in this chapter).

The Women of Lockheed

As we assess the multiple reasons for the stunning number of female officeholders in the Valley circa 1980, we must take note of Lockheed's impact. We can infer that the presence of thousands of female defense-contractor employees — all of whom were either salaried or union members with decent jobs to protect — must surely have contributed to the voting bloc that produced "the feminist capital." Moreover, many of the Lockheed wives, as well as women married to employees of other defense contractors or IBM employees, were themselves well educated and were prime candidates for community involvement leading to feminist convictions. There is at least one direct link between Lockheed and local politics: An early San Jose city councilwoman, Pat Sausedo, worked on an assembly line for the firm.[11] But the larger point is that there was an infusion of educated, impressive women into the Valley in the decades immediately prior to the birth of the "feminist capital."

From about 1960 to the very recent past, Lockheed Missiles and Space Company (LMSC) was the largest private employer in Santa Clara County. At the height of the firm's prosperity, it employed some twenty-five thousand employees, of whom 20 to 25 percent were female, depending on the year. That Lockheed employed a few women in highly responsible positions and that the firm had a ladder for encouraging those in secretarial or other hourly jobs to move into management suggests that LMSC may have inadvertently been a catalyst for social and political change.

By reading back issues of the employee newsletter the *Lockheed Star,* we learn that in 1961, a few years after LMSC had established its Sunnyvale plant, the firm began to hold special daylong programs for female high school students to interest them in a science career.[12] The columns of the newsletter also contain many accounts of skilled women operatives, such as Mary Tremper, who won an award as "Craftsman of the Month" in September 1969, because she wired two prototype black boxes, without error, on schedule, and below budget. (In this respect, LMSC seemingly bore a resemblance to Varian Associates in giving opportunity to women to perform skilled blue-collar jobs.) There are even a few accounts of pioneering women scientists employed by the firm, such as two LMSC employees who founded the first chapter of the Society of Women Engineers (SWE) in Southern California and then in Northern California when the firm moved to the Valley. [13]

One of the cofounders of the Society was Mary Ross, the first woman to receive the rating of "engineer" from Lockheed. Her route to this success was an unusual one. Of Cherokee heritage, Ross was born and raised in rural

Oklahoma. From the time of her birth in 1908 to when she launched a ca-
reer as a high school math teacher upon graduation from Northeastern State
Teachers College in Tahlequah, she had barely left her native state. But then
she decided to apply for a job working as a statistical clerk for the Bureau of
Indian Affairs in Washington, D.C., so she could see more of the world.
Along the way, she acquired a master's in math from the University of
Northern Colorado. When she applied for — and got — a wartime job with
Lockheed Aircraft in Southern California in July 1942, she had a background
that was unusual for a woman at that time. She began her job by analyzing
the problems of compressibility and aeroelasticity for a consulting engineer
at Lockheed. Hungry for talent, the firm gave her increasingly challenging
work and the opportunity to qualify as an engineer in 1944. When the war
ended, she continued to work for Lockheed and became the only woman in
a forty-person think tank for special projects — "the skunk works" — out of
which was born the missile and space division. When the firm launched
LMSC in Sunnyvale, she moved to the Valley and worked there till her retirement in 1973.

In 1999, Ross looked back over her career and emphasized how much fun
it had been. "You could just practically name what you wanted to do. It was
terribly exciting. They'd give us the mission, and we'd figure out how to accomplish it." Her work, much of which is still classified, included calculating
trajectories for spacecraft, "work that wasn't part of any university curricu-
lum. You had to dig it up for yourself."[14]

Her colleague both at Lockheed and in founding the Society of Women
Engineers sections was a metallurgist by the name of Esther Williams. Born
in Washington in 1913, Williams fell in love with physics and math in high
school and decided to major in physical metallurgy at Washington State
University. Before she was able to graduate, however, her father passed away.
During World War II, she found employment at Kaiser Shipyards in
Oakland and completed her undergraduate degree at the University of
California, Berkeley. She later recalled having been the only woman in
Berkeley's College of Engineering at that time. When the war ended, she
found a job at Douglas Aircraft in Southern California, analyzing plane
crashes, and then went to Lockheed. When the new Santa Clara Valley fa-
cility opened, the company transferred her to Sunnyvale to run its metallurgy lab, and she, too, stayed with Lockheed until retirement.

Asked about founding the two branches of SWE, Williams recalled the inspiration she felt when she read in the newspaper about the pioneering engineer Lillian Gilbreth and the Boston-based SWE. Williams decided to find out if there were enough women engineers in the Los Angeles area to warrant an organization. Securing publicity for the undertaking, she called a meeting, and to her delight, eighteen women came, one of whom was Mary Ross. When Lockheed transferred Ross and Williams to the Valley, it was a logical step for them to found a SWE section in the Bay Area and to launch the same recruiting efforts for young women in high school that the company had helped undertake in Los Angeles. In 1999, Williams speculated that Ross — "a great lady" — must have helped open eyes at Lockheed to what women are capable of.[15]

Perhaps even more noteworthy than the firm's willingness to employ and promote pioneering women scientists was its commitment to opportunity for hourly workers, including women, as expressed in the formation of an institutional ladder, the Lockheed Management Association. A former executive advisor to the Management Association, Joseph Reagan, explained that, despite its name, the group was not composed of managers, but rather of aspiring managers. Reagan remembered that many secretaries joined, received company-sponsored training, and were then able to move into administrative positions. Reagan's account was confirmed by the two women interviewed for this study who had been hourly employees and who had both been given the opportunity to move into the ranks of the salaried.[16] As further confirmation, the *Star* of April 25, 1986, reported that the LMSC Women's Seminar was about to celebrate its tenth anniversary with a luncheon. With space limited to five hundred attendees, the luncheon was sold out. According to the newsletter, the seminar was the only one of its kind in aerospace, and it had been started in February 1975 when Management Association members were invited to a goal-setting seminar for career women.

For some women, Lockheed (now Lockheed Martin) is still a good place to work. Marlene Zimmerman, who like Mary Ross was trained in math, has a job that she describes in glowing terms — though, in fact, she cannot discuss her highly classified work in any detail. Of a much later generation than the two pioneers, Zimmerman graduated from high school in 1967, at a time when obtaining a doctorate in math was a realistic possibility for a woman.

She successfully pursued her goal at the State University of New York, Buffalo, where she had also obtained her undergraduate degree. After teaching math at the Naval Academy for a few years, she went to LMSC in 1983. She started out doing math-oriented work, but over the years her job has evolved, so that as of 1999, she was the systems engineer — "the tech lead" — for an arms control group. Because the weapons systems that the United States builds are subject to treaty, LMSC must be meticulous in its compliance with treaty provisions; ensuring that that takes place is the assignment of Zimmerman's group. Of her work, she says, "Work is not my life." According to Zimmerman, the pace is humane, if not relaxed, which is in marked contrast to the typical pattern among professionals in the civilian high-tech industry.[17]

Why has Lockheed been, relatively speaking, a bastion of enlightenment? For example, how does Zimmerman's demanding job allow her to have a life? The answer lies partly in the fact that the job is, by nature, highly classified, which means that she cannot bring work home, nor can she discuss it with her fellow Lockheedian husband. One of the toughest aspects of the typical Valley high-tech professional job, by contrast, is that employees often feel that they are on call twenty-four hours a day and lack the downtime that Zimmerman finds so appealing. More fundamentally, there is the issue of the very different markets for a defense contractor versus civilian electronics. Firms in the latter sector have been in a far more competitive environment, and all of their employees are likely to feel the pressure.

Yet with the falling off of military spending after the end of the cold war and with Lockheed merging with Martin Marietta in 1994 to become Lockheed Martin, those Lockheed employees lucky enough to hold onto their jobs have begun to feel the pinch. At century's end, Lockheed Martin employed only 7,850 in the Valley, a big reduction from the high-water mark of 25,000.

In 1998, Theresa Perea described the arc of her job for Lockheed. Born in East Los Angeles in 1955, she married upon high school graduation. She and her husband then moved to the Valley, where she attended trade school in electronics. Her first job was at Fairchild, stuffing circuit boards. Laid off, she went back to trade school for more training and then got a job at LMSC. Once again she was laid off, but the firm called her back two-and-a-half years later in the late 1970s, and she has been there ever since. A prototype assembler, she builds flight boxes and does repairs. "I took every course Lockheed offered, and that made me versatile." She next attended school so as to enter management, a feat she was able to accomplish. When the layoffs started again in 1990 on a much bigger scale than before, she anticipated that salaried employees would be especially vulnerable and, thus, went back to being hourly.

However, Perea's second career as an hourly employee is much different from her first. She is now heavily involved with her local of the International Association of Machinists. A union steward, she has taken labor studies classes at San Jose State University and a special course for union activists in Maryland. Along the way, she has met a number of important people, such as California Governor Gray Davis. More importantly, she considers herself to be a resource for her coworkers, because of the knowledge of workmen's compensation and occupational safety and health issues that she has acquired. "The company is more money-hungry now. They try to get one person to do the job of three. . . . Stress me out, and I'll go on workmen's comp." Lockheed Martin sends more work out to subcontractors now, she states, and it often comes back to be redone. This forceful woman explains her philosophy as follows: "I like my steak at a hot dog price, and with patience you can get it."[18]

The stories of these high-achieving individuals suggest something about the pool of savvy, energetic women that Lockheed's presence and its employment of so many thousands helped call into being. Company policy encouraged and enabled personal advancement (in marked contrast to the chances for the thousands of nonunion assemblers in high tech). Though such women might not necessarily call themselves feminists, they have accomplished feminist goals. Their existence must be factored into any attempt to understand the origins of the "feminist capital."

The Politics of Change

The most important local harbinger of the changes that produced the feminist capital was the political arrival of a deeply conservative woman named Virginia Shaffer. Elected to the San Jose city council in 1962 as the first woman in that position, Shaffer and two male allies ran on an anti-incumbent platform, with the support of home owners' groups. At issue was the tax burden imposed by San Jose's extraordinarily rapid growth in the postwar period, rather than the environmental degradation the growth had created. In the years that followed the election of 1962, the relationship between gender and the politics of growth would continue, but the issues would become explicitly environmental in nature. In 1970, one year after antigrowth advocates were able to get City Manager Dutch Hamann fired, Janet Gray Hayes won election to the city council, though she had not yet fully emerged as the environmentalist leader she would become. Indeed, the early 1970s were years in which both feminism and environmentalism would develop into genuine grassroots movements and would provide a context for what would occur in the Santa Clara Valley by the mid-1970s. Women's organizations flourished in the Valley, both those with a long history, such as the League of Women Voters and the Young Women's Christian Association (YWCA), and those that were newly established, such as the National Women's Political Caucus, founded in 1971, with a branch established in the Valley a few years later.[19]

Scholars who have studied the emergence of antigrowth activism have noticed that there is a strong correlation between women finding a political voice and women using that voice to protect the quality of life in their communities. As one scholar of the Valley put it: "To a great degree, the revolt against development was led by women. . . . The construction companies, real estate developers, public works agencies, and building trades unions that formed the core of the dominant pro-growth coalition, by contrast, were overwhelmingly dominated by men."[20] Perhaps one can understand the emergence of the feminist capital as being what happens when an area with a strong tradition of female leadership undergoes one of the most explosive periods of growth of any region in the country in the twentieth century. The result was a combustion of female energy that was further fueled by the emergence of feminist issues on the national political agenda.

Another reason for women's extraordinary success in running for office is the strongly Democratic profile that the Valley has maintained since the 1930s. Said one observer, "This valley hasn't had much in the way of entrenched structure. To the extent that there was a Republican old guard, it identified with the small agricultural town, and it was swept away."[21] In November 1970, as the feminist revolution was gearing up, the partisan breakdown in Santa Clara County was 53.5 percent Democratic and 40.6 percent Republican. (Just before the March 2000 primary, it was 46 percent Democratic and 31.6 percent Republican, with the balance comprising those who belong to third parties or who are independent.) As has become well known, women officeholders have been disproportionately Democratic since 1970 — though this was not the case during an earlier time. Clearly, this long-standing partisan breakdown has been favorable for female officeholding.

"Extraordinary" is an extravagant word to use in characterizing female success, but it seems warranted in this case. In 1987, four years after leaving office as mayor, Janet Gray Hayes reminisced about her role as a pioneer and about the legacy she had helped to foster. She pointed out to the interviewer that as of the moment of their conversation, eight of the eleven San Jose City Council members were women, as well as three of the five Santa Clara County Supervisors, the County Executive, the San Jose City Attorney, the Superintendent of San Jose Unified School District, and one State Senator.[22] Clearly, "feminist capital" was not mere hyperbole.

There were indications of political change beyond the signal sent by Shaffer and her cohorts in 1962 and the election of Hayes in 1970. Most important was the passage of Measure B in 1973, which limited new zoning for homes where schools were overcrowded. The measure narrowly passed, despite the fact that its proponents were outspent by a 10-to-1 margin.[23] It was a clear signal that San Jose voters were increasingly disaffected by rampaging growth.

That same year saw the election of the third woman, Susanne Wilson, to the San Jose City Council. Wilson, born and raised in a small town in Texas, had moved to San Jose in 1960 with her IBM engineer husband and three children. She soon became deeply involved with the PTA, her Methodist church, and then the YWCA. During the civil rights era, she worked hard to bring minority women onto the YWCA board. Seeing the dedication and risks taken on the part of civil rights activists, she decided that she needed to be more willing to take risks herself. Therefore, she was receptive when she was approached to run for the council. With her record of activism, she was a credible candidate despite being one of a field of twenty. Once on the council, she became its strongest feminist voice.[24] Decades later, she spoke of the ways in which she believes she made a difference, such as by prompting the San Jose police to institute sensitivity training for police officers dealing with

"Before you decide
how to vote on the
Jail, take a look at
the issue from our
point of view."

Supervisor Dianne McKenna
Supervisor Susanne Wilson
Supervisor Zoe Lofgren

Figure 14. The three female supervisors in Santa Clara County in 1987. These women constituted the majority on the board and were not afraid to call attention to their clout in a political brochure advocating their position on the county jail. Courtesy of Susanne Wilson.

a rape victim. In 1978, she won a seat on the Santa Clara County Board of Supervisors, where her activism continued.[25]

In 1974, San Jose voters made history by choosing Hayes as the country's first woman mayor of a sizeable city, her success having been achieved with a campaign promise to "make San Jose better before we make it bigger."[26] With a background in the PTA and the League of Women Voters—a vigorous organization in the Valley then, with its own weekly public affairs television program—Hayes had also been active on behalf of open space and parks. Before becoming the wife of a physician and the mother of four children, she had acquired a master's in social services administration from the University of Chicago.[27] This impressive-sounding degree probably mattered less than her gender did, however. What Hayes and other women were finding was that "being a woman gave them a boost [with voters] in a county that valued clean government and honesty."[28] Indeed, a commentator writing in 1984 stated, "It is, after all, something of a women's game in Santa Clara County."[29] Worth noting is the fact that by the time of her election as mayor, Hayes already had a history of being the first woman in various capacities: She had been the first woman to serve on the San Jose Metro YMCA Board of Directors and the first to serve on the San Jose Redevelopment Agency, which she had even chaired.[30]

One other ingredient that must be mentioned in discussing the mix that produced a female majority on the San Jose City Council is the city's vote to switch to district elections in 1978, with the actual change coming in 1980. This mattered despite the fact that San Jose's women were not geographically concentrated. Above all, it lowered the cost of running for office, thus making candidacy more affordable for grassroots activists. Each of the five women who won election for the first time in 1980, thereby producing the female majority, said that she would not have run had she been required to run citywide.[31] Not surprisingly, district elections also helped empower people of color. When Blanca Alvarado won a seat in 1980, for example, representing a district in East San Jose, she became the first Latino on the council to be elected to that body, as opposed to being there by appointment.

With so many influential women in office, the next question becomes this: What did they do once there? Commenting on this issue, political scientist Janet Flammang, the author of a book largely focusing on the Valley as feminist capital says: "The same conditions that favored their election—slow-

Figure 15. Janet Gray Hayes, first woman mayor of San Jose
and the nation's first woman to be the mayor of a city of 500,000 or
more in population. Courtesy of Janet Gray Hayes.

growth environmentalism, desire for clean government, affluence, risk taking, absence of machine politics, the advent of district elections in 1980, and
effective women's organizations — also favored female officials' advocacy of a
women's policy agenda and expression of a distinctive political style."[32] Let
us turn to the content of that policy agenda.

The Santa Clara County Commission on the Status of Women

Even before women comprised the majority on the City Council and the
Board of Supervisors, there was innovative decision-making taking place

where women's issues were concerned, with hearty support from male feminist officeholders. In 1973, "in response to sustained grassroots feminist pressure," the then all-male Board of Supervisors established a Commission on the Status of Women that would play a significant role in many respects. With indirect subpoena power through a supervisor, the CSW had the capacity to conduct investigations and to hold hearings, complete with testimony taken under oath. Its charge was to eliminate sex discrimination in housing, employment, education, and community services. Its staffers went into the community and attended a host of meetings, not all of them specifically devoted to women's issues. In so doing, "[t]hey raised people's consciousness about what were women's issues."³³ Nearly twenty years after its founding, an annual report detailed the crisis intervention it had undertaken. With an average of five phone calls a day "from desperate women seeking answers," the CSW hotline had taken a total of about 32,400 calls in eighteen years.³⁴ In 1998, Norma Mencacci, the CSW director during a crucial period, reminisced about her work there and about the path that led her to feminist activism. Besides being valuable for her knowledge of the CSW, her story is revelatory of the new possibilities for women in those years. Raised in the Valley, she attended high school in San Jose, worked in the canneries in the summer, and even had a summer job performing computation for NASA at Moffett Field in Mountain View. She dropped out of the University of California, Berkeley, after one year to marry a man who worked for Food Machinery Corporation, and the firm then sent them to Belgium for sixteen years. Upon the couple's return to this country in 1970, she threw herself into activity with the League of Women Voters. After her divorce in 1974, she read about a Berkeley program in city and regional planning and decided to apply. Remarkably, a dean at the university looked at this re-entry woman in her forties, took cognizance of her community involvement, and admitted her to the program. "I passed my courses with flying colors." County Supervisor Rod Diridon, who had been seeing her in attendance at meetings for years and knew about her Berkeley study, invited her to be an intern in his office while she was completing her coursework. She became the liaison between Diridon, then the chair of the Association of Bay Area Governments, and the executive director of that organization. When Supervisor Susanne Wilson succeeded Diridon with ABAG, she said, according to Mencacci, "'I want Norma.'" Mencacci thus had a position of trust with two of the five supervisors. When the position of CSW director became available, she was a logical choice.

Mencacci recalled the CSW work as being compelling. "We put on day-long workshops on child support, domestic violence, and comparable worth." It was the issue of comparable worth that would be part of the Valley's history-making. When the Board of Supervisors agreed to study gender-based pay equity among county employees, the study was remanded to the CSW, with a task force that was chaired by Supervisor Wilson and that oversaw the staff work. Represented on the task force were, among others, various ethnic communities, the Service Employees International Union (SEIU), the League of Women Voters, and the Business and Professional Women's Club. At issue, Mencacci explained, was the problem of how to read the merit rules for employees. As it happened, the county staffperson with the greatest technical command of merit rules was a male, and he was very helpful. After nine months, the group produced a document called the "Women's Concerns Task Force Report," a document that recommended a comparable worth policy for county employees. Despite the fact that Sally Reed, the County Executive, disputed some of the statements in the document (in part because of budgetary shortfalls in those years), the Board of Supervisors accepted it by a vote of 5-0. The report was used as the basis for bargaining with SEIU Local 715, the union that represented county employees.[35] But even at this juncture, the county had already been moving in the direction of comparable worth in its contracts under prodding from the CSW.[36]

Comparable Worth

To understand the comparable worth history-making that took place in the Santa Clara Valley, it is necessary to examine yet another group of mobilized women in those years: the unionized female public employees and their male allies. One reason that the female majorities on the San Jose City Council and the Santa Clara County Board of Supervisors were making nationally significant decisions in this policy area was because they were being pushed in that direction by militant workers. Yet at the same time, it should be emphasized, the workers themselves drew inspiration from the election of so many women to office, and these workers used the "feminist capital" label in building a case for their comparable worth claims.[37] In essence, the workers' argument was that women employed by the city or county in the feminist capital should not be victimized by gender discrimination in pay. As Paul Johnston put it in his study of public-sector unions:

> The mobilization by the women of San Jose thus contained two inter-twined and ultimately inseparable strands: one asserting the economic value of the women's labor and demanding higher wages; the other asserting the value of women's work through city politics and grassroots movements.[38]

The emergence of vigorous public-sector unions in the Valley dates from shortly after the passage of new California legislation in 1968 mandating "that local governments grant exclusive recognition and 'meet and confer' in good faith with employee organizations."[39] Within a few years of this development, two of the Valley's most effective public-sector locals, SEIU Local 715 and AFSCME Local 101, had come into being, with the former having its base among county workers and the latter among those in the city of San Jose. Both locals replaced earlier, less-adversarial employee associations.

The divergent nature of their respective workforces has given these locals a quite different history. County workers included many in human services, which meant a disproportionately female workforce that began to shape the nature of Local 715 early on. The employee association for the city, on the other hand, had been dominated by the men in public works, who had established themselves as comfortable allies of the progrowth coalition and tended to be dismissive of the interests of the women in the city employ. Thus when the AFSCME local took shape in the city, its female members would have to battle the male old guard left over from the employee association, as well as the city itself.

In 1975, Local 715 led five thousand county employees on an eighteen-day strike that established its reputation for militancy. This local has continued to hang tough in negotiations. Thus while the city of San Jose negotiated over comparable worth to national fanfare in 1981 — to be discussed shortly — the county workers were quietly settling a new two-year contract that gave those in low-paid clerical jobs a disproportionately big raise: Entry-level clerks, for example, got a raise of 19 percent.[40]

The path to a similar level of success for women in pink-collar jobs contained more obstacles for San Jose workers. In this jurisdiction, the power of the men in public works constituted a large roadblock. Following the election of Hayes as mayor in 1974, women in two different sectors of city employment, City Hall and the libraries, organized to advance their interests and their agenda. In 1977, union officials appealed to the regional AFSCME office in San Francisco for help in dealing with the dissidents. The regional office dispatched a seasoned organizer, Maxine Jenkins, who, rather than working to quell criticism of the status quo in the San Jose local, helped abet it. In coalition with male custodians, who felt similarly marginalized by the ruling clique, the women staged a successful rebellion. Jenkins explained the situation this way to Paul Johnston: "There was a revolution in that union while I was there. The professionals run the union now, but it had been run by the public works groups, the engineering techs. They gave pretty short shrift to women."[41]

In 1978, the dissident group won control of Local 101, with large numbers of public works employees withdrawing in disgust. The following year — after California voters passed Proposition 13, which drastically undercut the funding for local government, endangered many services, and introduced a mood of panic about the future among public employees — Local 101 staged a one-day sick-in to try to induce the city to negotiate around comparable worth issues for nonmanagement workers. This event, on April 6, 1979, has been called "the first strike for comparable worth in the United States."[42]

With conflict over pay equity looming, the city commissioned a study by Hay Associates, a San Francisco consulting firm, so as to acquire data on the relationship between pay and gender. The Hay study rated 225 nonmanagement jobs in city government on the basis of their requirements for know-how, problem-solving, and accountability, and on the working conditions (such as a need for working with hazardous materials). Not surprisingly, the study uncovered a consistent pattern of gender discrimination in the pay for female-dominated jobs: Groundskeepers made $17,521 a year, for example, and clerk typists made $14,300. These two jobs were judged to be roughly equal on the basis of the aforementioned criteria, but the former was preponderantly filled by men and the latter by women.[43] There ensued a complicated series of maneuvers on the part of both the union and the city, but everyone was aware that the national spotlight would be on them should a strike result. When the strike, which lasted nine days, finally took place in early July 1981, both Mayor Hayes and the union's chief negotiator, William Callahan, flew to New York to appear on the *Today* show, and comparable worth in San Jose became, if only briefly, the talk of the nation.[44] The strike also received sympathetic coverage in the *San Jose Mercury News*, which had recently merged with the Knight chain and consequently had improved the objectivity of its reporting.[45]

In 2000, Joan Goddard, a librarian who was active in the 1981 strike and who later became president of Local 101, emphasized that though the public works men had been a roadblock for comparable worth issues initially, by the time of the strike, many male unionists were extremely supportive. The strike received official approval from the Central Labor Council, and the Teamsters — at that time not within the AFL-CIO fold — respected the picket lines.[46] Thus, the strike was significant not only because it enhanced pay equity, but also because it marked a moment in the education of the male labor movement about the importance of gender-based issues.

"I'm proud to be the mayor of the city that took the first giant step toward fairness in the workplace for women," Mayor Hayes proclaimed upon the settlement of the strike. The agreement included both general pay increases and additional specific ones for female-dominated jobs such as in libraries.[47] The agreement also helped enhance the area's reputation as feminist capital. In the years since 1981, Local 101 has continued to negotiate for pay equity, seeking improvements for pink-collar wages. As of 2000, the gap between male and female wages for the approximately seven thousand workers in the city of San Jose continues to narrow.[48]

Occupational Safety and Health

Like comparable worth, occupational safety and health issues have been of great concern to working women in the Valley, especially to those in high tech. Both Susanne Wilson and Janet Gray Hayes provided leadership in this arena — as did many other elected officials, though there is no single event that garnered so much dramatic media coverage as the strike of 1981. Therefore, occupational safety and health has not generated the same buzz about being within the purview of politicians in the feminist capital as has comparable worth.

As of 2000, there was a body of knowledge about occupational safety in electronics that had been accumulated over the previous thirty years. In 1998, a leading expert, Dr. Joseph LaDou, who is on the faculty of the University of California Medical School in San Francisco, explained how he gradually became aware of the health hazards associated with the semiconductor industry, which was at first thought to be clean and safe. A specialist in occupational medicine, he set up an industrial practice in Sunnyvale in 1969, with no notion that he would encounter anything untoward. Before long, his waiting room began to be filled with high-tech workers, primarily women, who were suffering from hydrofluoric acid burns, about twenty a day, according to his present recollection. In that early period, the health and safety protections were minimal, he was discovering, and when companies heard workers' complaints that they were being forced to use toxins, many firms charged that there was "mass hysteria" on the part of the workers. As LaDou started to speak out about the abuses he was uncovering, certain companies recommended that his practice be boycotted. In 1986 he affiliated with the University of California, San Francisco, and in 1988 he sold his practice, glad to be beyond reprisal and to be possessed of a "bully pulpit" from which to speak out about abuses.[49]

Ed Sawicki, Intel's first safety engineer, confirmed many of the details of LaDou's account. Coming out of military service circa 1970, Sawicki trained as an engineer at San Jose State University and has subsequently done graduate work in industrial toxicology at the University of San Francisco. In 1970, the Occupational Safety and Health Administration had been set up. In response, firms were looking for ways to improve their practices in that regard. In 1972, Sawicki heard that Intel needed someone in safety engineering; he applied for and got the job. There was little budget at first, he said, so a safety officer had to be resourceful. Intel was more receptive than some of its competitors, for which "[the issue of] safety and health was a joke." In general, he stated, the way these issues had been dealt with in the past was by "poster-hanging," whereby someone would plaster a plant with admonitions about being careful and consider that the problem had been solved. The hazardous nature of the chemicals being used to produce chips had been little studied, and many of the chemicals were nasty. In consequence, the workers' complaints tended to be genuine in his observation: "[A]bout 98 percent of workers' compensation cases were real."[50]

In 1999, Dee McCrorey described her own awakening to the hazards of wafer fabrication. Having gone to work for National Semiconductor in 1971, where she started by testing circuits on the wafers, she had become habituated to using a variety of chemicals and had accepted the usual company position that these chemicals would eventually work their way out of one's system. Some years later, she was working for a smaller firm and was exposed to traces of diborane gas, a slow leak that a coworker called to her attention.[51] When she went to the company clinic, "the doctor's eyes got big when I told him what I'd been exposed to. I asked how long it would take to leave my bloodstream. He replied, 'Are you kidding? No one knows. You're all guinea pigs.'" She subsequently became a trainer, committed to helping educate her fellow workers about the dangers they could face.[52]

Such testimony abounds. A great variety of chemicals was being used to clean or etch the chips. Ventilation was often primitive, and a worker was at constant risk both from liquids — a glove might tear, for example — and from fumes. So many substances were being used that even if a particular chemical had been certified as harmless by OSHA, there was no guarantee that it was safe in conjunction with all the others with which the workers in a clean room were being bombarded. That workers had no union protection made them all the more vulnerable. When workers would go to a company doctor or nurse, they often found that the health care professional evinced more enthusiasm for defending the interests of the company than for making an accurate diagnosis.[53] One analysis of the hazards, published in 1984, after the chemicals and their effects had begun to be studied, summed up the situation as follows:

> Organic solvents . . . are used extensively throughout the industry for cleaning, stripping, and degreasing operations. They are known to cause a range of health problems, including dermatitis; central nervous system effects such as nausea, dizziness, and headaches; liver and kidney damage; and even cancer. Corrosive acids are also commonly used and can cause serious burns when splashed on the skin and eyes, as well as lung damage when inhaled. (Acid burns are the most commonly reported occupational health problem in the industry.) Other toxic substances, including gases such as arsine and phosphine, metals such as lead and other solders, and epoxies, pose additional threats.[54]

By the late 1970s, the problem was coming to the attention of more and more people, even outside the industry. On February 18, 1978, in Sacramento, for example, the California State Federation of Labor convened a conference to tackle the occupational health of women workers, which marked the first time a state labor federation had taken on this issue. Co-sponsored by the national AFL-CIO and the Labor Occupational Health Program at the University of California, Berkeley, the conference featured a speak-out by workers, many in high tech, about what they were confronting on the job and an address by San Jose Mayor Janet Gray Hayes.[55]

The preceding year, a number of groups had come together to form a new organization, the Electronics Committee on Occupational Safety and Health. ECOSH comprised representatives from diverse groups, including the Santa Clara County Commission on the Status of Women, the American Friends Service Committee, and the United Electrical Workers Organizing Committee. Their goal was to learn as much as possible about high-tech hazards.[56]

Patricia Lamborn was the first staffer for ECOSH, and in 1999, she shared her personal story as well as her memories of activism around high-tech hazards. Pursuing her degree at the University of California, Santa Cruz, in the early 1970s, she worked on a Community Studies project in East San Jose. While there, she met a number of activists who were trying to organize for the UE (a later endeavor than that of Amy Newell and John Case, and one that will be discussed fully in Chapter 7). After graduating from college, Lamborn decided to get a job in electronics and to lend her energy to the unionizing effort. Having worked one summer in a cannery but with no technical background, she applied for and got a job at National Semi-conductor in October 1974.

The interest she would later take in protecting workers from chemicals came directly out of her own experiences. Working sixty hours a week assembling calculators, she and her colleagues were in a poorly ventilated room that had not been designed for such a purpose. "We were cranking out six thousand calculators a day, and there were lots of nauseous chemicals around." She soon broke out with cysts. Though her personal doctor told her to quit her job, she stuck it out, because she felt that she was making progress in building solidarity within her immediate group: She had organized lunchtime potlucks that broke down barriers among women who did not share a common language. By this means, "we got the Asian women to slow down, because they were setting a killing pace." Then National Semi shut the whole line down and moved it to Brazil. Her next job was in a stockroom, so she no longer had to confront the hazardous chemicals, though she did continue in her attempts to organize her fellow workers.

After working for National Semi for four years, she met fellow occupational safety and health activists Robin Baker and Amanda Hawes. They persuaded her to quit her job and to work for ECOSH. Looking back, she explained her decision as follows: "I had hoped for a full-fledged union, but it was very difficult, what with the high turnover. The UE is wonderful but small and is never going to have the resources to fund a successful effort. What's more, the union didn't have a strategy for dealing with companies shutting down an entire operation on the verge of a union success, and the workers knew it. . . . The workers *did* seem ready to act on the health issues."

The pioneers of ECOSH founded two separate, but related, organizations: One was dedicated to research and could thus receive federal funding, and the other was for advocacy. The former received OSHA money during the Carter administration — "We lost all funding three months after Ronald Reagan took office," Lamborn recalls. For the latter, the women raised money from foundations. "Hundreds of workers called our hotline, and we learned which chemicals to research. We hired young people as chemical detectives — the workers would give us the trade names of products they were using. We produced fifteen fact sheets with definitive data." These activities laid the groundwork for basic knowledge about what was going on with the chemicals in the semiconductor industry.

The next step was to push the county to set up a clinic for occupational safety and health problems. Lamborn said that she and other ECOSH staffers were repeatedly told about workers going to company clinics and getting a runaround, so they knew it was essential to make more fair-minded health care available. As it happened, there were several things operating in favor of a county clinic. In the first place, the county-run Valley Medical Center was expanding and looking for a new focus. In the second place, ECOSH received help from male trade unionists, who were encountering problems when they went to wire or plumb an electronics facility. "One injured worker was a plumber; he was shocked by the sloppy use of chemicals that he found." The plumbers' union then created a contract with the county to provide a health screening for their employees, she recalled, and that helped launch the new undertaking. Finally, Supervisor Susanne Wilson was a staunch ally.[57]

Though no one from the Valley was on the *Today* show with this issue, it was beginning to garner attention in the local media, especially in the reporting of Susan Yoachum of the *Mercury News*, the same reporter who would write the initial stories about the pollution of groundwater in the wells of the Great Oaks Water Company. It was Yoachum who broke the story of the "Signetics Three," three women who had become hypersensitive to chemical exposure as a result of their work at the local semiconductor firm. The story of these women provided a wake-up call to the area.

The women had developed a variety of symptoms, such as hallucinations, blisters in the mouth, and a weight gain of forty-five pounds for one of them. Without admitting responsibility, Signetics assigned them to sit in the company cafeteria while its staff investigated, an assignment that lasted more than a year. The women, restive after so many months of waiting, complained to the federal government, shortly after which they were fired.[58] In response to their complaints, the National Institute of Occupational Safety and Health (NIOSH) planned its first investigation of a Valley semiconductor firm — only to be met by Signetics' refusal to allow NIOSH staff access to the women's records.[59] Despite this, NIOSH doctors were able to determine that the women's complaints were valid.[60] Lamborn believes that this case was a turning point, not in solving the problem, unfortunately, but in raising public awareness.

Further developments in the occupational health of high-tech workers are discussed Chapter 7. For now, it is important to emphasize the gender ramifications of the issue: The victims were disproportionately female, as were the activists. Moreover, appropriately enough in the feminist capital, it was a woman supervisor, Susanne Wilson, who provided leadership for local government to begin playing a role in addressing the problem.

Working Women in a Quintessentially Man's World

"In Silicon Valley, muscling through sixteen-hour days is a badge of honor; being celled, faxed, phoned, and e-mailed at all hours of the day and night is a sign of prestige," said a 1999 article in the *San Jose Mercury News*, in which a Valley workaholic further explained that "[y]ou're so busy doing, you can't really feel happiness, or love or laughter."[61] As the world of Silicon Valley high tech has evolved, the work culture that has arisen has been described in such phrases as "by work obsessed," "addicted to work," "nerds in gilded cubicles," and "triumph of the nerds."[62] Whereas poorly remunerated assembly workers have demanding jobs because they must employ hazardous chemicals and perform repetitive tasks, highly paid professionals in the Valley function in a potentially toxic environment of their own. If these men and women do not internalize the mantra of "faster, cheaper, better" and drive themselves harder than required by any explicit, external set of controls, they may find themselves deemed to be losers and be bumped from the fast lane. This ever-present and unrelenting pressure to produce and produce quickly takes a fearsome toll on all personal relationships, but especially those with one's partner and children, as well as on the individual's own sense of psychic well-being. We are beginning to see a literature by social scientists that deals with such issues.[63] And journalists have, not surprisingly, had a field day describing some of the odder aspects of existence in the techie world, aspects that frequently reveal the tension between personal life and career. One could summarize the situation as it currently exists as follows: Women have begun to crack the glass ceiling, but they have only been able to nibble at the edges when it comes to changing the work culture. This culture makes it difficult for a person to combine job and family life, to the special detriment of women. In consequence, women are still markedly underrepresented in jobs that pay well and that entail creative responsibilities.

From the time that Hewlett-Packard and Varian Associates were founded to the early 1970s, there were few women in technical fields or in the upper reaches of business anywhere in the country. Indeed, in 1972, only slightly more than 1 percent of engineering degrees nationally went to women (a figure that had risen to 18.7 percent by 1988). Hence it is not surprising that the female employees in high tech in the early years tended to cluster among clerical workers or in personnel or marketing, although not necessarily in management positions in the latter areas.[64] We have seen that Varian and Lockheed hired a certain percentage of women in skilled blue-collar positions (the exact percentage has proven impossible to establish), and we have further seen that Lockheed employed a small number of women engineers and scientists very early on. But even these promising openings did not constitute precedents for progress until much later.

To understand how this could have been the case in the "feminist capital," it is important to note how male the founding myths of Silicon Valley have been. In the same decade in which Janet Gray Hayes was making history and the national news, two Valley men, Steve Jobs and Steve Wozniak, were making even bigger news by founding Apple Computers. They were archetypal figures: young, long-haired hackers who had flirted with making trouble with their skills before they made the first commercially viable personal computer.[65] Apple's rapid ascent from zero to FORTUNE 500 within five years of the firm's founding in 1977 was a phenomenon in American business history. As if the careers of David Packard and William Hewlett were not inspirational enough, the legend of Jobs and Wozniak has fueled thousands of dreams of start-ups and mega success. Yet the reputation for hacking and the unkempt personal appearance of Jobs and Woz when they first launched Apple were far removed from the fantasy world of the average young woman.[66]

Jobs and Woz represented the counterculture alternative to the established business culture of the Valley that, by and large, was not all that different from the "suits" who dominated other aspects of American business at the time. Although the "traitorous eight," who had spawned Fairchild and its progeny, had been innovative scientists and entrepreneurs, they were still "suits." Thus the two modal patterns in the Valley as of 1980 were male business-as-usual and male hacker. Not surprisingly, it would take time for women to participate in this world with any kind of competitive credibility, either for themselves or for others.

The first high-profile woman in the Valley's high-tech firmament was Sandra Kurtzig of the software firm, ASK Computer Systems. Because she has written an autobiography, we have a good account of her career. Starting as a contract programmer, she developed software useful for computerizing inventory and began to land regular clients. In 1974, the firm incorporated, and she started to work with Hewlett-Packard, whose managers saw the benefits of marketing her software along with their hardware. In 1976, this arrangement blossomed into a full-fledged cooperative sales agreement, whereby ASK personnel could accompany HP personnel on calls to prospects. Revenues reflected this advantage, going from $470,000 in 1978 to $2.5 million in 1979 and $8.3 million in 1980.[67] At this point, Kurtzig began to explore the feasibility of taking ASK public, an event that took place on October 1, 1981. The firm was sufficiently successful that Kurtzig could entitle her 1991 autobiography, *CEO: Building a $400 Million Company from the Ground Up* — an unusual financial achievement for a woman at the time.

By the 1980s, there had begun to be movement in the direction of greater opportunity for women. In 1970, women held 4 percent of professional jobs in the Valley and 0.5 percent of the managerial ones; in 1980, the figures were 17 percent and 14 percent, respectively.[68] At first, however, there was a glacial pace toward the top jobs. In a 1984 study, the authors reported that among the twenty largest publicly held firms in the Valley, there were 209 corporate officers, only four of whom were female. Those same firms had 150 directors, only one of whom was female.[69]

Nonetheless, some genuine progress was taking place. Significantly, Intel appointed its first female vice president, Carlene Ellis, in 1988. Trained in computer science, Ellis had been chosen to head the firm's administrative group.[70] Five years later, Dr. Jane Shaw, president and COO of ALZA Corporation, became the first woman to be elected to Intel's Board of Directors. An accomplished research scientist, she then had 12 patents and 110 publications to her credit.[71] The U.S. Census of 1990 revealed that women in Santa Clara County held 11 percent of the electrical/electronic engineer jobs, but 23 percent of computer systems analyst or scientist jobs (see Table 6.1). As of 1999, the chief technology officer for one of the Valley's most important firms, Cisco Systems, was Judy Estrin.[72]

It is instructive to follow the progress of women through the pages of various manifestations of the Apple Computers newsletter. A 1981 article featured Jean Richardson, for example: Five years earlier, she had been a housewife. As of 1981, she was running marketing services, with a mostly female staff of twenty. In on the ground floor with the firm, she recalled there being very few other women at Apple in the early days.[73] In 1986, a high-profile woman had a much bigger job: Thirty-three-year-old Debi Coleman had just been appointed the new head of worldwide manufacturing, after having joined Apple in 1981 as a project controller for the Macintosh.[74] Women also began to be singled out for their technical feats. In 1991, for example, an article trumpeted a new product, "the plug-and-play Ethernet card," which had been developed by a disproportionately female team, with a female lead engineer. This achievement, rare in "the primarily male world of R and D," was all the more noteworthy for having been pulled off in the fastest time to market of any finished hardware ever created by Networking and Communications.[75] Yet at a meeting of six hundred Apple women in 1992, it was conceded that women at that time had no presence either on the board of directors or in top management.[76]

TABLE 6.1

Gender Breakdown of Selected Jobs, Santa Clara County, 1990

	Male	Female
Aerospace engineers	37,024 (67%)	18,015 (33%)
Computer programmers	2,813 (72%)	1,093 (28%)
Computer systems analysts and scientists	4,790 (92%)	437 (8%)
Electrical/electronic engineers	17,800 (89%)	2,170 (11%)
Electrical/electronic technicians	11,316 (77%)	3,419 (23%)
Managers and administrators (salaried)	1,894 (68%)	876 (32%)
Managers and administrators (self-employed)	8,079 (78%)	2,238 (22%)
Supervisors and proprietors, sales (self-employed)	9,413 (70%)	3,969 (30%)

SOURCE: Equal Opportunity Data from http://govinfo.library.orst.edu.

Apple is also interesting because the firm has made efforts to humanize the work environment for its employees, as well as to offer resources for those under stress owing to personal matters. Such subjects received attention in a special family services supplement to the *Apple Five-Star News* of September 24, 1991, which announced a new comprehensive family leave policy whereby employees could take up to four months of consecutive unpaid leave for parenting, elder care, and the like. Moreover, there was a child care center at the main plant in Cupertino and a special program for helping employees who were adopting children. For reasons such as this, *Working Mother* magazine chose Apple as the number one company for working moms. Even with this corporate profile, however, problems remained. A Ford Foundation study had singled out Apple as one of three firms for in-depth research on family-friendliness and had discovered that "the cult of the macho workaholic is alive and well at Apple." The supplement reported that Ford researchers had encountered one engineer who put in eleven-hour days but felt guilty when he went home, because half of his coworkers were still hard at work.

That this work culture has taken a toll on family life can be empirically demonstrated. In her important book about the Valley, *Brave New Families*, Judith Stacey summarizes that toll circa 1990:

> Much of the data on local family changes represent an exaggeration of national trends. . . . For example, while the national divorce rate was doubling after 1960, in Santa Clara County it nearly tripled. By 1977 more county residents filed divorce papers than registered marriages. By 1980 the divorce rate in the county seat [San Jose] ranked ninth among U.S. metropolitan areas, higher than Los Angeles or San Francisco. Likewise the percentage of "nonfamily households" grew faster in the Silicon Valley than in the nation, and abortion rates were one and one-half times the national figures. . . . The high marriage casualty rate among workaholic engineers was dubbed "the silicon syndrome."[77]

Something else about the toll can be discerned in the stories of two high-achieving Valley women, each of whom has needed to take time off to restore a balance in her life. Susan Brown graduated from Mills College in Oakland in the 1960s, turning down a job with IBM to pursue a project (in those pre-Internet days) by which computers on all Bay Area campuses except U.C. Berkeley were linked, with Stanford acting as the hub. After a few years, she left to do graduate work in computer science at Northwestern University, from which she obtained a master's in 1974. This led to a job at the Bell Laboratories facility in Naperville, Illinois, where she worked for eleven years. "We had the best resources in the world." With a strong math background, she did well, despite encountering substantial gender discrimination, and moved into management. She then returned to the Bay Area and worked for a defense contractor in Sunnyvale, doing disarmament work. Her next move was to a start-up, which had been launched to develop improved voice-messaging. "I was back in product development, which I preferred to pure research." After six years, the position of vice president of engineering opened up, a position for which she knew she was qualified. When it went to a less-qualified man, she left the company.

Brown experienced little difficulty landing on her feet in the go-go atmosphere that existed in the Valley circa 1995. Becoming vice president of engineering for yet another start-up, one focused on desktop video conferencing, she soon discovered that "they hadn't done their science." Five weeks after she began, the company collapsed. But the job was not a total loss. While at the company, she encountered two impressive individuals, the CEO and a gifted engineer. The three of them spent time trying to create an idea for something else to manufacture and eventually came up with a plan to develop a cellular/wireless product. They launched a start-up, with Brown as the vice president of engineering, and devoted the first year to the basic science. But the system began to look increasingly complex to her — she had a background of working on switching at Bell Laboratories, and that gave her an expertise not shared by her colleagues. She began to disagree with her boss about how long it would take to bring the product to market. As a consequence, he replaced her as vice president of engineering and reassigned her to other duties. Events proved her to be right. As of February 1999, the firm had grown to 125 employees, but these employees had collectively been unable to meet their schedules, and the board decided to take the firm to bankruptcy.

A few months later, Brown tried to be philosophical about the situation: "It's common in the Valley to have firms go under, but usually in the first year and not after four years. I'd worked the last year for free, for stock options, and now that's all gone. I'll never work full-time again, if I can avoid it. I think that the kids suffer." The last is an issue, because she is the mother of two children. As of June 1999, this brilliant and accomplished woman was functioning as a full-time mom.[78]

Unlike Brown, Barbara Wakefield has worked for one firm, Hewlett-Packard, since high school. As her story unfolds, it becomes clear that the firm has been very good to her over the course of her more than twenty-five years there. "I've always been considered a high performer, so maybe HP has been extra willing to accommodate my needs." Nonetheless, she has needed to take advantage of this willingness by alternating between full-time and part-time employment. "I'm really intense," she explained. She has needed a break from time to time, not only because of her two children but also to recharge her batteries.

Raised in Palo Alto, where her father had a job at Pacific Bell, Wakefield first went to work for HP during the summer after her senior year of high school. Attending the University of California, Davis, for a year, she went back to work on a production line at HP the following summer. She then decided to drop out of college, get married, and work at HP full-time. But a regular assembly job was very different from her summer job, primarily because her immediate supervisor resented her desire to take initiatives. After five months, she transferred to an entry-level office job that, she laughingly explained, she got "on charm alone," because she could barely type. When she first started, she would stay late to retype on her own time. Despite so unpromising a beginning, the job proved to be a means of launching her career. Her assignment was in corporate college recruiting. With tens of thousands of résumés to track, Wakefield developed a method for computerizing the data. She has been in information technology ever since. Along the way, HP has paid for her to complete a degree at the University of Santa Clara, and various supervisors have shown an unusual sensitivity to the needs of her family life. "Lew Platt [who preceded Carly Fiorina and was heading HP at the time of the interview] gets it." Wakefield explained that she has not personally experienced a glass ceiling. Rather, people have been extremely supportive. But even so, she has felt constant stress — exhaustion, even — because of the conflict between personal life and job.[79]

In sum, each of these women has had to deal with such intense work pressures that she has occasionally found them to be overwhelming. Since the advent of e-mail, cell phones, and other means of working from home, the pressure has intensified. Particularly striking is the fact that Wakefield, employed by the firm that pioneered "the HP Way" of being considerate to employees, has nonetheless found the Valley work environment to be antithetical to her children's need for a mother who can fully engage with them. As of August 2000, she had embarked on a yearlong leave.

Anita Borg is doing something about all of this, not only by trying to recruit more women into scientific and technical fields, but also by trying to change the very culture of engineering itself to make it more woman-friendly. An accomplished computer scientist with a history of having worked in the Valley herself, Borg has persuaded a number of key individuals and firms to support her Institute for Women and Technology, housed at the Xerox Palo Alto Research Center. What has gotten favorable attention from Xerox, Sun Microsystems, Hewlett-Packard, Compaq, Lotus, and IBM as well as from a select number of research universities around the country has been her contention that high-tech firms are missing the boat by having a disproportionately male workforce that is unable — or at least unlikely — to dream up a full range of products appealing to women. The argument is "that the problem has become a vicious circle. Because male-dominated corporations don't understand what women want and underestimate the market clout of female customers, women largely are left out of the technological revolution, both as developers and consumers. And a large market goes untapped."[80]

Borg is, in short, a strategist in addition to being an activist. Calculating that the appeal of opening up a vast new market may be more efficacious in freeing up corporate resources for advancing women than a strict emphasis on the justice issue would be, she has mobilized and organized to the extent that there have already been two "Grace Hopper [an important pioneer computer scientist] Celebrations of Women in Computing," with another planned. Moreover, her organization, IWT, has held a number of workshops aimed at getting girls to brainstorm the technology of the future.[81]

The macho culture in the high-tech world has made such employment antithetical to many women. One woman who walked away from a high-tech job in the Valley explained her decision this way: "I got tired of working with men who appeared incapable of looking me in the eye when they spoke to me, who asked questions of male colleagues even though they knew I was most qualified to answer, or who seemed to resent the fact that I might be capable of coming up with better technical solutions on occasion." Quoting her, *Los Angeles Times* columnist Charles Piller asserted that "[w]omen are leaving or avoiding computer careers in droves, citing discrimination by male coworkers, few role models, family-unfriendly work environments, and a general sense that the field is irrelevant to their interests." Nationally, the percentage of computer programmers who are female has declined from 35 percent in 1990 to 29 percent in 1997.[82]

That some firms, Apple and Hewlett-Packard among them, have tried to palliate the atmosphere in the land of "faster, cheaper, better" and make it more family-friendly has been noted. A particularly striking example of such an attempt lies in Sun Microsystems' employment of an on-call lactation consultant for female employees who are new mothers.[83] Nonetheless, in November 1998, a team of three San Jose State University anthropologists who have been studying the Valley for the better part of a decade reported at a conference at DeAnza College that the frenzied schedule of "life in the fast lane" conduces toward relationships of a very instrumental nature: People tend to spend time with those from whom there is an immediate "pay-off."

In this scheme of things, parents may regard their children as obstacles in the path of a career, and "friends [unrelated to work] drop off the map pretty fast." One twenty-six-year-old man told a team member that he works seventy-hour weeks, but that he "cannot imagine being elsewhere than in Silicon Valley." As an example of how he sets priorities, he and his wife negotiated an agreement whereby there would be no laptops on vacation, "unless it's important."[84]

The final word on this subject belongs to Bonny Brown, a Stanford University psychologist who studies Valley entrepreneurs: "When work and play become interchangeable and everybody in your life becomes a colleague, you lose your ability to trust others' motives, and they lose their ability to trust yours. Ambiguity breeds confusion, and when you're confused as to who your friends are, your life is well on its way to losing meaning."[85]

The Valley's Female Power Elite

During the last quarter of the twentieth century, two parallel developments were taking place in the Valley: One was the construction of a mighty, male-dominated, economic engine that helped to propel the information age around the globe, and the other was the construction of as impressive a network of high-powered women officeholders as could readily be found anywhere. Until quite recently, however, these developments have been parallel rather than intersecting. It has only been at the dawn of the twenty-first century that the two developments are becoming less discrete. In other words, the Valley's high-powered women include leaders in the tech world. In addition, women leaders in other realms are becoming so numerous and so well-placed that it seems safe to predict that the Valley of the twenty-first century will be quite different as a result of their influence — though how much more humane remains an open question.

As we have seen, women officeholders in the feminist capital have not been shy about using their clout on behalf of other women on issues such as comparable worth and occupational safety. But that was not all they did for other women. That the network of high-powered women has so flourished over time owes to the work done by the network's pioneers. Susanne Wilson, for example, established a set of connections, which she called the Good Old

Gals, to foster female leadership. When it came time to appoint a new county executive in 1981, she and her two female colleagues on the Board of Supervisors, Zoe Lofgren (now in Congress) and Rebecca Morgan, dedicated themselves to seeing that the job went to Sally Reed, who was then an assistant city manager for San Jose. Lofgren had come to realize that Reed was a brilliant administrator with a rare ability to understand a budget, and she was able to convince Wilson and Morgan that Reed was the best person for the job. After the 3-2 vote that broke along gender lines, the *San Jose Mercury News* quoted one of the two male supervisors to the effect that he had nothing against Reed, but that he thought a particular male applicant had been stronger — with the clear implication that perhaps on this occasion feminism was running amok. Worth noting is the fact that Lofgren's judgment about Reed's abilities as an administrator has been borne out — Reed has gone from running Santa Clara County to running Los Angeles County to running the State of California's Department of Motor Vehicles.[86] This aside, Reed's tenure in the Valley solidified the "feminist capital" reputation.[87]

Another high-profile woman leader was the two-term mayor of San Jose, Susan Hammer. Having chaired Hayes's reelection campaign in 1978, Hammer then won election to the city council in 1980. In 1990, she won the mayoralty, with the support of both national and local women leaders, as well as the endorsement of AFSCME Local 101. Among her many accomplishments was a reinvigoration of the arts in downtown San Jose, a place that had suffered mightily from the expansion wrought by Dutch Hamann in the 1950s. Her immediate predecessor as mayor, Tom McEnery, had provided leadership for various redevelopment projects in the downtown but without Hammer's sensitivity to the involvement of various ethnic and immigrant groups. A visionary in her outreach to the Latino community, she also provided leadership to strengthen the high-tech presence in San Jose itself, such that there were approximately fifteen hundred firms within the city limits by the time she left office. Hammer identified her other issues as affordable housing, public transportation, and child care. Indeed, one of her supporters described her as bringing "mom into the mayor's office."[88]

If Hammer brought mom into the mayor's office, then Zoe Lofgren brought mom into the Board of Supervisors and the House of Representatives — in the former quite literally, because she gave birth twice while serving on the Board. When she was running for Congress for the first time, Lofgren attempted to be listed on the ballot as "County Supervisor, Mother."

Figure 16. Susan Hammer as mayor of San Jose. Courtesy of Susan Hammer.

When the California Secretary of State issued the opinion that this designation would be illegal, Lofgren received an immense amount of publicity from the ensuing flap, including an appearance on the *Today* show. Lofgren's career, in fact, is illustrative on the national level of a new breed of woman politician: One who is able to combine highly professional credentials with family credentials.

Raised in a blue-collar family in the Mayfield district of Palo Alto, Lofgren attended Stanford University on a scholarship and majored in political science. After graduation in 1970, she immediately went to work for Valley congressman Don Edwards, interweaving her work for him with study at Santa Clara University Law School, from which she graduated in 1975. Having established herself as a resident of San Jose, she successfully ran for a community college district board in November 1979 and for the Board of Supervisors in November 1980. In a 1994 interview, she gave some of the credit for her electoral success to Janet Gray Hayes, who had appointed her to two high-profile committees in San Jose, one of which she chaired.

Along the way, Lofgren had married a fellow lawyer, and she gave birth to their first child in February 1982. But how could this new role be reconciled with her supervisory duties? When she decided to breastfeed her daughter, her mother volunteered to help. During working hours, the baby stayed in a cradle in Lofgren's county office, and when she seemed hungry, Lofgren's mother would buzz the board room. "Then I'd say 'hold the vote, she's hungry.'" This occasioned a huge uproar in the press at the time, but after the birth of her second child in 1985, her breastfeeding breaks went unremarked. Lofgren was re-elected to the Board without opposition until her run for the House in 1994.

That she replaced Don Edwards in the House was an achievement of some note, because her opponent in the Democratic primary was former San Jose mayor (1982–90) Tom McEnery. The latter had most of the endorsements, including one from the *Mercury* and one from organized labor. He also held a double-digit lead in the polls at first. Lofgren's campaign drew on support from women but also captured support from blue-collar men, with the help of an advertisement that featured a picture of her father in front of the truck he had driven for a living. A career politician — unlike the pioneers Hayes and Wilson — she was nonetheless credible when she played up her credentials as a mother, and she put all of this together for a victory.[89]

As of 2000, there are a number of other Valley women officeholders of note, such as Congresswoman Anna Eshoo and San Jose City Councilwoman Cindy Chavez. One of the most effective feminists currently in office is County Supervisor Blanca Alvarado. (Alvarado has provided leadership on an array of issues in addition to those dealing with women.) Having moved from the San Jose City Council to the Board of Supervisors to succeed Lofgren, Alvarado put her energy into a new Office of Women's Advocacy to replace the moribund Commission on the Status of Women. To do so, she convened

Figure 17. Santa Clara County Supervisor Blanca Alvarado in
2000. Before being elected to the board, Alvarado had become, in
1980, the first Latino or Latina elected to the San Jose City
Council. Courtesy of Blanca Alvarado.

community leaders over a period of eight months to arrive at a job description for the OWA manager. In consequence, many women, such as those in the public-sector unions, are enthusiastic about her performance.[90]

Small-Business Owners

Yet another category of influential women — and one that has grown substantially without having garnered the same attention that has been accorded to the women in high tech — has been that of women who own or manage small businesses, such as real estate firms, restaurants, and retail outlets.[91] Such enterprises constitute the health of a downtown in particular and of a community in general, and those who run them are respected in the community.

Vicki Kwok Ching embodies this development. Born in China, Ching was raised in Taiwan. Having completed high school, she entered Taiwan University with the highest score on the entrance exam for her year, a feat that gave her celebrity status and enhanced her own self-confidence. She later moved to the United States when she transferred to Vassar College, from which she graduated. She then went on to do graduate work in history at Tufts University and to attend law school at the University of San Francisco.

Even with all this education in her background, it would be her skillful running of a restaurant that provided her with a métier. Ching's marriage ended in the early 1990s, at about the same time that California's economy was in its most serious slump in decades. As part of the divorce settlement, Ching acquired Palo Alto's best-known Chinese restaurant, Ming's, which was then in the throes of bankruptcy. As the economy improved, so, too, did Ming's bottom line. As of 2000, the restaurant is thriving, and owning it has afforded Ching the role of a player, both within the Chinese American community — she was president of the local Taiwan University Alumni Association — and in organizations for general community betterment, such as the Palo Alto Rotary Club and the Palo Alto Foundation.[92] It is only within the past half-generation that a Chinese American woman could occupy such a position.[93]

Amy Dean and Carly Fiorina

Whereas twenty-five years ago it was San Jose's pioneering women, in particular Mayor Hayes, who were making national news, now it is a woman labor leader and a woman CEO who are the Valley's top female newsmakers. Intense, extremely intelligent, and charismatic, they are breaking new ground in their respective fields.

When the *New York Times* ran a feature about Silicon Valley's AFL-CIO chief Amy Dean, the headline read: "The Most Innovative Figure in Silicon Valley? Maybe This Labor Organizer."[94] The article went on to state that "executives speak of Amy Dean with equal parts awe and anxiety." This might perhaps be discounted as press hyperbole, except for the fact that many other observers wax enthusiastic as well. A political scientist at San Jose State University referred to her, for example, as "one of the Valley's truly strategic thinkers."[95] Another academic commented in informal conversation that "when I'm around her, I feel like people must have felt around John L. Lewis in 1935." All of this is being said about a young woman who just turned forty in 2002.

Amy Dean was born into a family with deep roots in the labor movement in Chicago. She graduated with a degree in sociology from the University of Illinois, Urbana, in 1984. Her studies — as well as the ethical code of her Jewish religious background — convinced her of the importance of a vigorous trade union movement to creating a just society. Thus it was a logical next step for her to go to work for the International Ladies Garment Workers' Union upon graduation, at first as part of an internship program at the University of Chicago, where she had been accepted for graduate study in public policy, and then as a career commitment. Rising quickly to the position of Midwest Regional political education director for ILGWU, she moved to San Francisco in 1989 to work for ILGWU and to join her husband-to-be, who was working in Silicon Valley. Though she loved many things about San Francisco, she found the labor movement to be closed to advancement by newcomers, hence she moved to San Jose in 1990 as political director of the South Bay AFL-CIO Central Labor Council. In 1994, while still in her early thirties, she became executive director of the council, the fifteenth largest in the country. No one else had ever filled such a position so young in any of the country's six hundred labor councils.

"I'm not unique any more," she explained in 1998. "There are other young people. In fact, local labor councils are becoming the hot spot. What other institution sits at the crossroads of labor and community?" When John Sweeney was elected to head the national AFL-CIO in 1995, he appointed Dean to head a strategic planning committee aimed at putting central labor councils "back in business." Dean believes that this reinvigoration is beginning to produce results, hence her optimism about the future of the institution. As for the Valley itself, she assessed the strengths of local labor as follows: In the first place, there is vitality within the service employees (AF-SCME and SEIU) and the building trades, among others—though not in manufacturing. In the second place, there is "a wonderful culture of activism in this community that lives in the shadow of San Francisco. It's less flashy than theirs, but very solid."

Dauntingly, it is up to Dean and the team she has built to use those strengths to try to dent the anti-union monolith that is the Valley's high-tech industry. "SEIU and AFSCME are not going to jump off a cliff and start organizing in industries where they have no current base," she contended. Therefore, it is her job to come up with innovative alternatives. Not an easy task, but she was far from being discouraged during her 1998 interview. Pointing out that high tech is still very young, she argued that it should not be forgotten that "historically, industries have never organized in their infancy—only as they mature."[96]

An assessment of her successes so far is provided in Chapter 7. What is important for the current purpose is to point out that the "feminist capital" was the site for this breakthrough figure. Interestingly, one of Dean's chief aides, Bob Brownstein, was chief of staff for Susanne Wilson and budget director for Susan Hammer before joining her team, thus providing a human link among generations of women leaders.

Like Dean, Hewlett-Packard's Carly Fiorina is a prodigiously talented woman. And she has become an even bigger media star. Indeed, when she became president and CEO of the revered firm in July 1999, she was not only the first woman to head a blue-chip corporation but also the first outsider to run HP. Since taking over, she has continued to maintain a high profile, especially within the ranks of the eighty-three thousand–worker company.

Even before landing the HP post, Fiorina, then president of the global service providers operation at Lucent Technologies, had become known as the most powerful woman in American business. Her undergraduate training in medieval history and philosophy at Stanford University, from which she graduated in 1976, does not constitute a likely background for someone who would wind up in so powerful a position in the high-tech world, but Fiorina went on to earn an MBA at the University of Maryland, after which she launched her career as an account executive at AT&T. Her talent was quickly recognized, and AT&T sent her to a yearlong management program

Figure 18. The face of female power in the Valley in the early
twenty-first century: Amy Dean, executive officer of the South Bay
AFL-CIO. Courtesy of the South Bay Labor Council.

at the Sloan School of Management at MIT in 1988. Upon her return to the
firm, she enjoyed a rapid rise to a leadership position, so that when AT&T
spun off Lucent in 1995, she could emerge as a formidable figure within the
corporation.[97]

The period when Fiorina was ascending at Lucent was also the time when her immediate predecessor as CEO at HP, Lewis Platt, was changing the corporate culture to make HP friendlier to the needs of its female employees. According to the lore, Platt's conversion to this stance began when he lost his first wife in 1981. Left with two young daughters and filled with stress about fulfilling his parental duties to them while maintaining the pace in his already demanding job at HP, he developed insight into how tough it was for working mothers to do it all. Further, he realized that the firm was having a difficult time retaining many of its best women. When he became CEO of HP in 1992, he was in a position to do something about the situation. HP not only instituted a variety of flextime and job-sharing possibilities for men and women, but it also went so far as to encourage its employees to take advantage of them (as in the aforementioned case of Barbara Wakefield). Platt himself also began to go out of his way to encourage female ability.[98] Hence the firm that already enjoyed the reputation of being the best place to work in the Valley — especially for salaried employees — became an even better place to work. The HP Way now encompassed family-friendliness as well as a new willingness to dent the glass ceiling for women.

According to the analyses in the business pages, Fiorina's challenge in 1999 was to retain some of the aspects of the HP Way while shaking up the "stodginess" that was costing HP market share and profits. Known for her combination of sensitivity and toughness, she pledged that she would get HP to run on "Internet time" and to develop more products designed to support Internet use. In December 1999, *Forbes* ran a preliminary assessment of "the Carly Show."

> It is closed to outsiders, but Hewlett-Packard Co. is staging the greatest new show in corporate America. "Travels with Carly" stars Carleton S. Fiorina, who in July became the first outsider ever brought in to run the venerable citizen of Silicon Valley. After grabbing a torrent of media coverage upon her arrival, she disappeared from the public stage. But inside HP, Carly is on tour. She paces HP stages around the world, descending on twenty sites in ten countries to enlist rebels and battle resistance.
>
> Few executives anywhere push their style so forcefully, let alone at an outfit like HP, a place so low-key and humble that Japanese executives are shameless self-promoters by comparison. "Leadership is a performance," says Fiorina, 45. "You have to be conscious about your behavior, because everyone else is."[99]

It is not yet possible to gauge what Fiorina's success will be or what the costs may entail in lay-offs or additional stress to employees.[100] Even so, it is important, for our purposes, to take note of the fact that two women, a labor leader and the leader of a firm that has always been staunchly anti-union, are facing off, at least indirectly, in a battle to determine the shape of the Valley in the twenty-first century. Moreover, in July 2000, the *Mercury* ran a list of the forty most powerful people in the Valley and of that group, strikingly enough, thirteen were women, including Dean, Fiorina, Lofgren, and Eshoo.

From the late nineteenth century on, the Santa Clara Valley has had a sufficiently fluid social structure to foster mobility — access to the California Dream — for members of groups that had had a more difficult time gaining such access in other parts of the country. At first it was European Catholics who climbed the ladder with their fruit-growing skills and then, after the labor militancy of the 1930s, with their union-wage jobs. Then it was the tens of thousands who moved up with relatively well-paid aerospace jobs. That women from a number of backgrounds have progressed further in officeholding and in access to genuine community power than in most other parts of the country is not surprising. That the well-placed women have so far not succeeded in doing much to temper the most demanding aspects of life in the fast lane is equally unsurprising, because they are confronting both a potent culture and a potent source of economic might.

Historically, the counterweight to right the imbalance of power in the Valley would have been organized labor. Given its withering strength since World War II, however, labor is fighting an uphill battle to combat the massive concentration of power that the high-tech industry constitutes (a fact of which Amy Dean is clearly very well aware). The questions with which the next chapter deals are these: How severe has the maldistribution of resources become? What has happened to the fluidity? And what are the prospects for change?

SEVEN

The Global Economy on the Home Front:
A Tale of Two Valleys

At the dawn of the twenty-first century, there were few regions in the world so admired yet so envied as Silicon Valley. Each year in the late 1990s brought stories of increasing billions of dollars of venture capital being invested in the Valley and of firms arising out of virtually nowhere to assume a commanding position in a new market. Novel products, such as Internet networking systems, kept emerging that helped the Valley maintain its preeminence. Vast personal fortunes made by a few dazzled those on the outside looking in. Thoughtful observers had been, for some time, pointing out that there was a "dark side of the chip," a dark side encompassing such things as the Valley's high divorce rate, the great disparities in wealth and income created by the fabulous success of a few, and the toll on worker health of employment in high tech. But most Americans thought of the region in terms of its capacity to bestow riches on fortunate tech wizards.

In truth, even industry groups were beginning to take note of the growing gap between the Valley's haves and its have-nots and of the pernicious impact this would have on the quality of life for everyone. In the late 1990s, reports by the business-led consortium Joint Venture: Silicon Valley Network began to sound the alarm about the problem.[1] Startlingly, during a period of vast economic growth in the early 1990s, "real incomes for the poorest 20% of all households in the region fell by 8%, while rising by 2% in California overall."[2] Other statistics show a picture of the Valley that emphasizes its stark contrasts. For starters, in 1999, John Chambers, president and CEO of Cisco Systems and the Valley's most highly paid executive, made $121,701,629 in salary and stock options. Reporting this in its annual survey of the salaries of CEOs of large Valley companies (767 in 1999), the *San Jose Mercury News* further stated that the compensation for the group as a whole had gone up 70 percent in one year. "By contrast, the average annual wage around San Jose crept up a mere 5.87 percent to $51,509 from 1997 to 1998, [according to] the latest date available from the Bureau of Labor Statistics."[3] For those at the bottom of the ladder, for whom the average must seem almost as unattainable as Chambers' salary, the problem was especially harsh. Given that in 2000, the median price of a home in the Valley was in excess of $500,000, those who clean toilets or care for other people's children or assemble electronics components for a living have been condemned to a lifetime of being wretchedly housed. And those who have been solidly middle-class who lose a job or go through a divorce can experience painful downward mobility and can find themselves living in a mobile home or apartment rather than the suburban home to which they had become accustomed.[4]

The questions for this chapter are these: Why has the inequality been so extreme? How has the well-documented trend toward globalization in recent decades contributed to this situation? Finally, what are the prospects of halting or reversing the drift toward increasing disparities?

At "War" with Japan

To understand the increasing inequality in the Valley as of 2000, one must begin with the fierce competition with Japan that erupted in the 1980s. In the euphoria of flush times, it was seemingly forgotten that during the 1980s, firms in the U.S. semiconductor industry had been locked in what appeared to many as a fight to the finish with their Japanese competitors. The mid-1980s were the nadir, but as early as October 1980 Intel's Andrew Grove proclaimed: "We are at war ... with Japan."[5] Having pioneered the new technology, American firms such as Intel found themselves being outperformed, especially when it came to the relatively unspecialized "commodity chips." That same year, in fact, Hewlett-Packard announced that Japanese chips were preferable to American-made ones for the firm's needs.[6] In 1981, Intel's leadership opted to employ "the 125 percent solution:" "Grove decided that instead of laying off employees, he'd order Intel's staff to work 25% harder — two hours a day, every day, for free."[7] In 1986, Grove continued to employ dramatic language to characterize the semiconductor industry's problems: "There is a fire burning, threatening to destroy our industry." His anxiety is understandable in light of the fact that U.S.-based firms lost nearly $1 billion in 1985.[8]

Grim reports were emanating from throughout the Valley. At National Semiconductor, for example, there were losses totaling $165 million over a five-year period ending in May 1990. Between 1987 and 1990, the firm shut down four plants, laid off nearly six thousand workers, and sold off two divisions that accounted for nearly 43 percent of its business.[9] At Varian Associates, a key supplier of the equipment to manufacture the chips, the 1980s were rough, as well. Tellingly, in just one quarter ending in July 1986, the firm posted a loss of approximately $5 million, with the semiconductor equipment group primarily responsible for the misfortune.[10] In 1980, the United States commanded 57.2 percent of the world semiconductor market, yet it had only 35.9 percent of it in 1989.[11] In short, during the 1980s, the Valley was hurting, and industry leaders had to produce innovative ideas and make tough choices before a recovery could take place. "We were on the rocks," said Jerry Sanders of Advanced Micro Devices to characterize the period.[12]

One of the most important steps was to concede a certain market to Japan while bolstering what each company could do best. In Intel's case, their best bet was to produce pathbreaking "architecture" for ever-more powerful microprocessors. In fact, Grove led Intel out of commodity chips and into microprocessors that the Japanese could not match.[13] (So successful was that strategy that as of January 1998, Intel manufactured nearly 90 percent of the world's PC microprocessors.[14]) At National Semi the strategy, according to a company spokesman, was to focus on "high-complexity ... products of a proprietary nature that would be more resistant to Japanese intrusion. We embarked on an aggressive R & D investment program for the development of proprietary products that has totaled well over $1 billion in the [19]80s."[15] Yet another strategy was the one employed by T. J. Rodgers of Cypress Semiconductor. He positioned his firm to take advantage of a niche market by focusing on just a few products and by establishing a relatively small plant to keep costs down. In 1986, Cypress was the single most profitable U.S. semiconductor firm.[16]

But smart strategies were not enough. Success also required help from Uncle Sam in the form of subsidies and a tougher trade policy toward Japan. In particular, in 1987, key firms in the industry put together a research consortium called Sematech to reinvigorate semiconductor production. The group was financed with tens of millions of dollars worth of government help.[17] Though the consortium had its headquarters in Austin, Texas, Intel's Robert Noyce became its first CEO. (With the ever-advancing globalization in the late twentieth century, Sematech developed an international branch in 1999.) Through Sematech, the industry was able to develop more and more sophisticated and less error-ridden means of producing chips.

While the pressure from Japan was at its most intense, there were many attempts to cut costs, improve quality, and increase productivity. For example, in the late 1970s, Intel instituted "Intel Circles" whereby a group of four to ten people in the same department met regularly for problem solving.[18] Having adopted this quality circle approach, the firm went on to found a training program called Intel U to ensure that its employees would be able to burnish their skills. At first, the students were all managers, but over time the "student body" grew to include a broader range of employees. Intel developed these policies in response to the realization that in Japan production workers might well receive six months of training, while in the United States, assembly workers were typically receiving four or five days of training.[19]

Finding new ways to transfer the production work to lower-wage economies was clearly of supreme importance. As was mentioned in earlier chapters, companies outsourced abroad and built wafer fabs in less expensive areas of the United States. In April 1980, for instance, Intel announced the selection of Albuquerque as the site of its newest fab.[20] Since that time, an increasing number of production functions have been transferred out of the Valley, although other functions have often arisen to take the place of those being lost. Nonetheless, about thirty thousand jobs were lost in the 1980s, with production workers constituting 49.1 percent of manufacturing employment in the industry in 1977 but only 37.9 percent in 1987.[21] Summing up the effects of the 1985 slump, the scholar Ramon Sevilla stated: "As a result of the large number of permanent job displacements during the 1985 recession, working conditions of blue-collar workers, especially those who had built up seniority in the industry, have deteriorated due to the difficulty of finding meaningful employment alternatives."[22]

Another means of cutting costs and protecting oneself from excess capacity was an increasing reliance on contract manufacture. Says a scholar of this subject: "The mid-1980s are remembered as a cruel period in the electronics industry. . . . Faced with growing demand but still cognizant of recent problems with overcapacity in the industry, firms in the computer and data communications industries were reluctant to build new in-house manufacturing capacity and began to rely on their outside contractors even more heavily than before."[23]

And then there was the impact on the structure of compensation. Simply put, the already glaring contrast between the compensation for professionals and that for production workers became even more so. It was necessary to pay the former well enough to attract and maintain a high-powered workforce, but the latter represented a prime target for cutting costs. Absent the protection of a union and with thousands of newcomers arriving, as we learned in Chapter 5, production workers were in a poor — and deteriorating — bargaining position.

The larger meaning of the war with Japan is that an industry that was already hypercompetitive, with powerful imperatives to design new products and bring them to market as quickly and cheaply as humanly possible, became even more so.

The Offshore Imperative

Outsourcing abroad as a means of saving money is almost as old as the industry itself. Fairchild, the mother firm of the local semiconductor industry, came into being in 1957 and built an assembly plant in Hong Kong as early as 1963.[24] But even before that, as we learned in Chapter 4, the pioneering electronics firm Varian Associates had begun to establish an overseas presence.[25]

Varian helped lead the parade toward high-tech globalization because it was Russell Varian and his colleagues who had developed the klystron. In the early stages of the postwar electronics industry, this tube was invaluable to the nascent industry throughout the world. The firm's newsletter of November 1957, for example, trumpeted a trip to Japan by then-president Myrl Stearns and his wife. They went to Japan to explore the technical capabilities of Japanese business "in anticipation of licensing agreements." A number of large Japanese electronics companies were already using the klystron, the newsletter explained. Ten years later, a newsletter listed the places at home and abroad where facilities, both plants and sales operations, were located: San Carlos, Monrovia, Walnut Creek in California; Beverly, Massachusetts; Union, New Jersey; Salt Lake City, Utah; Lexington, Kentucky; Portland, Oregon; and small towns in Illinois and New York — plus a plant in Ontario, Canada. Overseas there were Varian outposts in Paris, Zurich, London, Inverkeithing (Scotland), Turin, Rome, Stockholm, Amsterdam, Stuttgart, Sydney, and Melbourne. As of 1989, 40 percent of the firm's business came from outside the United States.[26] As of 1992, there were manufacturing facilities in seven countries on three continents, offices in nineteen countries, and sales being made in more than one hundred countries.[27] Over the years, many other American-made goods that were as stellar as the klystron had been in its day would contribute to a similar pattern for other firms.

Valley firms have turned to overseas markets and overseas production at a fraction of the cost of domestic production, especially that in the Valley itself. As the last half of the twentieth century amply demonstrated, the electronics industry was particularly well adapted to separating management/ development from production. The chips themselves — and chip-based products — are small, and the cost of transporting them is cheap. Although professionals, especially talented scientists and engineers, are often recruited by the promise of the good life in a desirable location — such as the Valley of Heart's Delight — the cost of living in such a place makes it a poor choice for concentrated production. Thus, the separation of design from production was possible, it was desirable from the companies' standpoint, and, for many firms, it happened very quickly.

Those high-tech companies not so swift to effect the separation as were such companies as Intel, which was manufacturing in Penang within a few years of the firm's founding, have complained of being at a competitive disadvantage. Apple Computers constitutes a prime example. Taking over as

CEO of Apple in 1992, Michael Spindler amplified an earlier statement he had made: "What I said was that relative to our global competitors in Taiwan, Texas, and elsewhere, we were at a disadvantage in facilities costs and costs of living because of the large proportion of our workforce located in the Santa Clara Valley [83 percent in 1992]. . . . We have to consider relocating functions in order to remain competitive."[28]

Articles in the *San Francisco Examiner* and the *San Jose Mercury News* document a similar problem at IBM. In 1995, the firm brought in a new executive to run the San Jose operation. Big Blue had been losing market share of its disk drive business, headquartered in San Jose, to upstarts such as Seagate. San Jose employment had peaked at around ninety-five hundred in 1985, but it was down to around five thousand ten years later as IBM "finally mimicked competitors by shifting jobs to Southeast Asia."[29] Four years later came the announcement that IBM would transfer its entire San Jose disk drive operation to Japan and complete the transfer of its tape drive assembly from San Jose to Guadalajara.[30]

Another aspect of high-tech globalization that has been an important factor in the Valley has been foreign investment. By the mid-1980s, there was an infusion of capital from Korea and Japan, as well as from the Netherlands and France.[31] To cite just one example of this phenomenon, in 1979, the French firm Schlumberger bought Fairchild.

By 2000, the big story was the amount of collaboration and integration between the Valley and Taiwan. Concerned about the loss of many of its most talented offspring, Taiwan developed strategies to reverse the brain drain to Silicon Valley and the rest of the United States. Taiwanese officials began to include overseas Taiwanese in their plans and to solicit ideas from them, with the result that there has been a considerable amount of reverse migration, in some instances of people who have lived in the Valley for ten or fifteen years. Indeed, homes in the Hsinchu Science Park have been built to resemble suburban homes in the Santa Clara Valley, apparently so that the returnees will feel at home.[32]

To give an accurate assessment of the costs and benefits to Valley residents of the global economy is challenging, because many generalizations must be nuanced or qualified. It is certainly true that tens of thousands of production jobs vanished as companies built assembly plants or fabs elsewhere. On the other hand, as of 2000, most observers felt that the Valley's biggest problem was not a dearth of jobs — as seemed to be potentially the problem in the 1980s — but rather an excess of them, considering the supply of housing stock. Between 1995 and 2000, about 168,000 jobs were created in Santa Clara County, as opposed to 28,000 new dwellings. This resulted in a ruinous inflation in home prices.[33] As this is written, the dot-com downturn has begun to reverse the situation whereby there is an overabundance of employment, but it has not yet brought down the price of housing significantly.

The downturn notwithstanding, what seems most problematic is not so much that the process of globalization has shrunk the volume of employment.[34] Rather, it is, as we will learn, that the blue-collar work that is left is often of a contingent nature — working for a subcontractor, for example, or even performing highly exploitative industrial homework. Either that or the blue-collar employment requires a level of training that places it out of reach of the many thousands of poorly educated newcomers to the Valley, about whom we read in Chapter 5. This means that the gap between haves and have-nots exists within the ranks of production workers as well as between workers and professionals.

The UE Takes Another Shot

That the high-tech industry in the Valley has so successfully resisted the inroads of labor organizing is clearly one of the major factors in the growing gap between haves and have-nots, inasmuch as production workers currently have few protections from the ravages of market forces. We have seen that the Valley's vigorous labor movement of the 1930s lost steam and became much weaker during the cold war–obsessed 1940s and 1950s — as happened in most of the rest of the country. We have further seen that the first serious attempt in the early 1970s to organize in high tech on behalf of the United Electrical Workers bore no permanent fruit. The globalizing economy was implicated in that failure, both because of the influx of immigrants in a poor position to defend their interests and because of runaway production. There were a number of subsequent attempts to organize during the adolescence of the industry, most notably another by the UE. Though none was successful, these attempts bear scrutiny for what they tell us about the clout of high-tech employers and the consequent situation of workers.

By the mid-1970s, the activities of Amy Newell and John Case were winding down, with Newell departing for the East Coast in 1975. It would not, however, be long before there was another concerted effort by UE activists. It has been possible to learn a great deal about this second endeavor through interviews with many of those mostly closely involved. Moreover, there is also a written record because of the publicly identified misconduct of one firm, Signetics, against which a fired UE activist successfully pursued a complaint with the National Labor Relations Board.

One of the key activists, David Bacon, explained how he came to work on behalf of the UE. Having been an organizer for the United Farm Workers, he decided to switch his focus to electronics and secured employment as an engineering technician with National Semiconductor in 1978. Lacking any prior experience, he landed the job by telling the interviewer that he would troubleshoot the "fabulously complicated" machines by checking to see if they were plugged in! He now says that he began to understand the level of inequity in the industry when he met a Filipina coworker with an advanced degree from her homeland who was making about half what he, a white male, made with qualifications that included neither experience in the industry nor a college degree.[35]

By that time, there was a small core of "a couple of dozen" activists, including Bacon, who reconstituted a UE organizing committee. The committee's greatest triumph came early on when its members mounted a campaign at National Semi and at Signetics to achieve a cost-of-living raise. Bacon, at this juncture their president, got the idea from a UFW campaign in which he had participated. Committee members surreptitiously plastered yellow stickies throughout the plants calling for a raise. So ubiquitous were the stickies, and so successful were they in stirring up worker anger over wages (during a time of high inflation in the late 1970s), that National granted an across-the-board raise of thirty-five cents an hour.

Unlike the earlier effort by Newell and Case, this second committee then decided to operate more openly and to struggle for legitimacy. They published a newsletter (with funding from the national UE and an Oakland local) that community supporters distributed at the gates of selected plants during shift changes. At first, the actual employees at the various firms remained under cover, but as a result of testifying about occupational safety issues, Bacon went public, and others soon followed in his wake. He now says, "I felt like I was painting a big target on my back."[36]

By the time the committee was distributing its newsletter, the Electronics Committee on Occupational Safety and Health was also in operation, with much communication and some overlap in personnel between it and the UE group. ECOSH leaders decided to launch a campaign to get the dangerous chemical trichlorethylene (TCE) banned from the chip production process. They needed a "worker" to testify about its hazards at a press conference, and Bacon found himself in that role. Soon thereafter, another committee member, Signetics employee Pat Sacco Woods, spoke out about TCE also, becoming the second activist to go public. In the latter case, Woods had become so sensitive to chemicals as a result of working with TCE that she was unable to walk down a supermarket aisle containing household chemicals without distress.[37]

At this point, there was much to encourage the UE group. The cost-of-living campaign had borne fruit, the activists had gone public with impunity — at least to date, the campaign against TCE was successful, and it began to be possible to attract workers to house meetings. A key recruit at this time was Romie Manan, a man who had been a union activist in his native Philippines and had then found employment with National Semiconductor fairly soon after arriving in the Valley in 1979. In Bacon's judgment, Manan helped substantially in giving the UE effort credibility with his fellow Filipinos, which was then the largest single ethnic group in the workforce at the plants being targeted. "When he joined, we could do the newsletter in English, Spanish, *and* Tagalog." Finally, in 1980, the national UE invested in a full-time organizer, Michael Eisenscher, sent on permanent assignment to the Valley.

Bacon explained the developments that took place, which coincided with the belt-tightening set in motion by the "war with Japan:"

> We never really thought that we were in the position to fight for union recognition; we knew it'd be a long drawn-out process. The companies cranked up the discipline as a means of reducing the workforce while not technically laying workers off. Foremen were enforcing these disciplinary measures, and it was tough. By 1982 we had a few hundred members, many of whom were Filipino. We were pretty close to the Human Relations Committee of Santa Clara County. We convinced them to hold a hearing on the issue of racism in electronics, launched a big campaign about racism, in fact, and that's when lots of us were fired — though not Romie.[38]

One other source of provocation must be mentioned in the litany of what activists did to render themselves personae non gratae to their employers, and that is the campaign they launched to establish their right to leaflet in the National Semiconductor cafeteria. The organizers' position was that they were not interfering with anyone's work, that the leafleting was being done on their own time, and that therefore it was legal. It seemed to the activists that the company responded to this by broadcasting videos in the cafeteria about the competition with Japan. The videos featured exhortations by CEO Charles Sporck to "team up to win." In short, the two sides were engaged in a turf war for the cafeteria, a war that the company obviously had no intention of losing. One by one, the activists began to be fired or to quit because "they'd [the company] figure out how to make your work life horrible." In an ironic twist, Bacon himself was fired over a violation of health and safety rules.[39]

The accuracy of this account by activists is borne out by a contemporary article by Susan Yoachum in the *San Jose Mercury News*. Describing Bacon's firing, Yoachum said that she had seen a notebook handed out at an American Electronics Association seminar in May 1980. In this document, attorneys warned high-tech supervisors of the potential hazards of "the failure to remove misfits." In other words, they warned against any laxness about allowing identifiable union activists to retain their jobs.[40] Clearly, the warning fell upon receptive ears.

The case of Rachel Marshall offers the strongest evidence of the lengths to which employers were willing to go to keep out those they saw as troublemakers. In 1978, Marshall landed a job with Signetics as a telecommunications operator. Working swing shift, she took breaks with production workers, one of whom told her about the union. Marshall was soon a convert and began attending UE meetings, which were held at a small Catholic Church in East San Jose. Before long, she was handing out leaflets herself and working with Pat Sacco Woods. Eventually, the two women decided to start wearing buttons that said "United Electrical Workers Organizing Committee." It did not take long for the company to respond. One evening, Marshall came to work to find that a coworker, Esther Singh — with whom she had been repeatedly sparring, since Singh had metamorphosed from a union supporter to an antagonist — seemed eager to pick an argument with her. As a consequence of the argument, Marshall was placed on suspension and guards immediately marched her out. She was subsequently fired, at which point she filed a complaint with the NLRB alleging unwarranted termination. In the text of the NLRB decision is the description of an affidavit from Singh, in which she repudiated earlier testimony of hers that had damaged Marshall:

> This final affidavit was a total about-face, and depicted Singh as having deliberately orchestrated, with [Mary] Monfared's [a supervisor in industrial relations] conniving knowledge and assent, a series of confrontations with Marshall that were designed to show the insufferableness of working in proximity to Marshall. Singh expressly told of how her bona fide interest in a departmental transfer was cleverly deflected by Monfared into a vehicle for spawning the notion that Marshall was exasperatingly antagonistic, disruptive, and uncooperative in work-related matters. Singh explained that from an opening suggestiveness to full-blown confirmation, Monfared induced and encouraged her to vex Marshall, while at the same time acting victimized by the process.[41]

This evidence plus the fact that Marshall herself was "a superbly convincing witness" persuaded the Board to find in her favor. She received a cash settlement, which she used to finance her own law school education, and the company was required to post a notice to its employees about the disposition of the case.[42]

When the dust settled, however, the efforts to form a union under UE auspices had been seriously weakened. Most of the activists had been purged. Lacking a foothold within the various plants, the UE went into a hiatus and then tried to organize a "nonunion union" from the outside, to no great effect.[43] The good news for the organizing committee was that Pat Sacco Woods and Romie Manan were able to keep their jobs. Woods was a single mother who worked assiduously to learn all the company rules so as to protect herself. Manan, however, had the help of the activists who mobilized to protect his job with National Semi.[44]

Other organizing efforts included one by the Glaziers' Union at Atari in 1983, with the union losing by a vote of 143 to 29. An Atari worker told a reporter, "Unions are outdated; we don't need them."[45] The International Brotherhood of Electrical Workers lost a vote at Raytheon in Santa Clara by a margin of 284 to 219.[46] Then there was a similarly unsuccessful attempt by the United Auto Workers to organize Intel's Livermore fab. Intel responded to the attempt with a massive campaign of its own to persuade workers that they were better off without a union, in part by discerning and responding to grievances that seemed to the firm to be legitimate. In this instance, only one in five employees voted for the union. "In the end, the ballot result was proof that Intel knew its own workers better than the outside organizers of the labor union," according to the author of a book about Intel.[47] The firm's Robert Noyce told the authors of another book: "Remaining nonunion is an essential for survival. . . . If we had the work rules that unionized companies have, we'd all go out of business. This is a very high priority for management here."[48]

By happenstance, the high-water mark of the union exertions coincided with the height of the competition with Japan. Many firms were mounting drives to convince their workers of the need for extra effort and for special loyalty, even without the threat posed by organized labor. Thus the firms were in fighting mode and had a ready-made argument to deflect the activists' contentions. This attitude no doubt figured into the various defeats, in addition to the more heavy-handed tactics that were being employed by firms.

In addition to the other determinants that have been adduced to account for the labor failure, there is the fact that the union that showed the greatest vigor in attempting to organize high tech in the Valley — the UE — had long been marginalized by the AFL-CIO and its constituent elements. As a consequence, little support was forthcoming for UE activists from the Santa Clara County Central Labor Council — though David Bacon does recall expressions of solidarity at the time of the campaign against racism. What's more, the established unions with the strongest local presence, above all the International Association of Machinists with its base at Lockheed, showed little interest in organizing a workforce largely composed of immigrant women.[49] There is a tantalizing bit of evidence in a newspaper article from 1980 with the headline, "Unions Urge Silicon Valley Organizing Drive." Both Michael Nye of the Central Labor Council and David Bacon appeared at a press conference to announce the new drive, along with representatives from the UAW and ECOSH.[50] But this drive ran into the buzz saw about which we have already learned.

Furthermore, some analysts believe that certain employers, especially Hewlett-Packard, have treated their employees well enough in such matters as benefits, stock options, and basic respect that not only have their own employees shown no interest in a union, but also employees at other less-desirable companies daydream about getting a job at HP, "the Cadillac plant," rather than working toward the advantages that could be derived from joining a union.[51]

Finally, there are a variety of cultural factors that have been a barrier to unionization. Women workers, in particular, may be so overstressed by the demands of family and job that they find it difficult to devote time to an inchoate union. One woman told Karen Hossfeld:

> [The union organizers] kept asking me, "Why don't the other Mexican women come to the meetings? They have just as much to gain." I kept telling them — they're afraid of deportation, they can't afford the dues, they've got to take care of their kids, and their husbands won't let them. And they don't understand English good. And all [the organizers] said was, "But it's in their own best interests." . . . Eventually, they got Spanish-speaking organizers, but it's like they didn't even consider the other barriers. They kept asking me, "Why don't they come?"[52]

The Decline of Blue-Collar Employment

In discussing the decline of blue-collar work in the Valley, there are several threads to be followed. These include the diminution of aerospace work, the disappearance of the fruit industry, and the degradation of electronics assembly work as more and more of this work was performed by contingent workers. The first two instances have also meant a decline in unionized manufacturing jobs. The net result is that there has been a shrinkage of opportunity in the Valley for those who want to build stable lives on the basis of production work.

In his memoir of growing up in a Lockheed family, David Beers writes about the current period: "But there are no husks of factories or rows of boarded-up houses to inspire folksongs about hard luck aeronautical engineers. Where blue sky culture fades, the suburban veneer remains implacably pastel."[53] In fact, because the cost of housing in Silicon Valley is so high, there are unlikely to be boarded-up houses as a consequence of aerospace lay-offs. Some families might have to scale back their type of residence after a job has been lost. On the other hand, there are families in which either a blue- or a white-collar breadwinner has been laid off from an aerospace job but who can afford to retire on the proceeds of selling a Valley home — as long as they relocate elsewhere.[54]

Lockheed, for decades the Valley's largest employer, has had an especially tough time. In addition to the reduction of military spending after the end of the cold war, which was a challenge for all defense contractors, the firm lost a number of its remaining military contracts in the late twentieth century. Moreover, several high-profile Lockheed products had spectacular public failures, with the result that Lockheed Martin's stock fell 70 percent in the two years ending with March 2000.[55] Not surprisingly, morale has plummeted, as we learned in Chapter 6 from the reflections of Lockheed employee Theresa Perea. Where once the mighty firm employed upward of twenty-five thousand in the Valley alone, the total was less than eight thousand in early 2000.[56] Though many observers believe that the firm can come back, it will never again offer the thousands of union-wage jobs that it did in its prime. To work at Lockheed in 2000 is to fear for one's job and to cope with relentless cost-cutting. Tempering this anxiety is the fact that aerospace workers are much likelier to have skills of use to high tech than are displaced fruit industry workers.

As for the fruit industry, the year 1999 witnessed the end of an era. The last major cannery in San Jose, Del Monte Plant No. 3, located just west of downtown and employing nearly fifteen hundred people, closed its doors to move to Modesto. A sad event for the workers and for the community, this development provided the occasion for a great deal of retrospective coverage in the *Mercury News*, coverage that underlined how serious a loss it truly was. "People, like crops of fruit, return summer after summer. The median age at the plant is 50, and 75 percent of the work force is female."[57] In fact, full-time employees had averaged twenty-five years of service with the plant, and seasonal ones had averaged twelve years.

The larger meaning of this pattern can be simply put: In the case of hundreds of women and a smaller number of men, the plant had been the focal point of their lives for decades. It is not too much to say that for some people the Del Monte cannery had played an extraordinarily positive role. Irma Balderas, in 1999 an elementary school principal in East San Jose, was the first woman in her family to attend college, an achievement financed in part by her summer job at Plant No. 3. Frances Cefalu worked at the plant for forty-five years before retiring with a diamond pin in 1978: "I was the first female regular employee to get five diamonds [for forty-five years of employment]." Jesus Carrasco liked his work so well that at age eighty-one he was still employed there part-time, hosing off waste fruit from the cannery equipment.[58] Telling these stories and others, the *Mercury News* reporter commented: "Each of these seemingly different people from all over Silicon Valley shares a common endowment. They are graduates of a certain tough school in San Jose. Each has worked for Del Monte cannery, which is closing this fall after an 82-year run."[59] It is impossible to imagine a similarly sentimental story about a hypothetical wafer fab closing, among other reasons because people tend not to have this kind of job tenure in electronics. Nor can one readily envision a poem about assembly work such as the one written by Sofia Curiel about her cannery job, a poem that concludes:

Gracias a mis compañeras
Gracias a mis compañeros
Gracias a mis mayordomos (bosses)
Que yo a uno que otro los quiero (I love each and every one)[60]

Because most of them had worked together for many years, the plant's closing was emotionally fraught:

Usually workers have in-plant parties to celebrate the end of a run.
There was one such event last week where poignancy hung heavy.
　　In a dim room filled with 30 tons of fresh pears still waiting to be
canned, warehouse workers held a goodbye party. Wearing hard hats,
they danced to Spanish polka music. They ate a potluck supper topped
off by corn on the cob doused with butter and hot sauce. Then back
to work, the pears calling.
　　"Every year when we say goodbye, we know we will see each other
again. But not this year," said Hortensia Montes, a 22-year plant vet-
eran. "It's sad. I pass by whole departments that already are completely
empty. It brings tears to my eyes."[61]

What makes this set of developments especially poignant is the fact that there is little similar employment left in the Valley. Del Monte offered a job that was unionized, stable, and available to people with poor or middling skills in English, people who may well have arrived from a peasant background. For the Del Monte employees who did not take up the offer to relocate to Modesto, and for the ongoing stream of immigrants who once could have secured this type of employment, it is hard to envision what will take its place. In response to the situation, Working Partnerships USA (an affiliate of the South Bay Central Labor Council), the Silicon Valley Private Industry Council, and the city of San Jose have jointly undertaken a retraining program for displaced cannery workers, with five or six hundred workers having gone through the program as of September 2000.

There have even been attempts to gear the workers up for high-tech jobs. For example, Dora Perez, who worked at Del Monte for twenty-seven years, and about a half-dozen of her former coworkers have received training in the use of personal computers at the Biblioteca Latinoamericana near downtown San Jose. Their teacher explained to a reporter, "It's hard for them . . . they can lose the cursor and get frustrated. You can see they have trouble, but they're so persistent." As of May 2000, counselors had helped place two hundred former Del Monte workers in other jobs, including in electronics.[62]

Dora Perez and another former Del Monte worker undergoing retraining shared their stories, remarkable in both cases. In the first instance, Perez told of being born in Mexico and coming to the United States as an undocumented worker at the age of seventeen, having obtained only a sixth-grade education. She was able to get employment at Del Monte immediately, because her father and her uncles had jobs there. Starting as a sorter, she worked her way up the ladder: She moved to a position greasing the machines and next to performing the work of a light mechanic. With this background, she then taught herself how to operate a forklift and was able to move into year-round work in a warehouse, a job paying $42,000 a year at the time the plant closed. The mother of four children, she proudly explained that she and her husband (through whom she obtained citizenship) have been able to send their oldest two to college and to subsidize their children's multiple sports activities — as well as to own a home that is fully paid for. In the fall of 2000, many years after Perez left school, she was back in the classroom. But she acknowledged that the computer training would be unlikely to result in a job that paid as well as the one she left.

Maria Antonieta Hernandez came from Mexico in the early 1950s. For a number of years, she and her former husband ran four tailor shops. Then in 1975, she went to work for Del Monte, where she spent the preponderance of her time assigned to a warehouse. So devoted was she to her job and her coworkers that she has made two photo albums to preserve her memories of her "beloved job:" "*Recuerdos de mi querido trabajo*, Del Monte Foods," says the introductory page. She has included photographs she took of the machines, of the plant after the machines had been moved to Modesto, and of workers on all three shifts. She has also written of her feelings about the plant's closing, including the following: "*Estoy llorando al escribir estas lineas; mi corazon siente que algo muy triste esta a punto de pasar en mi vida, pero fueron tantos y tantos los momentos felices que pase aqui.*" ("I'm crying as I write these lines; yet my heart feels that however sad it is to go through this moment in my life, there were many, many happy moments here.")[63]

Said Sergio Perez, who chaired the Silicon Valley Private Industry Council task force set up to deal with the retraining of cannery workers: "It's like a death in the family, losing Del Monte. There is anguish, like if your spouse died. What kind of jobs can people get that will pay them anything like as much as they made in the cannery?"[64] No one yet knows the answer to that question.

Exploitation of Electronics Workers

Over the years, there has been a degradation of electronics assembly work, employment that was typically not that wonderful to begin with. One telling example of how hypercompetitive the industry has become and the impact this has had on workers was the strategy adopted by IBM in 1996 for one of its Valley operations: "IBM, the world's largest computer maker, imports Mexican workers from its Guadalajara plant to labor seven days a week on its San Jose disk-drive assembly line." Paying the Mexican workers about $1.40 an hour and bringing them in on the type of visa issued for training — though the workers were doing exactly the same work as they did at home — the firm could afford to pay their living expenses and still enjoy a bargain, since it would have had to pay American workers $8.00 to $9.00 an hour.[65]

Perhaps the most exploited workers in the Valley have been those who perform piecework at home, a form of exploitation that is rendered all the easier because electronics components are small and can be delivered surreptitiously in a suitcase. As early as 1980, journalists were reporting a black market in such work, fueled by the desire to cut costs in the competition with Japan: "Widespread underground employment of housewives, aliens, and welfare recipients for less than minimum wage labor by peninsula electronics firms is being investigated by a new local team of investigators from the State Division of Labor Standards."[66] People were assembling circuit boards at home for fifty cents apiece or so and being paid under the table. Worst of all was what this meant for health and safety issues. A home worker might well have been keeping a pot of solvent boiling on her stove, so as to be able to clean components at will. Moreover, sometimes people were able to collect welfare or unemployment while working off the books at below the minimum wage.[67]

Despite this investigation, which did not result in any fines or charges after leaders of the industry promised to police themselves, the problem has persisted.[68] In June 1999, the *Mercury News* ran a series about the extent to which even some large and well-regarded firms, such as Hewlett-Packard and Sun Microsystems, have used components produced via piecework at home. The large firms purchased the components from contract manufacturers, which were characterized by the fact that they make no products under their own brand names. Alleging that "there is a hidden, low-tech underbelly: a loose network of Asian immigrants who are paid by the piece to assemble electronics parts in their homes for some of high tech's major companies, in apparent violation of labor, tax, and safety laws," the paper provided impressive detail about the abuses, especially given the fact that reporters had interviewed more than seventy people who had either done such work themselves or had firsthand knowledge of it.[69] The more recent variant of the practice has seen employers assigning regular employees additional work to be performed after hours, with little regard to whether the work will be performed safely or whether it will involve children.

Essential to the rationale for requiring workers to take tasks home with them is the chronic Valley need for maximum speed coupled with its drive to produce goods as cheaply as possible. In fact, certain contract manufacturers claim that sending work home is necessary from time to time. "Sometimes when the job is so hot . . . even if you add OT [overtime] you can't make the schedule," said one longtime production manager for Solectron, a leading contract manufacturer. "So we give the workers 100 boards and the next day they have to bring back 100 boards. Maybe at home they do it faster if they have brothers or sisters helping out."[70]

Another significant aspect of the situation is the fact that this work is often done by relatively recent immigrants, who know little of their rights under American labor law. Nor do they know of the long struggles earlier in American history to end such abuses. Where others see exploitation, they may see opportunity:

> Quyen Tong's hand trembles slightly, just enough to make it difficult for the 51-year old to line up two prongs of a tiny transistor so they fit into pindot holes on a printed circuit board. It takes him three tries to get it right.
>
> Tong, a Vietnamese immigrant, leans over the family dining table to inspect his work as his 10-year-old son, Nam, piles a handful of transistors by his side. Nam has bent each transistor wire into a tiny U-shape. . . .
>
> In the living room a few feet away, Tong's 18-year-old son Viet and a friend have flopped belly down on blue-and-white plaid sofas and are loading transistors on two other boards. Down the back hallway, Tong's daughters — three of them teenagers — can be heard, chatting and moving about the family bedrooms. They are working on boards, too.

By the time the article was due to appear, Tong had landed a better job, one that did not require much take-home work. "When I was in high school, I dreamed of this; I dreamed of coming here," he told the reporter who had been interviewing him.[71]

Interestingly, one of the firms implicated in the practice of employing home assemblers was Cisco Systems, whose president and CEO was the Valley's highest paid executive in 1999. The company apparently relied on its ability to fudge what an "independent contractor" is; that is, if the home workers are legitimately independent contractors, then the practice might be considered legal. A follow-up story in October 1999 reported that "Cisco Systems, Inc. is an example of a company taking a closer look at its practices. It has halted work with four assemblers who operate their businesses in residential areas."[72] The story reported a general decline in work done at home since the June series had run, owing both to public scrutiny and to yet another investigation by the state. "'We are investigating every employer mentioned in the [*Mercury News*] articles,' [Miles] Locker [chief counsel for the state's Division of Labor Standards Enforcement] said."[73] In December 1999, the California Labor Commissioner fined three Bay Area companies as a consequence of the investigation.

To police this arena adequately is no easy undertaking, and therefore there is room for skepticism about how much permanent change has really taken place. The problem is that contract manufacturers use subcontractors who may themselves have subcontractors, so that accountability is difficult to establish. Further, one of the ways in which immigrant entrepreneurs launch themselves into business is by setting up a small-scale "assembly house," at which they employ co-ethnics. "In the past, Asian immigrants looking to start a business might have opened a restaurant. Today, they'd rather own an assembly house. It's the new American dream."[74] Undercapitalized and lightly regulated, these assembly houses often engage in practices that fly in the face of American law governing wages and hours, health and safety, and child labor.

And then there are the large contract manufacturers, such as the aforementioned Solectron, a Milpitas company that was generating billions of dollars of annual revenue by the late twentieth century while remaining virtually unknown to the public because it produces no brand-name items. Founded in 1977 to develop products using solar energy, Solectron evolved into performing assembly work for such giants as IBM and HP. By 1984, the firm had annual revenues of $54 million. Until 1992, it confined its operations to Silicon Valley. That year, it acquired facilities in Charlotte, North Carolina, from IBM. "By 1995, Solectron had grown to more than $2 billion in annual revenues and had plants in North Carolina, Washington State, Texas, Malaysia, Scotland, France, and Germany."[75] As of late 2000, it had close to thirty-five thousand employees worldwide and was the biggest such firm on the planet. It has kept up with the demand for its services by "[d]ipping into the second and third tier of contract manufacturing — using companies such as Top Line or its own employees-cum-independent contractors."[76]

Solectron has clearly played a major role in habituating Valley workers to piecework and contingent employment — though it has announced that it is attempting to move away from the former practice, according to newspaper accounts. Solectron was, in fact, one of those investigated as a consequence of the *Mercury News* exposé, but the state found no violations.[77] What's clear is that there are many well-established relationships that might favor the continuation of abuses. In the 1999 exposé, for example, there was an article about a young Vietnamese Chinese immigrant by the name of Bryan Lam. For four years, Lam had been undertaking rush jobs for Solectron by deploying a team of home assembly workers he had put together, a connection that had been fostered by the fact that his brother-in-law had founded Top Line Electronics, a Solectron subcontractor. "During these four years Lam has never had a contract with Solectron, but individual managers in different divisions would call him when they had work, he [Lam] says."[78]

In 1996, Working Partnerships published a report attempting to establish the extent of all forms of contingent employment in the Valley, or employment that lacks the characteristics of stability and a full array of benefits, including pensions, that have become the hallmarks of American employment in the postwar years. When the number of temporary workers is added to those who are part-time, self-employed, or performing business services for more than one employer, the estimates for all types of contingent employment in the Valley range from 27 to 40 percent.[79] Of course, many of the people who are self-employed or who are legitimate independent contractors do well for themselves, so these estimates should not be read as a gauge of misery. Nonetheless, the numbers do suggest something about the growth in vulnerability of workers in the area.

The life of contingent work can be difficult, however, even for those with professional training and experience. At a meeting of contingent workers held at the Valley's Labor Temple in December 1998, Julian Cornejo told his story.[80] A mechanical designer, he had been temping for twelve years and had seen working conditions decline in that period. For him and his family, the worst moment came when he was injured on the job. While the process of securing a settlement from an insurance company was unfolding, the family was forced to give up its home. Because the temp agency is the employer of record, he explained, it was difficult to establish responsibility for a work-related injury, given the fact that the incident occurred at a firm that was *not* the employer of record.

A New Era in Occupational Safety

A continuing thread through the chapters dealing with electronics workers has been the issue of occupational safety and health. Following the issue over time makes it possible to discern that there are two, seemingly contradictory, truths. On the one hand, there has been real and important progress in making the workplace safer; on the other, the problem is still serious.

In their reminiscences, most of the labor activists point to the area of occupational safety as the one place where they feel their efforts paid off, absent a union being founded. As a result of their agitation, TCE was banned, companies began to improve ventilation, and companies no longer maintain that a worker who feels lousy is suffering from hysteria. But what the companies have yet to concede, and what current litigation is attempting to establish, is that high-tech workers may be at risk for long-term health problems, up to and including death. Furthermore, no matter how good a job an Intel may have done in cleaning up the workplace, there are so many marginal operations that routinely cut corners that any given day in the Valley there are thousands of workers at risk of damage to their health, at least on a short-term basis. Finally, companies innovate so constantly that it is difficult for those monitoring the situation to stay abreast of the hazards posed by chemicals, particularly as they interact with one another.

As this is written, a very important and potentially precedent-setting case has been filed against IBM and is working its way through the legal system, with claimants in several parts of the country, but focused primarily in upstate New York and Silicon Valley. One of the lead attorneys, Amanda Hawes, who is internationally known for her work representing electronics workers and who was one of the founders of ECOSH, provided background on the case from the plaintiffs' perspective. By the mid-1980s, both the National Institute of Occupational Safety and Health and the Occupational Safety and Health Administration (OSHA) were becoming concerned about the hazards of glycol ethers, she explained. "We wanted a ban, but the attitude of industry was 'Where's the body count? Without a body count, you got nothing; we're not talking to you.'"

Despite foot-dragging by the industry, the empirical data began to be collected. A Massachusetts study documented an elevated rate of miscarriages among production workers in clean rooms, for example, though its findings were based on a relatively small number of workers. IBM then launched its own study, looking at both women workers and wives of male workers, a study that found a correlation between miscarriages and working with glycol ethers. These studies did not look at cancer and only collected information about birth defects along the way.[81] In response to the findings, the industry began trying to use less toxic solvents, but did not go so far as completely eliminating the use of dangerous chemicals. Moreover IBM has been extremely guarded about releasing information it has collected about the incidence of occupational health problems.

Then in 1996, a man who had worked at IBM's Fishkill plant and who had developed testicular cancer came forward. Of crucial importance is the fact that his job involved applying photo resist, a compound that contains glycol ethers, to wafers. Trying to fathom what had happened to him, he looked around at his coworkers and found that he was not alone in his health problems. Out of this discovery came the litigation, which originally involved seven workers in New York. Reporting on the case in its early stages, the *New York Times* explained that this would be the first concerted attempt to try to nail down liability for chemical exposure in the high-tech industry.[82] By 2000, the suit had grown to encompass in excess of one hundred adult plaintiffs and more than twenty-five children.

Among the plaintiffs are a number in San Jose, with many observers maintaining that they can discern the presence of a cluster of cancers in the Valley. For example, Frederick Tarmaun, a retired chemist, worked on developing plastics for the industry. He has seen six of eleven men who worked alongside him at IBM contract cancer and die.[83]

Though companies have been willing to take some steps to remedy the situation, they have not been willing to see the Environmental Protection Agency sponsor a study to establish whether there is truly a correlation between the incidence of cancer and work in electronics. In 1997, California's Department of Health Services developed a proposal to use California's Health Registries to study the rates at which disease occurs among electronics workers and their families.[84] An industry group unanimously opposed the proposal, which had been made to the EPA. "[T]he high-tech industry has declined to cooperate with the Environmental Protection Agency in studying whether electronics workers in California have higher rates of cancer and birth defects than the public. 'There is no scientific basis to justify a study,' said Lee Neal, health and safety director for the Semiconductor Industry Association. 'We use chemicals in work environments two to three times cleaner than the typical operating room.'"[85] And that is where the matter stands as of this writing.

One of the most consequential developments from the standpoint of worker safety has been the level of international exchange, both of information and of strategies, among professionals and activists in a number of countries. For example, Amanda Hawes has spent time in Malaysia and represents some of the workers at a National Semiconductor plant in Scotland. Dr. LaDou gives papers at conferences abroad and corresponds with his counterparts in other countries. In short, in the globally interconnected world of the twenty-first century, capital is not the only sector to form such links.

Asked what she hopes to achieve with the IBM litigation, Hawes replies that she is hoping to prove that "so-called low level exposures are real, and they really hurt. There's nothing else like a clean room anywhere. . . . The new generation of clean rooms is different, though, than they were for the folks now battling cancer. People don't go in them — people are an intolerable source of contamination."

New Union Strategies

Unions are using innovative new strategies, both locally and nationally, to fight back from the loss of power and influence they had suffered relative to their glory days of an earlier era. In the first place, as is the case with the occupational safety activists, union activists are increasing their contacts with their counterparts around the world. For example, in the wake of the passage of NAFTA in the early days of the first Clinton administration, the UE (now the United Electrical, Radio and Machine Workers of America) has formed a "strategic alliance" with an independent federation of Mexican labor unions and cooperatives, the *Frente Autentico del Trabajo* (FAT). Like the UE, the FAT opposes NAFTA. The two unions "have supported each others' organizing campaigns, and solidarity of this sort has been an important factor in several victories," according to a UE brochure.

Another national development with local ramifications, which are of the highest importance in the Valley, has been the change of policy enunciated by the AFL-CIO in early 2000 with respect to immigrants. With its new doctrine calling for amnesty for undocumented workers (a change we have already discussed in Chapter 5), the national group has enabled the local labor movement to intensify its outreach to the immigrant community.

Given the composition of the Valley's working class, this was a change that was as essential as it was overdue.

And then there are the new strategies of a purely local nature, many of which have been undertaken by South Bay labor leader Amy Dean. New ideas and the dynamism to sell them to potential allies continue to flow from the South Bay Central Labor Council, which is no doubt why Dean has received so much admiring coverage from the local and national press.

But the resurgence of energy and ideas began even before Dean assumed leadership of the Central Labor Council in 1994 (although not before she had gone to work for the Council). The Justice for Janitors campaign was sparked by a combination of activism from the Mexican American community and Local 1877 of the Service Employees International Union. Activists were responding to testimony that had been given at a 1990 hearing to the effect that many of the Valley's working poor were too destitute to have health insurance but had too much income to qualify for Medi-Cal, the state's provision of medical help for the poor. The testimony also established that these Valley working poor came from the ranks of low-paying service jobs, in high tech and other industries.

In response to the testimony, an organization called Cleaning Up Silicon Valley Coalition came into being. The group launched itself by organizing public events and marches to call attention to the plight of poorly paid janitors. For its initial drive to improve the lives of janitors, the coalition decided to target Apple Computers, which had a contract for its janitorial services with a nonunion firm called Shine. As part of the campaign, the coalition picketed the home of then-Apple CEO John Sculley, after which Apple pressured Shine to negotiate with the union. A majority of Shine workers chose the union in an election in early 1992, providing a historic victory for the local labor movement.[86] There have since been follow-up victories for janitors, such as a very favorable contract in June 2000 for Local 1877, which now represents several hundred janitors in the Valley, many of whom work for companies that contract with high-tech firms.[87]

When Dean became head of the Council in 1994, innovative ideas began to pour out. In the first place, the CLC founded a research and policy component, the aforementioned Working Partnerships USA, in 1995. In the ensuing years, Working Partnerships has published a number of studies of the local economy, funded by grants from progressive foundations (including both the Hewlett and the Packard Foundations). In particular, the research has focused on the problems of the most vulnerable of the Valley's workers, above all, those with contingent employment.

With this research in hand, Dean and her colleagues are trying to dent the anti-union monolith that is the Valley's high-tech industry. Though the CLC represents 110,000 workers, they are found among the ranks of nurses, teachers, carpenters, grocery clerks, and city and county employees, with dwindling numbers in manufacturing and, as we have seen, almost none in electronics. To plan her attack, Dean seized on the issue of the tech industry's contingent workers. For example, the CLC has created its own nonprofit personnel agency to serve as an alternative to those that allegedly exploit workers. The Council is also planning a campaign similar to the national campaign directed at Nike to embarrass the shoe firm about its products being manufactured under exploitative conditions abroad. The CLC campaign aims to champion a corporate code of conduct for high-tech companies in the Valley.

Another innovation occurred when Working Partnerships created an Interfaith Council for Social Justice to add moral urgency to the campaign to better the lives of the working poor. On Labor Day weekend in 1998, pastors and rabbis in the San Jose area asked congregants to support plans for requiring that a "living wage" be paid by the city of San Jose's contractors. The pleas resulted in more than four thousand postcards being sent to the city.[88] The lobbying effort was part of the Dean-led CLC's greatest success to date. In late 1998, the City Council did, in fact, mandate a wage of $10.75 per hour (or $9.50 with benefits) for employees who work for city contractors, a political coup for labor. Though it did not touch the high-tech industry directly and though it provided certain exemptions, it sent a signal that the South Bay labor movement was in a fighting mood and could win significant battles. It also provided an interesting coda to the story of Valley labor in the twentieth century, a story that had begun with labor leader Walter Mathewson's election to the City Council in 1906 on a platform of ensuring that city work would be performed only by union labor — as we learned in Chapter 1.

To understand how this measure could be successful in the face of strong opposition from the local Chamber of Commerce, it is important to bear in mind the leadership record of then-Mayor Susan Hammer. As we read in

Chapter 6, Hammer was a can-do politician with an impressive ability to put coalitions together to advance her goals. Where the living wage proposal was concerned, Hammer's budget director, Bob Brownstein, helped draft it, and it received the strong support of the mayor herself. Hammer explained that the debate in the City Council "turned the corner" upon the release of a report from Working Partnerships entitled "Growing Together or Drifting Apart?" The report provided compelling empirical data about growing economic inequality in the Valley. The data and a "full-bore effort" by Dean and her cohorts proved convincing, and the proposal passed by a vote of 7 to 3. In addition, shortly before the living wage vote, there was an all-out effort by labor in the November 1998 election that succeeded in electing Cindy Chavez to the City Council, despite the best efforts of the business community to elect someone else.[89]

In 1999, the second "labor in the pulpit" campaign had pastors and rabbis in thirty-five participating houses of worship calling attention to the plight of the Valley's most vulnerable residents and asking congregants to fill out postcards directed to Santa Clara County, asking the Board of Supervisors to adopt a code of conduct for agencies deploying temporary workers.[90]

There are glimmerings of hope for Valley labor in developments that have been taking place in other parts of the country. In the fall of 2000, for example, the National Labor Relations Board gave temporary workers the right to join a union. The Board's decision took note of the tremendous growth of the temporary workforce nationally. Shortly thereafter, Microsoft's temporary workers — perhaps as many as eight thousand — won an important legal battle. The giant software company agreed to settle the class-action suit *Vizcaino v Microsoft* by paying the plaintiffs $97 million. "Plaintiffs' attorneys successfully argued that Microsoft had misclassified thousands of long-term contractors as 'temps' when they were in fact 'common-law' employees of Microsoft, and then used that misclassification to illegally prevent them from participating in an employee benefit plan."[91]

The last word on this subject belongs to Louis Rocha, president of Local 9423 of the Communication Workers of America and member of a Mexican-American family that has been in the Valley for seventy years. Rocha, in fact, tells a family history that recapitulates many an immigrant success story from the first three-quarters of the twentieth century, in particular, the boost that people got from working in food processing. For his father, mother, grandmother, and aunts, the cannery work they performed represented a step up from the work in the fields that had been the lot of those who went before. The family owned land in Sal Si Puedes on which they grew vegetables. The household economy was based on land ownership, food cultivation, and food processing work (his father was also a union carpenter), as the household economies of the Italian immigrants had been a generation earlier. Rocha dropped out of the University of California at Santa Cruz to help his mother financially. He went to work as a telephone lineman and has been with the phone company ever since. After a few years, he became active in the union, and he eventually ran for president as part of a slate dedicated to rejuvenating the local, which has about thirty-two hundred members in several counties. As it happens, the national CWA has developed a plan for reaching out to potential tech workers by offering training for the job of networking specialist, a plan that Rocha is eager to see implemented at the local level:

> We have a program: we're organizing, and we're going to be reaching out to workers at all the big companies. It's never been easy; we just have to figure out how it can be done. There *will* be a way to organize.
>
> I'm on the board of the United Way, so I sit elbow to elbow with representatives of some of the giants — from IBM, Cisco, Intel, HP, all of them, but they *are* people. Sometimes we lump them together and paint them with this brush and make them evil. But the fact is that labor's a force to be reckoned with here — they *have* to partner with us.
>
> Right now the bubble has burst. People are reassessing. There isn't that blinding strike-it-rich mentality. We reach out in different ways. People have to join the union to receive our training, but with low dues. This has been well received by people in the Mayfair district [in East San Jose]. Almost every business now has to have a networking specialist, so there's a high demand for this job.[92]

The Valley labor movement is fighting back, bolstered by developments on the national labor scene. The business community has demonstrated an awareness that the growing inequality is a concern, though not to the point of welcoming collective bargaining for high-tech workers. The likelihood of meaningful redress any time in the near future can seem like a remote dream, however. Says Bob Brownstein about the dilemma in 2000: "The great threat to this valley, if you want to use the metaphor of the hourglass economy, is that huge numbers of people will be trapped in the bottom of the hourglass with low pay and a poor future. In particular, the housing problem has the potential of destroying the openness and fluidity that everybody treasures. At this point, the public policy solutions would require sacrifice from people who are not the victims." During the Great Depression, enough people were victims of economic distress that the public would support innovative solutions for the poor and the unfortunate, both locally and nationally. That was far from being the case in either California at large or in Silicon Valley in 2000. And therefore, it is difficult to envision how the needs of the thousands of the working poor, many of whom toil in high tech, can be met.

Yet the area that has seen so much explosive change over the course of the twentieth century may prove that it can change in this respect, too. In particular, any national reforms to the laws governing immigration that make newcomers less vulnerable in the workplace, coupled with the new stance toward immigrants on the part of organized labor, may help to level the playing field in Silicon Valley.

Moreover, the city of San Jose, with its tradition of innovative leadership, may provide a source of renewal. During the course of the twentieth century, the city's downtown virtually died. When redevelopment restored downtown, it had been reinvented as a capital of diversity as well as the capital of Silicon Valley. The political forces that created that eventuality may also be able to redress the problem of inequality. Clearly, the labor movement cannot do it alone, but in coalition with progressive local politicians, social justice–oriented religious institutions, environmental groups, grassroots community activists, and other nodes of strength, there may be the possibility of improvement. And because San Jose was home to nearly one million people as of 2000, that would be a significant achievement.

Afterword

In the preceding chapters, we have taken a journey through the history of the Santa Clara Valley, from the late nineteenth century to the end of the twentieth century. We have focused particular attention on the situation of the working-class women, primarily immigrant, who have been the backbone of the production workforce, both in the fruit industry that dominated the Valley in 1900 and the electronics industry that dominated in 2000. We have learned about valiant efforts by women to build lives for themselves and their families, about courageous struggles in the face of great difficulty, and about hard-won victories for those who seemed too vulnerable to have the capacity to be victorious, even in the eyes of their potential allies.

In particular, all cannery workers achieved a union in the 1930s and women cannery workers achieved reform of the union in the 1970s, reform that ultimately meant that they could obtain better jobs than they had previously been able to hope for. Though middle-class people with good access to education would not necessarily have viewed such jobs as desirable, the jobs, in fact, afforded generations of newcomers from southern Europe, the southwestern United States, and Mexico a shot at having stable lives. This could occur even if they arrived without good English skills or a good educational background.

Another substantial group of working women were employed in the Valley's aerospace industry, although this group did not include new immigrants. These women were employed as secretaries, in security, as technicians. All belonged to a union and enjoyed a union wage, except for those who were salaried and on a ladder of professional advancement.

Women who come to the Valley as immigrants in the early twenty-first century are confronting two developments that make access to the California Dream as difficult as ever. In the first place, they must deal with the degradation of blue-collar employment and the disappearance of many of the jobs that paid a union wage. In the second place, they must try to find lodging in an area where home prices and rents are among the highest in the United States. So severe is the problem, in fact, that an article in the *New York Times* of February 20, 2000, proclaimed: "Many in Silicon Valley Cannot Afford Housing, Even at $50,000 a Year." The article went on to explain that some of the Valley's working poor are forced to spend all night riding a bus, because they cannot come up with enough money to find housing.

> Most of them [the people on a particular bus] work full time. One is a cashier at a toy store. Another works at a box factory. Another says he juggles three part-time jobs. But in the dot-com land of milk and honey, where the median family income, $82,000, is the highest in the nation (and an average of 63 people hit the millionaire mark every day), non-tech jobs do not pay the rent.

What the reporter, Evelyn Nieves, missed is the fact that there are many thousands of tech jobs that do not pay the rent either.

Earlier, before the land became among the most expensive on the planet, immigrants might have had to struggle with jobs that paid poorly or were exploitative, but they could usually afford to save enough for home ownership. Owning a home — particularly since they did not have to sacrifice the education of their children to do so, as often happened in other parts of the country — gave them a chance to build a future. In fact, all the evidence suggests that the southern European immigrants one hundred years ago were able to pass on middle-class status to their children to a remarkable extent because they owned a home.

It is impossible to predict the fate of the descendants of those who come now. Though a study of history may allow us to make educated guesses about the future, if something truly new under the sun occurs, a knowledge of the past will not have prepared people for it. Who in the 1920s, for example, whether historian or otherwise, could have anticipated the turbulence of the 1930s that destabilized the status quo and paved the way for real change in the Valley? What is clear is this: In the early twenty-first century, Silicon Valley's rewards are so disproportionately going to the haves at the expense of the have-nots that it may take another shakeup of some magnitude to extend the benefits of the California Dream of prosperity more broadly.

INTRODUCTION

1. See Lenny Siegel and John Markoff, *The High Cost of High Tech: The Dark Side of the Chip* (New York: Harper & Row, 1985) for an important critique of the Valley.

2. By prune tree, I mean a variety of plum grown exclusively for drying.

3. Indeed, the boundaries of what could be considered "Silicon Valley" expand all the time. High-tech firms have traveled around the bottom of the San Francisco Bay and up into southern Alameda County. They have also located in San Mateo County to the north of Palo Alto. Strictly speaking, these areas are not part of the Santa Clara Valley.

4. See, for example, *Silicon Valley 2010* (San Jose: Joint Venture: Silicon Valley Network, 1999). The report's data confirm that the area is dealing with an increase in inequality.

5. See, for example, Jonathan Keats, "It's the End of Work as We Know It," *San Francisco* (December 1998). As another instance of someone making this point, I attended a conference entitled "Life in the Fast Lane," which was held at DeAnza College, Cupertino, on November 13, 1998. The conference featured the research of three San Jose State University anthropologists (Charles Darrah, James Freeman, and Jane English-Lueck). I was sitting with the anthropologist Lee Davis of San Francisco State University. As one speaker after another described the extraordinary pressures middle-class people accept, Davis stated, "Only a religious system could command this type of loyalty."

6. Outstanding works on immigrant women include Miriam Cohen, *Workshop to Office: Two Generations of Italian Women in New York City, 1900–1950* (Ithaca, NY: Cornell University Press, 1992); Hasia Diner, *Erin's Daughters in America* (Baltimore: Johns Hopkins University Press, 1983); Donna Gabaccia, *From the Other Side: Women, Gender, and Immigrant Life in the United States* (Bloomington: Indiana University Press, 1994); Susan Glenn, *Daughters of the Shtetl* (Ithaca, NY: Cornell University Press, 1990); Vicki L. Ruiz, "The Flapper

and the Chaperone: Historical Memory Among Mexican-American Women," in *Seeking Ground: Multidisciplinary Studies of Immigrant Women in the United States,* ed. Donna Gabaccia (Westport, Conn.: Greenwood Press, 1992); Judy Yung, *Unbound Feet: A Social History of Chinese Women in San Francisco* (Berkeley: University of California Press, 1995).

7. See, for example, Glenna Matthews, "Ethnicity and Success in San Jose," *Journal of Interdisciplinary History* 7 (Autumn 1976): 305–18.

8. See Stephen Pitti, "Quicksilver Community: Mexican Migrations and Politics in the Santa Clara Valley" (Ph.D. diss., Stanford University, 1998); Timothy J. Lukes and Gary Okihiro, *Japanese Legacy: Farming and Community Life in California's Santa Clara Valley,* Local History Studies, vol. 31 (Cupertino: California History Center, 1985); Connie Young Yu, *Chinatown San Jose, USA* (San Jose: San Jose Historical Museum, 1993).

9. Kathleen Neils Conzen, "Mainstreams and Side Channels: The Localization of Immigrant cultures," *Journal of American Ethnic History* (Fall 1991): 13.

CHAPTER I

1. On this subject see Matthew Frye Jacobson, *Whiteness of a Different Color: European Immigrants and the Alchemy of Race* (Cambridge: Harvard University Press, 1998).

2. Kevin Starr, *Americans and the California Dream, 1850–1915* (New York: Oxford University Press, 1973), 192.

3. Matthews, "Ethnicity and Success."

4. Ibid.

5. See Glenna Matthews, "Forging a Cosmopolitan Civic Culture: The Regional Identity of San Francisco and Northern California," in *Many Wests: Place, Culture, and Regional Identity,* ed. David M. Wrobel and Michael Steiner (Lawrence: University of Kansas Press, 1997).

6. See Douglas Monroy, *Thrown Among Strangers: The Making of Mexican Culture in Frontier California* (Berkeley: University of California Press, 1990), and Tomas Almaguer, *Racial Fault Lines: The Historical Origins of White Supremacy in California* (Berkeley: University of California Press, 1994).

7. Remarks given by William Deverell to the California Studies Seminar, University of California, Berkeley, February 22, 1999.

8. Frederic Hall, *The History of San Jose and Surroundings* (San Francisco: A. L. Bancroft, 1871), 284, 285.

9. Pitti, "Quicksilver Community," 98. Pitti says that the majority of these miners had been born in Mexico rather than California.

10. Ibid., 150.

11. Yvonne Jacobson, *Passing Farms, Enduring Values: California's Santa Clara Valley* (Los Altos, Calif.: William Kaufmann, 1984), 89.

12. Yu, *Chinatown San Jose*, 8, 9.

13. See the authoritative work by Peter Philips, "Towards a New Theory of Wage Structure: The Evolution of Wages in the California Canneries, 1870 to the Present" (Ph.D. diss., Stanford University, 1980).

14. Clyde Arbuckle, *Clyde Arbuckle's History of San Jose* (San Jose: Smith & McKay, 1986), 156.

15. Yu, *Chinatown San Jose*, 103.

16. Lukes and Okihiro, *Japanese Legacy*, 19.

17. See M. F. Jacobson, *Whiteness of a Different Color.*

18. As quoted in M. F. Jacobson, *Whiteness of a Different Color,* 56.

19. Mary Bowden Carroll, *Ten Years in Paradise: Leaves from a Society Reporter's Notebook* (San Jose: Popp & Hogan, 1903).

20. See Alexander Saxton, *The Indispensable Enemy: Labor and the Anti-Chinese Movement in California* (Berkeley: University of California Press, 1971). For San Jose, see Yu, *Chinatown San Jose.*

21. Yu, *Chinatown San Jose*, 15.

22. On Heinlenville, see Yu, *Chinatown San Jose.*

23. See Sucheng Chan, *Asian Americans: An Interpretive History* (Boston: Twayne, 1991) for details on the various means used to achieve access to land.

24. On the Japanese in the Santa Clara Valley, see Lukes and Okihiro, *Japanese Legacy.*

25. The Japanese students were by far the most numerous group of students of color.

26. Bruno Lasker, *Filipino Immigration* (New York: Arno Press, 1969), 15. Lasker doesn't give precise figures for the size of the Filipino population in the Santa Clara Valley, but from other data I have, I would estimate it to have been a few hundred in 1930.

27. See Pitti, "Quicksilver Community," 10, for the maintenance of tradition argument and 151 for the statistics.

28. Pitti, "Quicksilver Community," 190–5.

29. See Silvano M. Tomasi, "The Ethnic Church and the Integration of Italian Immigrants in the United States," in *The Italian Experience in the United States,* eds. Silvano M. Tomasi and Madeleine H. Engel (Staten Island, NY: Center for Migration Studies, 1970), 183, for information about ethnic parishes in general and about Bishop Scalabrini in particular. I also learned about the San Jose parishes from Brother Tom Marshall, S.J., Assistant Archivist, the California Province of the Society of Jesus, in a letter of August 22, 1977, in my possession.

30. As quoted in M. F. Jacobson, *Whiteness of a Different Color,* 81.

31. Robert Thorpe, "Council-Manager Government in San Jose, California" (master's thesis, Stanford University, 1938), 44.

32. Kimball Young, *Mental Differences in Certain Immigrant Groups: Psychological Tests of South Europeans in Typical California Schools with Bearing on the Ed-*

ucational Policy and on the Problems of Racial Contacts in This Country (Eugene: University Press of Oregon, 1922), 21, 76.

33. Paul Davis Chapman, *Schools as Sorters: Lewis M. Terman, Applied Psychology, and the Intelligence Testing Movement* (New York: New York University Press, 1988), 123.

34. This generalization is based on many sources. In the first place, my own interviews with retired cannery workers produced one person after another talking about "my son, the engineer" or "my daughter, the teacher." In the second place, it is based on Micaela di Leonardo's ethnographic findings about Italian Americans in Northern California, in *The Varieties of Ethnic Experience: Kinship, Class, and Gender Among California's Italian-Americans* (Ithaca, NY: Cornell University Press, 1984). Thirdly, a special series entitled "Voices of Diversity" in the Sunday supplement of the *San Jose Mercury News* in the mid-1990s dealt with eight different ethnic groups in the Valley. The article devoted to the Valley's Italian Americans begins this way: "From the orchards and vineyards that first brought Santa Clara Valley prominence as an agricultural power, to the universities that have helped make the South Bay a cultural center, to the urban development that's the foundation of San Jose's future growth, Italian-Americans have played major roles in shaping the region" ("Shapers of a Better Life," *San Jose Mercury News, West Magazine*, 12 November 1995, 15). One interviewee is quoted as saying, "Maybe it's a classist comment, but I think the affluence that the families were able to gain had to do with the loss of the cultural things. As you become more affluent, you become able to move. Money allows you to leave your roots." Finally, and most compellingly of all, Rich Lovelady of the California Department of Finance provided me with data drawn from the 1990 U.S. Census and presented in the Public Use Microdata File. Of the sample of those of Italian ancestry that year in Santa Clara County, 35.9 percent were employed as managers or professionals and another 35 percent in sales and administrative support; 31.7 percent had achieved college degrees, as opposed to 21 percent of Italian Americans nationally. In short, the group was overwhelmingly white-collar.

35. Jan Otto Marius Broek, *The Santa Clara Valley: A Study in Landscape Changes* (Utrecht, The Netherlands: N.V.A. Oosthoek's Uitgevers-MIJ, 1932), 125f.

36. I. G. "Slugger" Ficarrota, interview by author, 13 May 1986, San Jose, California. Ficarrota was a cannery business agent for thirty-two years.

37. Stephen Thernstrom, *Poverty and Progress* (New York: Atheneum, 1969), 157.

38. Joel Perlmann, *Ethnic Differences: Schooling and Social Structure Among the Irish, Italians, Jews, and Blacks in an American City, 1880–1935* (Cambridge: Cambridge University Press, 1988), 83.

39. Ficarrota, interview.

40. There is no monograph on San Jose's Italian community. I base my gen-

eralization on the home provinces of those I interviewed, on the lists of fraternal organizations and their provincial identifications, and on the previously cited *San Jose Mercury News* series on the area's Italian Americans.

41. See, for example, Edward Banfield, *Moral Basis of a Backward Society* (New York: Free Press, 1958), and Herbert Gans, *Urban Villagers: Group and Class in the Life of Italian Americans* (New York: Free Press, 1962).

42. di Leonardo, *The Varieties of Ethnic Experience*, 95.

43. *San Jose Mercury News*, 12 November 1995.

44. John Bodnar, *The Transplanted: A History of Immigrants in Urban America* (Bloomington: Indiana University Press, 1985), 140.

45. Theresa Chiechi, a retired cannery worker who was one hundred years old at the time of the interview. *San Jose Mercury News*, 12 November 1995.

46. For the experiences of the Mountain View Spaniards, who immigrated via Hawaii, see Ann Yards Cozzolino, "The Mountain View 'Sugar-Boat' Spanish Family of Juan Larez Lopez," ms. in the possession of the author. Dora Peregrina Ferri (a cousin of Cozzolino's), interview with the author, 18 September 1999, Redwood City, California.

47. Lasker, *Filipino Immigration*, 15–8.

48. Pitti, "Quicksilver Community," 178, 184f.

49. Rudy Calles, *Champion Prune Pickers: Migrant Worker's Dilemma* (Los Alamitos, Calif.: Hwong Publishing, 1979).

50. Jaclyn Greenberg, "Industry in the Garden: A Social History of the Canning Industry and Cannery Workers in the Santa Clara Valley, California, 1870–1920" (Ph.D. diss., University of California, Los Angeles, 1985), 111.

51. On the peculiarities of California agriculture in this regard, see Carey McWilliams, *California: The Great Exception* (New York: A. A. Wyn, 1949), especially chapter 7. But see also David Vaught, *Cultivating California* (Baltimore: Johns Hopkins University Press, 1999).

52. *Western Canner and Packer*, June 1929.

53. "Adventures of Del Monte," *Fortune* 18 (November 1938); Philips, "Towards a New Theory of Wage Structure," 145–53, 270.

54. Robert Couchman, *The Sunsweet Story* (San Jose: Sunsweet Growers, 1967), 48–50. There is a splendid new book on the cooperative movement in the raisin industry: Victoria Saker Woeste, *The Farmer's Benevolent Trust: Law and Agricultural Cooperation in Industrial America, 1865–1945* (Chapel Hill: University of North Carolina Press, 1998). Says Woeste (p. 4): "The history of the cooperative movement supplies a case in point of this idea [of unintended consequences]. Cooperation embodied a series of puzzling incongruities. It combined the ideologies of self-help and agrarian self-sufficiency, even as it embraced the trend toward combination and consolidation. . . . The movement was born out of farmers' protests against monopolies and trusts, yet it staked its own existence on a privileged use of monopoly and the trust."

55. Bureau of the Census, *Agriculture* II (3), 580–1.

56. Couchman, *The Sunsweet Story*, 71.

57. Broek, *The Santa Clara Valley*, 112.

58. Canneries' report to the National Recovery Administration, National Archives, Record Group 9, Boxes 1231, 1232.

59. California Packing Corporation, "An Industry That Sprang from a Kettle," *San Francisco*, 1928.

60. For background and a guide to the literature on this subject, see Glenna Matthews, "'The Los Angeles of the North': San Jose's Transition from Fruit Capital to High-Tech Metropolis," *Journal of Urban History* 25 (May 1999): 459–76.

61. On the waitresses' union in San Francisco, see Dorothy Sue Cobble, *Dishing It Out: Waitresses and Their Unions in the Twentieth Century* (Urbana: University of Illinois Press, 1991). On San Francisco labor history in general, see Michael Kazin, *Barons of Labor: The San Francisco Building Trades and Union Power in the Progressive Era* (Urbana: University of Illinois Press, 1987), and Michael Kazin, "The Great Exception Revisited: Organized Labor and Politics in San Francisco and Los Angeles, 1870–1940," *Pacific Historical Review* 55 (August 1986): 371–402.

62. Ira Cross, *A History of the Labor Movement in California* (Berkeley: University of California Press, 1935), 144–98.

63. Donald Anthony, "Labor Conditions in the Canning Industry in the Santa Clara Valley of the State of California" (Ph.D. diss., Stanford University, 1928), 18.

64. On the relative harmony among white workers in San Francisco, see William Issel and Robert Cherny, *San Francisco, 1865–1932: Politics, Power, and Urban Development* (Berkeley: University of California Press, 1986), 204–7. See Saxton, *The Indispensable Enemy*, on the racism of white workers.

65. See, for example, Vicki L. Ruiz, *Cannery Women/Cannery Lives: Mexican Women, Unionization, and the California Food Processing Industry, 1930–1950* (Albuquerque: University of New Mexico Press, 1987), on the "cannery culture" of these workers in Southern California.

66. A special report from the California Bureau of Labor Statistics in 1913, *Labor Conditions in the California Canning Industry*, provides statistical data on the age of women in the canneries. The report states that "women employed in the canneries are notably older than those in other industries" (34). See also Carole Turbin, "Beyond Conventional Wisdom: Women's Wage Work, Household Economic Contribution, and Labor Activism in a Mid-Nineteenth-Century Working-Class Community," in *To Toil the Livelong Day: America's Women at Work, 1780–1980*, ed. Carol Groneman and Mary Beth Norton (Ithaca, NY: Cornell University Press, 1987), for an account of a community and an industry with some interesting parallels to San Jose and its women cannery workers. In

Troy, New York, women collar makers moved in and out of the workforce according to their stage in the life cycle. Daughters followed their mothers into the industry. Turbin argues that these factors conduced toward unionization.

67. Dorothy Navarro and Dadie Lorente, interview with the author, 21 November 1974, San Jose, California; Elizabeth Nicholas, interview with the author, 13 November 1974, Mountain View, California.

68. Lorente and Navarro, interviews. Videotaped interviews with cannery workers, California History Center, DeAnza College, Cupertino.

69. Cobble, *Dishing It Out*, 6.

70. Carole Turbin, *Working Women of Collar City: Gender, Class, and Community in Troy, 1864–86* (Urbana: University of Illinois Press, 1992), 166.

71. On the subject of piece rates for cannery workers, see Martin Brown and Peter Philips, "The Decline of the Piece-Rate System in California Canning: Technological Innovation, Labor Management, and Union Pressure," *Business History Review* 60 (Winter 1986): 564–601.

72. The workers' letters, many handwritten scrawls, are scattered throughout the canning industry files in the National Recovery Administration (NRA) collection, National Archives, Record Group 9, Boxes 1228–32. The testimony given to the NRA is contained in National Industrial Recovery Administration, "Hearing on Code of Fair Practices and Competition, Canning Industry," 281–3.

73. Elizabeth Reis, "Cannery Row: The AFL, the IWW, and Bay Area Cannery Workers," *California History* 64 (Summer 1985): 181.

74. Ibid., 187. On the Toilers, see also Greenberg, "Industry in the Garden;" Department of Labor, *Labor Unionism in American Agriculture*, by Stuart Jamieson, bulletin no. 836, 1945; and Kenneth Hugh Smith, "Industrial Relations in the California Fruit and Vegetable Canning Industry" (master's thesis, University of California, Berkeley, 1949).

75. James McLoughlin, interview with the author, 30 October 1974, San Jose, California. The head of the Retail Clerks' local for many years, McLoughlin is the widower of Myra Eaton McLoughlin, the only woman in the AFL cannery workers' leadership in the 1930s.

76. Elizabeth Nicholas, videotaped interview, California History Center, De Anza College, Cupertino.

77. *Union Journal*, 1 September 1910.

78. This generalization is based on a reading of scattered issues of *The World* for 1908. There are no extant issues of any analogous publication for the Santa Clara Valley itself, at least that I have been able to discover.

79. *Organized Labor*, 23 May 1908; *Palo Alto Times*, 19 May 1908; *San Francisco Call*, 19 May 1908; *San Jose Mercury*, 19 May 1908.

80. Thorpe, "Council-Manager Government," 10.

81. *San Jose Mercury Herald*, 20 April 1915.

CHAPTER 2

1. *Western Canner and Packer,* October 1929.
2. Dewey Anderson, interview with the author, 24 October 1974, San Jose, California.
3. *Western Canner and Packer,* May 1931.
4. *Western Canner and Packer,* May 1932; January 1933. The reports were based on a census of the industry.
5. Smith "Industrial Relations," 117f.
6. Ibid., 117–27.
7. *San Jose Mercury Herald,* 17 May 1932.
8. *San Jose Mercury Herald,* 1 November 1937; 4 November 1937.
9. Carey McWilliams, interview with the author, 5 November 1975, New York, New York.
10. Caroline Decker Gladstein, interview with the author, April 18, 1974, San Francisco, California.
11. Anderson, interview.
12. Roger Baldwin to Al Meyer, telegram dated 29 August 1933, ACLU papers, State Historical Society of Wisconsin, vol. 649.
13. Nicholas, interview. Nicholas told me that she first joined the Communist Party in the early 1920s and that she had been a member through the date of the interview. Living in the Valley for decades, she was an excellent source for information on local Communist Party activities. Professor Robert Cherny, of San Francisco State University, shared with me copies of the notes he took in the Comintern Archives in Moscow on the activities of the Communist Party in the United States. Though he was primarily interested in maritime organizing (he was a biographer of Harry Bridges of the International Longshoremen and Warehousemen's Union), he took a few notes that reveal a strong Party concern about California agriculture.
14. Dorothy Healey, interview with George Ewart, Phonotape 49A, Bancroft Library, University of California, Berkeley.
15. Department of Labor, *Labor Unionism,* 84. "Spanish" refers to immigrants from Spain.
16. Healey, interview. Healey, herself an organizer, acknowledged that the strike was spontaneous. In a later interview, Healey provided the following recollection of the strike:

> In the beginning of the strike, we could not rent a single hall in San Jose. It was very much like the unemployed demonstrations. There was nothing which was legal, where people could gather together. The police brutality was of a far greater level than anything that the people have seen in later years, because there was no consciousness on the part of anybody else in the public that there was anything wrong in what they were doing. So we would hold these street meetings — I mean park meetings, strike meetings — at St. James Park, and the police would break them up.

Dorothy Healey, "Tradition's Chains Have Bound Us," interview by Joel Gardner, UCLA Oral History Program, 1972, 59f.

17. *San Jose Mercury Herald*, 30 July 1931.

18. *Daily Worker*, August 8, 1931. See also Cletus E. Daniel, *Bitter Harvest: A History of California Farmworkers, 1870–1941* (Berkeley: University of California Press, 1982), 128.

19. *Daily Worker*, 3 August 1931.

20. *San Francisco News*, 1 August 1931.

21. Stuart M. Jamieson, "Labor Unionism in Agriculture" (Ph.D. diss., University of California, Berkeley, 1943). Page 212 makes this point.

22. Porter M. Chaffee, "A History of the Cannery and Agricultural Workers Industrial Union," Federal Writers Project Papers, Carton 35, Bancroft Library. Using the hall for this meeting represented an achievement, given Dorothy Healey's recollection of having no place but St. James Park in which to hold meetings. See also the *San Jose Mercury-Herald*, 4 August 1931.

23. *San Jose Mercury-Herald*, 31 July 1931.

24. *San Jose Mercury-Herald*, 4 August 1931.

25. *San Francisco News*, 1 August 1931.

26. Chaffee, "A History of the Cannery and Agricultural Workers Industrial Union."

27. *People v Matt Huotari and Elizabeth Nicholas*, Superior Court, County of Santa Clara, case no. 242251/2 (1933).

28. Jamieson, "Labor Unionism," 43.

29. Gladstein, interview.

30. There are several sources about these strikes. See Jamieson, "Labor Unionism," 99, 231–3; *Western Worker*, 24 April 1933; *San Jose Mercury-Herald*, 15 June 1933, 17 June 1933, 18 June 1933; Ella Winter, "For the Duration of the Crop," *New Republic*, 25 October 1933; Addison Keeler, "Report of Agricultural Workers Union," Federal Writers Project Papers, Carton 13, Bancroft Library; Norman Lowenstein, "Strikes and Strike Tactics in California Agriculture" (master's thesis, University of California, Berkeley, 1940), 75–8.

31. Gladstein, interview.

32. A copy of this letter is in the Federal Writers Project Papers, Carton 13, Bancroft Library.

33. Ibid.

34. Chaffee, "A History of the Cannery and Agricultural Workers Industrial Union."

35. Federal Writers Project Papers, Carton 13, Bancroft Library.

36. Fond 515, Opis 1, File 3295: District 13 Correspondence, Comintern Archives. From the files of Professor Robert Cherny.

37. See Harry Farrell, *Swift Justice: Murder and Vengeance in a California Town* (New York: St. Martin's Press, 1992). Royce Brier of the *San Francisco Chronicle* won a Pulitzer Prize for his coverage of the lynching in San Jose. When I was

doing the research for my dissertation, I conducted several interviews, such as one with Robert Couchman (on 19 November 1974), who was there watching from a pepper tree. Despite my research and Farrell's, much of the case is shrouded in mystery and likely to remain so. No one was ever tried for his/her role in the lynching, hence there is no public record that would indicate who was primarily responsible.

38. "Governor Lynch and His Mob," *The Nation*, 13 December 1933; *San Jose Mercury-Herald*, 28 November 1933.

39. The ACLU sent two men to San Jose to investigate the lynching, but the investigation produced no meaningful results. On this subject, see Glenna Matthews, "A California Middletown: The Social History of San Jose in the Depression" (Ph.D. diss., Stanford University, 1977), chapter 5.

40. Clarke A. Chambers, *California Farm Organizations* (Berkeley: University of California Press, 1952), 110.

41. *San Jose Mercury-Herald*, 6 March 1934.

42. There are many accounts of the strike that had been precipitated by militant longshoremen. See, for example, Bruce Nelson, *Workers on the Waterfront: Seamen, Longshoremen, and Unionism in the 1930s* (Urbana: University of Illinois Press, 1988).

43. *Union Gazette*, October 9, 1936.

44. John Terry, "The Terror in San Jose," *The Nation*, 8 August 1934.

45. *Union Gazette*, 13 November 1936.

46. Daniel, *Bitter Harvest*, 252–4.

47. See Ellis M. Hawley, *The New Deal and the Problem of Monopoly: A Study in Economic Ambivalence* (Princeton: Princeton University Press, 1966).

48. See Glenna Matthews, "The Apricot War: A Study of the Changing Fruit Industry During the 1930s," *Agricultural History* 59 (January 1985): 25–39.

49. Ibid. See also "Large Scale Organization in the Food Industry," TNEC Monograph no. 35, 76th Congress (Washington, D.C.: GPO, 1940).

50. *San Jose Mercury-Herald*, 22 June 1937; see also Herbert William Free, "California Apricot Growers Union" (master's thesis, University of California, Berkeley, 1941), 3.

51. *San Jose Mercury-Herald*, 17 June 1939.

52. *San Jose Mercury-Herald*, 13 July 1939.

53. Free, "California Apricot Growers Union," 63.

54. Carey McWilliams, *Ill Fares the Land* (Boston: Little, Brown, 1942), 21. See also *Fortune*, 1938.

55. For the march inland, see Harvey Schwartz, *The March Inland: Origins of the ILWU Warehouse Division, 1934–1938* (Los Angeles: Institute of Industrial Relations, 1978).

56. See Stuart M. Jamieson, "The Origins and Present Structure of Labor Unions in Agricultural and Allied Industries of California," in Senate Subcomit-

tee of the Committee on Education and Labor, *Hearings Pursuant to S. Res. 266, Violations of Free Speech and Rights of Labor,* 74th and 76th Cong. 1936–40, part 62, 22531–41.

57. As quoted in Daniel, *Bitter Harvest,* 274.

58. Nelson, *Workers on the Waterfront,* 196.

59. J. Paul St. Sure, "Some Comments on Employer Organizations and Collective Bargaining in Northern California Since 1934," interview by Corinne Gilb, Institute of Industrial Relations Oral History Project, University of California, Berkeley (1957): 141–7.

60. Schwartz, *The March Inland,* 134–7.

61. I. G. "Slugger" Ficarrota, interview with the author, 9 June 1975.

62. Elizabeth Nicholas, interviews with the author, 13 November 1974; 30 July 1980, Mountain View, California.

63. See Gerald A. Rose, "The March Inland: The Stockton Cannery Strike of 1937," *Southern California Quarterly* 54 (Spring 1972): 67–82; (Summer 1972): 155–76.

64. St. Sure, "Some Commments," 168, 169, 182.

65. Elizabeth Nicholas, interview with the author, 30 July 1980.

66. Marjorie Howell, "California Cannery Unions" (master's thesis, Stanford University, 1946), 25.

67. These events preceded the formation of the CIO's United Cannery and Agricultural and Packing and Allied Workers of America (UCAPAWA) in Denver in July 1937. Radicals were still working within existing AFL locals in the spring of 1937.

68. *Union Gazette,* 29 January 1937; 26 February 1937.

69. *Union Gazette,* 4 June 1937.

70. *Union Gazette,* 11 June 1937.

71. Angelo Ghirlanda, interview with the author, 19 July 1980, Gilroy, California. Ghirlanda was not part of the mobilized group of warehousemen who were in touch with militants in San Francisco. But he did tell me that Vandeleur had designated him as a leader of what would prove to be the emerging company union. Obviously, he didn't say this in so many words. But he did say that the leader of the California State Federation sought him out for a leadership role shortly before 20852 went public.

72. St. Sure, "Some Comments," 173.

73. *UG,* 23 July 1937; *San Jose Mercury-Herald,* 20 July 1937.

74. Don Sanfilippo, interview with the author, 15 July 1980, Sunnyvale, California. These leaders were all men, except for Myra Eaton, who had died by the time I began my research.

75. Don Sanfilippo spoke as if the local had been a closed shop. Yet St. Sure recalled that California Processors and Growers had been quite careful not to grant a closed shop, because leaders knew that they would have been on shaky

legal ground. (St. Sure, "Some Comments," 171, 172). To make matters even more confusing, Stuart Jamieson, at the time a leading authority on agricultural unionism, testified to the LaFollette Committee that the closed shop and the check-off had been very effective in stifling CIO competition against the AFL in Northern California canneries. See Jamieson, "The Origins and Present Structure of Labor Unions," 22539.

76. 22 NLRB, 29 March 1940, 250.

77. Walter Jones, interview with the author, 6 August 1980, Sunnyvale, California.

78. Gladstein, Leonard, Patsey, and Anderson, Attorneys at Law, Papers, Carton 59, #2061, Bancroft Library.

79. *San Jose Mercury-Herald*, 22 July 1939.

80. *San Jose Mercury-Herald*, 29 July 1939

81. *San Jose Mercury-Herald*, 19 May 1941.

82. Kenneth Cameron, Jr., "Association Bargaining in the California Canning Industry" (master's thesis, University of California, Berkeley, 1949), 183.

83. On the organization of dried fruit packers by the CIO, see Glenna Matthews, "The Fruit Workers of the Santa Clara Valley: Alternative Paths to Union Organization During the 1930s," *Pacific Historical Review* 54 (February 1985): 51–70.

84. Michael Paul Rogin and John L. Shover, *Political Change in California: Critical Elections and Social Movements, 1890–1966* (Westport, Conn.: Greenwood Publishing), 115.

85. *San Jose Mercury-Herald*, 10 October 1930.

86. Dewey Anderson and Percy E. Davidson, *Ballots and the Democratic Struggle* (Stanford: Stanford University Press, 1943), 115, 357. This book studies Santa Clara County to test the impact of the New Deal on voting.

87. Professor James Gregory of the University of Washington is working on what will no doubt be an authoritative scholarly account of Sinclair's campaign and its impact on the electorate.

88. For a fuller discussion of these issues and the empirical basis for these generalizations, see Matthews, "A California Middletown," chapter 8.

89. The CAWIU went out of its way to recruit Mexican Americans, for example. See Pitti, "Quicksilver Community," 231.

CHAPTER 3

1. Roger Lotchin, *Fortress California, 1910–1961: From Warfare to Welfare* (New York: Oxford University Press, 1992).

2. Carl Abbott, *The Metropolitan Frontier: Cities in the Modern American West* (Tucson: University of Arizona Press, 1993), 8.

3. Lotchin, *Fortress California*, 56. Lotchin says that there was a coalition of Bay Area cities to get the dirigible base for Sunnyvale.

4. *San Jose Mercury*, 23 April 1940.

5. See Al Campbell and Mimi Real, *Growing Orbit: The Story of FMC Corporation* (Chicago: The FMC Corporation, 1992), 77. The original contract was for amphibious landing vehicles. By the end of the war, the firm was also supplying bomb hoists, aviation parts, box-making machines, and special-purpose pumps.

6. *San Jose Mercury-Herald*, 23 November 1940.

7. Rebecca S. Lowen, *Creating the Cold War University: The Transformation of Stanford* (Berkeley: University of California Press, 1997), chapter 1.

8. Gerald D. Nash, *World War II and the West: Reshaping the Economy* (Lincoln: University of Nebraska Press, 1990), 4.

9. As events played out, aircraft building was carried on in Southern California and ships were built along San Francisco Bay.

10. Abbott, *The Metropolitan Frontier*, 10.

11. Frank Taylor, "Factory in the Country," *Saturday Evening Post*, 13 April 1946.

12. Though Hendy was sold to Westinghouse after the war, which then sold the facility to Northrop Grumman, there was, as of 1999, an Iron Man Museum in the plant. The museum honored the contribution made by the company to the war effort. I was able to visit the museum and consult its archives.

13. "The Joshua Hendy Iron Works, 1906–1946, Sunnyvale, California," brochure from the American Society of Mechanical Engineers, 14 December 1978.

14. Lola Vaughan, interview with the author, 30 May 1999, Sunnyvale, California.

15. The *Union Gazette* of July 28, 1944, reported that the International Association of Machinists had a membership of 11,400 in the county.

16. S. L. Wykes, "Preserving a City's Story," *San Jose Mercury News*, 30 September 1987.

17. Pitti, "Quicksilver Community," 250.

18. Ibid., 203.

19. Varden Fuller et al., "Domestic and Imported Workers in the Harvest Labor Market, Santa Clara County, California," California Agricultural Experiment Station, Giannini Foundation of Agricultural Economics, Report no. 184, January 1956, 9 (Frank B. Duveneck Papers, Box 1, Hoover Institution Archives).

20. See, for example, Albert S. Broussard, *Black San Francisco: The Struggle for Racial Equality in the West, 1900–1954* (Lawrence: University Press of Kansas, 1993), and Gretchen Lemke-Santangelo, *Abiding Courage: African American Migrant Women and the East Bay Community* (Chapel Hill: University of North Carolina Press, 1996), for a discussion of the way in which arriving African Americans from the South troubled those already present in San Francisco and Oakland.

21. Pitti, "Quicksilver Community," 222f.

22. See David G. Gutierrez, *Walls and Mirrors: Mexican Americans, Mexican Immigrants, and the Politics of Ethnicity* (Berkeley: University of California Press, 1995), 151.

23. Pitti, "Quicksilver Community," 207.

24. Armand Juarez Sanchez, "An Analysis of the Barrio as a Socio Cultural Environment and Its Informal Needs-Meeting Resources" (Ph.D. diss., University of California, Berkeley, 1977), 80.

25. See Margaret Clark, *Health in the Mexican-American Culture* (Berkeley: University of California Press, 1959), 33. Clark says that a sense of group loyalty within the *colonia* is fostered by such factors as common language, kinship, and so forth.

26. As quoted in Sanchez, "An Analysis of the Barrio," 75. Sanchez calls the period from 1928 to 1960 the "height of the autonomous barrio."

27. Walter Jones, interview with the author, 6 August 1980, Sunnyvale, California.

28. These contracts first came to my attention in Halle G. Lewis, "Comparing AFL and CIO Representation of California Cannery Workers During World War II," unpublished seminar paper, San Francisco State University, 1995. Consulting the contracts myself, I agreed with Lewis' judgment. See Agreement Between the Grower-Shipper Vegetable Association and United Cannery, Agricultural, Packing, and Allied Workers of America, Local 78, 11 June 1943, Grower-Shipper Vegetable Association file, Case No. 111-7377-D, Box 5, Clark Kerr Collection. See also Collective Bargaining Agreement Between California Processors and Growers and the American Federation of Labor and California State Council of Cannery Unions, as amended 10 July 1943. California Processors and Growers file, Case No. 111-7430-D, Clark Kerr Collection, Labor Archives and Research Center, San Francisco State University.

29. Cameron, "Association Bargaining," 129.

30. *AFL Proceedings*, 1940, 276–7.

31. *AFL Proceedings*, 1941, 286–7.

32. See *Union Gazette*, 9 March 1945, 11 May 1945 (for the election).

33. Consult the *Union Gazette* of 19 October 1945, 26 October 1945, 5 April 1946, 23 August 1946, and 6 September 1946 for these events.

34. St. Sure, "Some Comments," , 227–9.

35. Ibid., 235f.

36. Ibid., 237.

37. Jones, interview.

38. Patricia Zavella, *Women's Work and Chicano Families: Cannery Workers of the Santa Clara Valley* (Ithaca, NY: Cornell University Press, 1987), 54, 55.

39. For an excellent, balanced account of the impact of Taft-Hartley on organized labor, see Robert Zieger, *The CIO, 1935–1955* (Chapel Hill: University of North Carolina Press, 1995).

40. Elizabeth Faue, *Community of Suffering and Struggle: Women, Men, and the Labor Movement in Minneapolis, 1915–1945* (Chapel Hill: University of North Carolina Press, 1991), 14.

41. Nancy F. Gabin, *Feminism in the Labor Movement: Women and the United Auto Workers, 1935–1975* (Ithaca, NY: Cornell University Press, 1990), 130.

42. Paul Pinsky, *Economic Material on California Canning Industry* (San Francisco: Research Department of California CIO Council, 1946), II-B-3f.

43. Brown and Philips, "The Decline of the Piece-Rate System," 574.

44. Ibid., 585.

45. Lukes and Okihiro, *Japanese Legacy*, 118f.

46. Ibid., 120.

47. These newsletters can be found in the archives of the Santa Clara County Office of Education.

48. "San Jose's Master Plan," Institute of Governmental Studies Library, University of California, Berkeley, 1958, 17.

49. George Starbird, "The New Metropolis," transcript of a talk given to the San Jose Rotary Club, San Jose Public Library, 1972.

50. Charles Davidson, interview with the author, 11 October 1996, San Jose, California.

51. Philip J. Trounstine and Terry Christensen, *Movers and Shakers: The Study of Community Power* (New York: St. Martin's Press, 1982), 97. See also Joel Garreau, *Edge City: Life on the New Frontier* (New York: Anchor Books, 1992), 224–7, for a similar point about sewers.

52. See Charles Harry Benjamin, "School District Reorganization in California: A Study of State Politics of Education" (Ph.D. diss., Stanford University, 1980), chapters 3–5, for a discussion of AB1.

53. Ibid., 19

54. Glen W. Vance, "School District Organization in the Metropolitan Area of Santa Clara County, California" (Ed.D. diss., University of Arizona, 1966), 141.

55. Tri Commission, "Housing Patterns, Zoning Laws, and Segregated Schools in Santa Clara County," Report on Public Hearings, California Room, San Jose Public Library, August 4–September 21, 1975.

56. "San Jose's Master Plan," 85–8.

57. Kenneth Jackson, *Crabgrass Frontier: The Suburbanization of the United States* (New York: Oxford University Press, 1985), 266.

58. Richard Reinhardt, "Joe Ridder's San Jose," *San Francisco* 7 (November 1965).

59. See Karl Belser, "The Making of Slurban America," *Cry California* 5 (Fall 1970); Rebecca Conard, "Slurbanizing the Valley of Heart's Delight: Origins of Agricultural Land Protection in California" (master's thesis, University of California, Santa Barbara, 1983); George Goodrich Mader, "Planning for Agricul-

ture in Urbanizing Areas: A Case Study of Santa Clara County, California" (master's thesis, University of California, Los Angeles, 1956). Conard points out that the largest operators with the most to protect were the most likely to resist the blandishments of developers.

60. Reinhardt, "Joe Ridder's San Jose."

61. Paul F. Griffin and Ronald L. Chatham, "Urban Impact on Agriculture in Santa Clara County, California," *Annals of the Association of American Geographers* 48 (September 1958): 203.

62. Karl Belser, "Orderly Development of the Suburbs," Catherine Bauer Wurster Papers, Box 7, Bancroft Library, February 10, 1966.

63. Philip Hamburger, *The New Yorker,* 4 May 1963.

64. Republican though he was, Jones had also been the point person for trying to get the state legislature to repeal the criminal syndicalism act at the behest of the Valley's liberals and its labor movement. See Herbert C. Jones Papers, Folder 900, Stanford University Archives, Stanford University, for correspondence to this effect.

65. Herbert C. Jones, "Herbert C. Jones on California Government and Public Issues," Regional Oral History Project, Bancroft Library, 1958, 256–8. Before passage of the Jones Act, water districts were set up under the Wright Irrigation Act, designed for districts with only one source of water.

66. See Jones, "Herbert C. Jones on California Government and Public issues;" Herbert C. Jones, "Water for the Valley: A Quarter-Century Record of the Santa Clara Valley Water Conservation District, 1929–1954," pamphlet, Stanford University Archives; Seonaid McArthur, ed., *Water in the Santa Clara Valley,* Local History Studies, no. 27, (Cupertino: California History Center, 1981); Albert Henley, interview with the author, 28 October 1996; Richard A. Walker and Matthew J. Williams, "Water from Power: Water Supply and Regional Growth in the Santa Clara Valley," *Economic Geography* 58 (April 1982): 95–119; A. P. Hamann, "Water Importation Program for Santa Clara County Cities," *Western City* (October 1965). On the new state role in water that developed in the 1930s, see Norris Hundley, Jr., *The Great Thirst: Californians and Water* (Berkeley: University of California Press, 1992). I also consulted archival materials in the library of the Santa Clara Valley Water District.

67. Harry Farrell, *San Jose Mercury,* 29 July 1961; Harry Farrell, "The San Felipe Story," pamphlet from the Santa Clara Valley Water District, 1987; Harry Farrell, interview with the author, 9 October 1996; Robert Rue Lee, "Local Government Public Works Decision-Making" (Ph.D. diss., Stanford University, 1964).

68. For a fuller discussion see Matthews, "'Los Angeles of the North'," 459–76.

69. Josephine Whitney Duveneck, *Life on Two Levels,* (Los Altos, Calif.: William Kaufmann, 1978), chapter 25. See also the discussion of the California

Federation for Civic Unity in William Issel, "Jews and Catholics Against Prejudice: Interfaith Cooperation in the San Francisco Civil Rights Campaign, 1940–1960," Forthcoming in *California Jews*, eds. Ava Kahn and Marc Dollinger, Brandeis Series in American Jewish History, Culture, and Life (Jonathan D. Sarna, general editor).

70. Duveneck, *Life on Two Levels*, chapter 25.

71. As quoted in Richard Griswold del Castillo and Richard A. Garcia, *Cesar Chavez: A Triumph of Spirit* (Norman: University of Oklahoma Press, 1995), 25.

72. Ibid., 23.

73. Pitti, "Quicksilver Community," 290.

74. Ibid., 373.

75. Ibid., 350.

76. Ibid., 340.

77. Ibid., 336–40.

78. Taylor, "Factory in the Country."

79. Ibid.

80. Lukes and Okihiro, *Japanese Legacy*, 122.

81. Ibid., 137, 138.

82. Fuller, "Domestic and Imported Workers."

83. Dorothy Goble, "Education Today — Self-Sufficiency Tomorrow," report on the Educational Project for Seasonal Farm Families, Santa Clara County, California, 1955–1960, Frank B. Duveneck Papers, Box 1, Hoover Institution Archives, October 1960.

84. Ibid.

85. Starbird, "The New Metropolis."

86. The *Union Gazette* contained a number of articles in these years that suggest that the local AFL was nearly as eager as the Chamber of Commerce was to woo business to the area. The *Gazette* of January 12, 1945, for example, reported that unions were joining with the Chamber in an effort to bring new industry to the county. Five labor leaders were on the newly formed Industrial Committee, and the labor movement was even pledging money to the drive. What its members had at stake was more jobs that would pay year-round wages.

87. See the article about the Lester brothers and their orchard in the *San Jose Mercury News*, 5 April 1998. My comments are also based on a field trip around the Valley that I conducted for the "Green and Gold" conference, held at the University of California, Santa Cruz, in August 1998. We visited the Lester ranch, and the brothers explained their operation.

CHAPTER 4

1. Tim John Sturgeon, "The Origins of Silicon Valley: The Development of the Electronics Industry in the San Francisco Bay Area" (master's thesis, Uni-

versity of California, Berkeley, 1992), 11. See also Arthur L. Norberg, "The Origins of the Electronics Industry on the Pacific Coast," *Proceedings of the Institute of Electrical and Electronics Engineers, Inc.* 64 (September 1976): 1314–22. On the industrialization of the Bay Area, see Richard Walker, "Industry Builds the City: The Suburbanization of Manufacturing in the San Francisco Bay Area, 1850–1940," *Journal of Historical Geography* 27 (January 2001).

2. Sturgeon, "The Origins of Silicon Valley," 5.

3. Ibid.

4. Frederick Seitz and Norman G. Einspruch, *Electronic Genie: The Tangled History of Silicon* (Urbana: University of Illinois Press, 1998), 154.

5. Sturgeon, "The Origins of Silicon Valley," 32.

6. Ibid.

7. AnnaLee Saxenian, *Regional Advantage: Culture and Competition in Silicon Valley and Route 128* (Cambridge: Harvard University Press, 1994); Sturgeon, "The Origins of Silicon Valley," 66, 67.

8. Lowen, *Creating the Cold War University*, 37.

9. John M. Findlay, *Magic Lands: Western Cityscapes and American Culture After 1940* (Berkeley: University of California Press, 1992), 124.

10. Dorothy Varian, *The Inventor and the Pilot* (Palo Alto, Calif.: Pacific Books, 1983), 53, 54.

11. The quote is from Ward Winslow, *Varian: Fifty Years of Innovative Excellence* (Palo Alto: Santa Clara Valley Historical Association, 1998), 4. My account is drawn from Winslow; Lowen, *Creating the Cold War University*; Varian, *The Inventor and the Pilot*; and the Varian Associates newsletters and magazines in the Stanford University Archives.

12. Lowen, *Creating the Cold War University*, 41.

13. Winslow, *Varian*, 6.

14. Lowen, *Creating the Cold War University*, 118.

15. Herbert J. Cabral, "To the End of the Rainbow: The Evolution of the Westinghouse Marine Division," pamphlet published by the Iron Man Museum, Sunnyvale, xiii.

16. Ibid., 2–7

17. *Union Gazette*, 2 November 1945.

18. *San Jose Mercury*, 8 July 1948.

19. *San Jose Evening News*, 31 March 1949.

20. Ruth Milkman, *Gender at Work: The Dynamics of Job Segregation by Sex During World War II* (Urbana: University of Illinois Press, 1987), 2. See also Ronald Schatz, *The Electrical Workers: A History of Labor at General Electric and Westinghouse, 1923–1960* (Urbana: University of Illinois Press, 1983).

21. This account is based on Zieger, *The CIO*, 255–85.

22. See UE Papers, Box 9, Folder 16, Labor Archives and Research Center, San Francisco State University, for one account of the cost of red-baiting in the Valley: "[W]e've been red-baited to a fairtheewell [sic]."

23. Says Zieger, *The CIO:* "Communist-influenced unions such as the ILWU, the FTA, and the UE were notable for fair and efficient administration, innovative cultural and educational programs, and positive responses to the distinctive problems of minority and female members." 255.

24. See Milkman, *Gender at Work*, on women in the United Electrical Workers. See also a UE Local 1008 Information Bulletin in the UE Papers, Box 9, Folder 8, LARC, contrasting the International Association of Machinists with the United Electrical Workers on gender equity.

25. *Lockheed Star*, 11 May 1979, special commemorative issue in honor of the twenty-fifth anniversary of the founding of the missile division. On August 24, 1999, I interviewed E. Lewis Nichols, the attorney who purchased the land on behalf of Lockheed. He told me that Cyril Chappellet, a colleague who had graduated from Stanford, was pitching the Santa Clara Valley to the firm as the place for a science-oriented facility to be located, and that these views prevailed.

26. Walter J. Boyne, *Beyond the Horizon: The Lockheed Story* (New York: St. Martin's Press, 1998), 275.

27. David Beers, *Blue Sky Dream: A Memoir of America's Fall from Grace* (New York: Doubleday, 1996).

28. Arline Smith, interview with the author, 31 August 1998, Sunnyvale, California.

29. These figures are based on Bureau of Labor Statistics (BLS) figures for the missile and space industry as a whole. The BLS economist with whom I consulted advised me that since there were so few players in the industry, the figures would be an accurate gauge for Lockheed. The Lockheed Martin Public Relations staff advised me that the firm had a 25 percent female workforce at the Sunnyvale facility as of 1999.

30. Giving Lockheed its due as an employer, it is also true that the Lockheed Minority and Female Coalition, alleging discrimination, won a class-action lawsuit against the firm in 1973 (Beers, *Blue Sky Dream*, 254, 255).

31. There is one commonsensical explanation for this phenomenon. Lockheed was the only missile company in the Valley, so to change jobs would have meant relocating. This aside, even the lower-level workers seem to have been remarkably loyal. Arline Smith, for example, commented on how little turnover there was among her immediate coworkers. The *Lockheed Star* included pages of pictures of employees being feted for their twenty or twenty-five years plus anniversaries with the firm.

32. In 1966, our family bought a four-bedroom suburban dream home in Sunnyvale for $26,300, my Lockheed-employee husband having just been promoted from hourly to salaried, but at the low end of the scale. We sold it for $92,000 in 1978. Today that model commands at least $500,000.

33. Beers, *Blue Sky Dream*, 151.

34. Michael S. Malone, *The Big Score: The Billion-Dollar Story of Silicon Valley* (Garden City, NY: Doubleday, 1985), 61.

35. John F. Keller, "The Production Worker in Electronics: Industrialization and Labor Development in California's Santa Clara Valley" (Ph.D. diss., University of Michigan, 1981), 57–9. Keller points out that the Santa Clara Valley was strategically located for electronics. With Lockheed Missiles and Space in its midst, the Valley was between the aeronautics manufacturing in Southern California and Seattle.

36. *San Francisco Examiner,* 1 October 1995.

37. Ramon C. Sevilla, "Employment Practices and Industrial Restructuring: A Case Study of the Semiconductor Industry in Silicon Valley, 1955–1991" (Ph.D. diss., University of California, Los Angeles, 1992), 151. Sevilla provides a valuable discussion of the Valley's labor movement on the eve of Silicon Valley, though his account of the cannery union is inaccurate.

38. Stanford University Archives has a substantial Varian Associates collection. In addition, I visited the firm's headquarters in Palo Alto, where I received every consideration. I was able to examine every issue of the newsletter or the subsequent magazine, as the firm grew in size, from the earliest issue through to the 1990s.

39. Varian, *The Inventor and the Pilot,* 234–42.

40. Winslow, *Varian,* 8–15; *Varian Associates Magazine,* December 1968, Stanford University Archives.

41. "Varian Associates Newsletter," November 1956, Stanford University Archives.

42. Varian Papers, VA, Box 2, Stanford University Archives.

43. Winslow, *Varian,* 60.

44. Statement of company philosophy written by Russell Varian, Varian Papers, VA, Box 2, Stanford University Archives, March 10, 1953.

45. "Varian Associates Newsletter," December 1958, Stanford University Archives.

46. Winslow, *Varian,* 37.

47. *Varian Associates Magazine,* March 1972, Stanford University Archives.

48. See the November 1961 issue of the Varian Associates newsletter, Stanford University Archives, for a discussion of the Job Interest Forum, a cornerstone of Varian personnel philosophy. After six months of service in a capacity, an employee could fill out a form to apply for a step up, so as to enhance the possibility of promotion from within.

49. *Varian Associates Magazine,* August 1978, Stanford University Archives.

50. Lowen, *Creating the Cold War University,* 114.

51. See the discussion of Stanford Industrial Park in Findlay, *Magic Lands,* chapter 3.

52. Winslow, *Varian,* 50.

53. Ibid., 40–42. Edward Ginzton was eager that the firm not be overly reliant on any one product or market.

54. "Varian Associates Newsletter," December 1963, Stanford University Archives.

55. Varian has hardly been alone in this difficulty. Discussing the decline in industrial research in general, Richard S. Rosenbloom and William J. Spencer say: "Unfortunately, technological fecundity and scientific distinction did not always carry through to the corporate bottom line." *Engines of Innovation: U.S. Industrial Research at the End of an Era*, ed. Rosenbloom and Spencer (Boston: Harvard Business School Press, 1996), 2.

56. Winslow, *Varian*, 29. My generalization is also based on a reading of the newsletters for the history of the firm. A September 1984 issue, for example, contained a letter from Tom Sege, the president, saying that the firm's profits were respectable, but still not keeping pace with the industry's leading companies, such as Hewlett-Packard.

57. *Varian Associates Magazine*, February 1972, Stanford University Archives.

58. *Varian Associates Magazine*, May 1980, Stanford University Archives.

59. *Varian Associates Magazine*, March 1971, Stanford University Archives.

60. "Varian Associates Newsletter," January 1958, Stanford University Archives.

61. *Varian Associates Magazine*, February 1973, Stanford University Archives. See also a number of other issues of the newsletter/magazine for more information about women and Varian. The April 1962 issue, for example, described how 115 members of the Women's Association of the Electronics Industry met and toured Varian. Eighteen of the group worked at Varian. The July 1982 issue had an article, "Women, Careers, and Success," featuring a number of women, one of whom was Ruth Davis of the Varian Board of Directors, a woman who had had a career of designing software systems for the Navy. Finally, the November 1985 issue featured Varian Success Stories, including two women who'd risen through the ranks, such as from secretary to software engineer.

62. "Varian Associates Newsletter," January 1963, Stanford University Archives.

63. Gordon E. Moore, "Some Personal Perspectives on Research in the Semiconductor Industry," in *Engines of Innovation*, ed. Rosenbloom and Spencer, 166.

64. Ibid. The eight decided to work within the corporate framework of Fairchild Camera and Instrument, which then founded the Fairchild Semiconductor Corporation.

65. Pamphlet prepared for the Tech Museum of Innovation, San Jose, 1999, 2. I took my granddaughter to the museum, and a docent responded to my inquiries about semiconductors by very helpfully photocopying the material he was using. This proved to be the most lucid exposition of the mysteries of the chip that I have yet encountered.

66. Robert Howard, *Brave New Work Place* (New York: Viking, 1985), 141.

67. Tim Jackson, *Inside Intel: Andy Grove and the Rise of the World's Most Powerful Chip Company* (New York: Dutton, 1997), 71.

68. George MacLeod, interview with the author, 20 September 1998, Kenwood, California.

69. Paul Pinsky, *Economic Material*, chapter 2.

70. Stephen M. Payne, *Santa Clara County: Harvest of Change* (Northridge, Cal.: Windsor Publications, 1987).

71. Zavella, *Women's Work*, 54.

72. Ibid.

73. Amanda Hawes, interview with the author, 5 June 2000, San Jose, California.

74. Zavella, *Women's Work*, 27 (for home-owning); 134, 135 (for college). As further confirmation of the fact that the cannery workers then lived in single-family homes, there are many letters from the families in the Sam Kagel Collection at the Labor Archives and Research Center, San Francisco State University. Mr. Kagel was an expert witness in an important civil rights case respecting these workers. A perusal of the addresses of these letters reveals no apartment complexes, the place where assembly workers tend to live in current times. I should explain that these papers have been accessioned but not yet catalogued. I was allowed to look through boxes that seemed relevant, so that I could evaluate their significance for labor history.

75. Hawes, interview.

76. Ted Smith, interview with the author, 1 March 1999. Smith had been an attorney for the dissident cannery workers. He recalls that the United Farm Workers general counsel, Jerry Cohen, was eager to open up a second front against the Teamsters.

77. *San Francisco Chronicle*, 25 June 1976.

78. This is based on my reading of the *Alaniz* decision in the Sam Kagel Collection, LARC, as well as other written materials there, including court testimony and correspondence. See also Zavella, *Women's Work*, 64–9, and "Reform Faction Seeks Canners Union Control," *San Jose Mercury News*, 30 September 1975.

79. Findlay, *Magic Lands*, 32.

80. RoseAnne Dominguez, "The Decline of Santa Clara County's Fruit and Vegetable Canning Industry, 1967–1987" (master's thesis, San Jose State University, 1992), 62f.

81. Ibid., 48.

82. Zavella, *Women's Work*, 163.

83. *San Jose Mercury News*, 20 January 1984. It's not clear to me whether this particular project ever actually got built. Others surely have been built on such land.

84. Keller, "The Production Worker in Electronics," 110.

85. Myra H. Strober and Carolyn L. Arnold, "Integrated Circuits/Segregated Labor: Women in Computer-Related Occupations and High-Tech Industries," in *Computer Chips and Paper Clips: Technology and Women's Employment,* ed. Heidi Hartmann et al., (Washington: National Academy Press, 1986), 154.

86. Sevilla, "Employment Practices," 279.

87. Keller, "The Production Worker in Electronics," 129.

88. Sevilla, "Employment Practices," 296. Sevilla argues that the reason prized engineers have to be paid so well is to keep them. Therefore, it's all the more necessary to hold down the wages of production workers.

89. Patricia Lamborn, interview with the author, 12 March 1999. See also Strober and Arnold, "Integrated Circuits/Segregated Labor."

90. Pat Sacco Woods, interview with author, October 18, 1998.

91. Manuel Castells and Peter Hall, *Technopoles of the World: The Making of the 21st-Century Industrial Complex* (London: Routledge, 1994), 17.

92. Dan Walters, *The New California: Facing the 21st Century* (Sacramento: California Journal Press, 1986).

93. *San Jose Mercury News,* 20 February 1985.

94. Presentations by Chuck Darrah, Jan English-Leuck, and James Freeman, "Life in the Fast Lane: The Environment Called Silicon Valley," California Studies Conference, California History Center, DeAnza College, Cupertino, 13 November 1998.

95. Castells and Hall, *Technopoles of the World,* 23.

96. In the economic downturn of the early twenty-first century, newspaper reports have indicated that there has been a diminution of the HP Way, apparently because of competitive pressures.

97. David Packard, *The H-P Way: How Bill Hewlett and I Built Our Company* (New York: HarperBusiness, 1995), 136. On the H-P Way, see also Castells and Hall, *Technopoles of the World,* 23, and Malone, *The Big Score,* 34–6.

98. Macleod, interview.

99. Malone, *The Big Score,* 134.

100. *San Jose Mercury News,* 20 February 1985.

101. Moore, "Some Personal Perspectives," 168.

102. *San Francisco Chronicle,* 23 September 1980.

103. Judith Stacey, *Brave New Families: Stories of Domestic Upheaval in Late Twentieth-Century America* (New York: Basic Books, 1991), 25.

CHAPTER 5

1. There are a small number of high-profile women entrepreneurs in the Valley, about whom we'll learn in Chapter 6. One big barrier to female entrepreneurship is that the world of venture capital remains very much an old boys network. According to an article in the *San Jose Mercury News* (24 January 2000), the

Forum for Women Entrepreneurs released statistics saying that as of that date there were 75 women among a group of 1,112 venture capitalists "currently active nationally." Although low, the figure represented a significant growth from the nine female venture capitalists in 1994. Interestingly enough, the *San Francisco Chronicle* had a story about a conference, called Springboard 2000, which brought together would-be women entrepreneurs and venture capitalists. Some 350 applications came in, and 27 women made the cut. Those women featured in the article — fewer than ten — included three with Indian surnames. See San Francisco *Chronicle*, of 2 February 2000.

2. Mike Cassidy, *San Jose Mercury News*, 9 March 2000.

3. According to the "Summit on Immigrant Needs Newsletter," published by Santa Clara County, July/September 2000 edition, "Santa Clara County is the first of 999 counties in the U.S. to comprehensively analyze immigrant lives and contributions."

4. Y. Jacobson, *Passing Farms, Enduring Values*, 235.

5. Jeff Goodell, "The Venture Capitalist in My Bedroom," *The New York Times Magazine*, 28 May 2000. The author, who had moved to a suburban Sunnyvale home near Vallco Village with his family in 1963, had returned to find that the home is now a dormitory for young Asian American professionals, who live there while launching a career.

6. Edward Jang-Woo Park, "Asian Americans in Silicon Valley: Race and Ethnicity in the Postindustrial Economy" (Ph.D. diss., University of California, Berkeley, 1993), 85.

7. As of 1990, there were 27,873 persons of Japanese descent in Santa Clara County. Of these, nearly three-quarters were U.S.-born.

8. Reed Ueda, *Postwar Immigrant America: A Social History* (Boston: Bedford Books, 1994), chapter 2. I also consulted David M. Reimers, *Still the Golden Door: The Third World Comes to America* (New York: Columbia University Press, 1992), and Alejandro Portes and Ruben G. Rumbaut, *Immigrant America: A Portrait*, 2nd ed. (Berkeley: University of California Press, 1996).

9. Talk by David Gutierrez at Stanford University, January 18, 2000. Professor Gutierrez is writing a book-length study of this subject.

10. See Ueda, *Postwar Immigrant America*, 45, for various refinements and changes to the 1965 law that were added in 1976 and 1978.

11. See, for example, the article on the Valley and the politics of the election in 2000 in the *San Francisco Chronicle*, 20 January 2000.

12. Reimers, *Still the Golden Door*, 124, 125.

13. Donna Gabaccia discusses Dominican women in this regard. Gabaccia, *From the Other Side*, 58. I was particularly struck by what Gabaccia reported, because I have assigned oral history interviews to students for which they have talked to immigrant women family members and encountered a similar delight in American domestic appurtenances.

14. Nazli Kibria, *Family Tightrope: The Changing Lives of Vietnamese Americans* (Princeton: Princeton University Press, 1993), 19. See also the discussion of Mexican immigrant women in Pierrette Hondagneu-Sotelo, *Gendered Transitions: Mexican Experience of Immigration* (Berkeley: University of California Press, 1994), 10. See, too, Gabaccia, "Immigrant Women: Nowhere at Home," *Journal of American Ethnic History* 10 (Summer 1991): 68, 69.

15. Gabaccia, *From the Other Side*, 29f.

16. Bernard Wong, *Ethnicity and Entrepreneurship: The New Chinese Immigrants in the San Francisco Bay Area* (Boston: Allyn and Bacon, 1998), 87, 88.

17. John Keller, "The Production Worker in Electronics" (Ph.D. diss., University of Michigan, 1981), 224.

18. *San Francisco Chronicle*, 4 June 1999.

19. Dee McCrorey, interview with the author, 1 June 1999.

20. Sevillla, "Employment Practices," 282.

21. Ibid.

22. Dr. Joseph LaDou, interview with the author, 21 September 1998, Woodside, California.

23. Charles Piller, "High-Tech Model of Inconsistency" *Los Angeles Times*, 9 January 1998.

24. George Vernez, "Mexican Labor in California's Economy: From Rapid Growth to Likely Stability," in *The California-Mexico Connection*, ed. Abraham F. Lowenthal and Katrina Burgess (Stanford: Stanford University Press, 1993), 156, 157.

25. Hondagneu-Sotelo, *Gendered Transitions*, 34–8.

26. Warren Mar, interview with the author, 24 September 1998, Oakland, California. Mar described this as a trajectory for both Latino and Asian immigrants who arrive with poor English skills. Mar, a bilingual Chinese American, delineated the trajectory by way of explaining why his work as an organizer for the Hotel and Restaurants Workers' Union has been so intertwined with the experiences of new immigrants in the Bay Area.

27. Keller, "The Production Worker in Electronics," 226–37.

28. Hondagneu-Sotelo, *Gendered Transitions*, 62.

29. Wong, *Ethnicity and Entrepreneurship*, 37.

30. Vicki Kwok Ching, interview with the author, 2 December 1999, Palo Alto, California. The quote and the observations are from the interview. For more on Ching, see the discussion in Chapter 6. Worth noting is the finding by Hondagneu-Sotelo for an unnamed Mexican community somewhere in the Bay Area: "I discovered that, regardless of the years or even decades of continuous residence in the U.S., men are more apt than women to say that they wish to return to Mexico" (*Gendered Transitions*, 98).

31. AnnaLee Saxenian, *Silicon Valley's New Immigrant Entrepreneurs* (San Francisco: Public Policy Institute of California, 1999), 13.

32. Aryn Baker and Lyssa Mudd, "In Land of Opportunity, Joblessness Frustrates Newcomers," *Los Angeles Times*, 29 August 2000.

33. *San Jose Mercury-Herald, West Magazine*, 4 December 1994.

34. See Kibria, *Family Tightrope*, and James Freeman, *Hearts of Sorrow: Vietnamese-American Lives* (Stanford: Stanford University Press, 1989).

35. Ruben Rumbaut, as quoted in Freeman, *Hearts of Sorrow*, 18–20.

36. *San Jose Mercury-Herald, West Magazine*, 4 December 1994.

37. Freeman, *Hearts of Sorrow*, 17, on the success stories and 8, on their effect on downtown.

38. *San Jose Mercury News*, 19 March 2000.

39. Park, "Asian Americans in Silicon Valley," 90.

40. According to the *San Jose Mercury News* (28 August 1999), for all voters in Santa Clara County, 47 percent were Democratic; 32 percent, Republican; and 21 percent, declined to state or third party. For Vietnamese Americans, the figures were 28 percent Democratic, 39 percent Republican, and 33 percent decline to state.

41. Freeman, *Hearts of Sorrow*, 14.

42. Also noteworthy is the fact that the people who have told me these stories have expressed no resentment about what this practice might do to property values. Rather, they've expressed admiration for how hard the newcomers are working to get ahead.

43. Park, "Asian Americans in Silicon Valley," 90.

44. "The Filipinos in Mountain View, California: Summary Report," Pacific Studies Center Archives, Mountain View.

45. Romie Manan, interview with the author, 29 September 1998, Sunnyvale, California.

46. Park, "Asian Americans in Silicon Valley," 120.

47. Ibid., 110.

48. As quoted in Park, "Asian Americans in Silicon Valley," 118.

49. Ibid., 107.

50. This quote furnishes the title of Hossfeld's forthcoming book. See Karen J. Hossfeld, "Divisions of Labor, Divisions of Lives: Immigrant Women Workers in Silicon Valley" (Ph.D. diss., University of California, Santa Cruz, 1988).

51. See Park, "Asian Americans in Silicon Valley," chapter 6, for a discussion of this subject.

52. Saxenian, *Silicon Valley's New Immigrant Entrepreneurs*, viii.

53. *San Jose Mercury News*, 4 January 2000. The article lists five Vietnamese entrepreneurs of note.

54. *San Jose Mercury News*, 6 March 2000.

55. Saxenian, *Silicon Valley's New Immigrant Entrepreneurs*, viii.

56. Bernard Wong, presentation to California Studies Seminar, University of California, Berkeley, November 17, 1999.

57. Saxenian, *Silicon Valley's New Immigrant Entrepreneurs*, 38.

58. Rafael Alarcon, "From Servants to Engineers: Mexican Immigration and Labor Markets in the San Francisco Bay Area," working paper, Chicano/Latino Policy Project, University of California, Berkeley, 1997, 10.

59. *San Francisco Chronicle*, 14 December 1999.

60. Correspondence with Boy Luethje, February 9, 2000. Professor Luethje has published a book in Germany about Silicon Valley.

61. Jackson, *Inside Intel*, 144.

62. David Lazarus, "A Question of Fraud," *San Francisco Chronicle*, 21 September 2000.

63. *San Francisco Chronicle*, 5 October 2000.

64. Sevilla, "Employment Practices." Sevilla says that between 1962 and 1966, there were "perfunctory attempts" by the UAW to organize Fairchild and by the IAM to organize National Semiconductor (154). I want to point out that Robert Garcia was also part of this effort, but since I was unable to interview him, I cannot give him his due.

65. Amy Newell, interview with the author, 10 May 1999. John Case, interview with the author, 29 May 1999. In addition, Amy Newell was kind enough to photocopy her correspondence with UE headquarters for my use.

66. Newell, interview.

67. *New York Times*, 2 December 1977.

68. Sevilla, "Employment Practices," 156; Martha Reiner, "Unions Gather for Organizing Effort in Electronics Industry," *San Francisco Business Journal*, 1 June 1981.

69. David Bacon, "Union-Busting in the Valley," *In These Times*, 23 November 1997.

70. Saxenian, *Regional Advantage*, 183, n. 61.

71. Park, "Asian Americans in Silicon Valley." According to Park, "the industry's managers decided to abandon the Fordist social equation. From its inception, one of the central elements in this effort has been a vigorous resistance to labor unions. To do this, the industry has avoided the traditional labor force that has had historical ties with labor unions. Instead the industry has relied on a labor force whose social marginality alienated them from labor unions" (179).

72. Jackson, *Inside Intel*, 139. An article in the January 1979 *Inteleads* magazine described the launching of the Penang operation in 1972. I should say that I was granted access to the Intel archives so as to read the publication there.

73. Case, interview.

74. Jesus Martinez Saldana, "At the Periphery of Democracy: The Binational Politics of Mexican Immigrants in Silicon Valley" (Ph.D. diss., University of California, Berkeley, 1993), 125.

75. Ann Gibbons, "U.S. Intensifying Raids Against Illegal Aliens," *Peninsula Times Tribune*, 17 April 1984.

76. *San Jose Mercury News*, 25 April 1984.

77. Martinez Saldana, "At the Periphery of Democracy," 126.

78. *San Jose Mercury News*, 16 April 1999.

79. Martinez Saldana, "At the Periphery of Democracy," 99f.

80. Ibid., 100; Joseph A. Rodriguez, "Becoming Latinos: Mexican Americans, Chicanos, and the Spanish Myth in the Urban Southwest," *Western Historical Quarterly* 29 (Summer 1998): 185.

81. Martinez Saldana, "At the Periphery of Democracy," 113f.

82. Professor Ramon Chacon of Santa Clara University has analyzed the politics of Quetzlcoatl.

83. *San Jose Mercury News*, 19 August 1999.

84. Wong, California Studies Seminar.

85. Zachary Coile, *San Francisco Examiner*, 20 February 2000. This in-depth feature on Cupertino and Asian Americans in California politics argues that the fund-raising scandal of 1996 involving Chinese Americans has served to depress current involvement.

86. Richard Magat, *Unlikely Partners: Philanthropic Foundations and the Labor Movement* (Ithaca, NY: Institute of Labor Relations Press, 1999), 175, 176.

87. Ted Smith, interview with the author, 1 March 1999, San Jose, California.

88. See *San Jose Mercury News*, 2 February 1982, for the original story about Lorraine Ross' letter to Great Oaks. *San Jose Mercury News* (10 July 1983) contained several pages about the problem, including detailed information about the problem plants. I also relied on information from Ted Smith. My son David Matthews went to work for the Santa Clara Valley Water District in the summer of 1984 as part of the effort to seal old wells.

89. Terry Christensen points out that David Packard led his colleagues to found what was first called the Santa Clara Valley Manufacturing Group (and is now the Silicon Valley Manufacturing Group) so as to represent the industry's "interests and negotiate reasonable regulation" after these revelations began to be made. See Christensen, "San Jose Becomes the Capital of Silicon Valley" in *Reflections of the Past: An Anthology of San Jose*, ed. Judith Henderson (Encinitas, Calif.: San Jose Historical Museum and Heritage Media Corporation, 1996), 209.

90. Worth noting is the fact that in his Congressional race in 2000, the Japanese American Mike Honda used "Si, se puede" on his yard signs — in a district that encompasses Latino neighborhoods. As it happens, Honda is fluent in Spanish, because he served as a Peace Corps volunteer in El Salvador.

91. I attended the meeting. The crowd estimate comes from the coverage in the *San Jose Mercury News*, 30 April 2000.

92. Kenneth Meinhardt, M.D., Soleng Tom, M.D., Philip Tse, M.P.H., and Connie Young Yu, *Santa Clara County Health Department Asian Health Assessment Project*, August 3, 1984. Yu shared her copy with me.

93. Connie Young Yu, interview with the author, 7 February 2000, Los Altos Hills, California.

94. These figures are in the report. See "Bridging Borders in Silicon Valley: Summit on Immigrant Needs and Contributions," San Jose: Office of Human Relations, Santa Clara County, December 2000. I had access to the findings before the December 6 summit, because I participated in the Wages and Working Conditions Work Group, which helped formulate and analyze the findings in that area.

95. From a fund-raising letter the Center mailed out in December 1997. The letter goes on to say that law students have won lawful status for immigrants from Cambodia, China, Colombia, Cuba, El Salvador, Georgia, Guatemala, Honduras, Iran, Laos, Mexico, Nicaragua, and Somalia. The above account is also based on the Center's brochure and on an interview with Stevenson at the Center, on November 2, 1999.

96. Doris Y. Ng, "From War on Poverty to War on Welfare: The Impact of Welfare Reform on the Lives of Immigrant Women" (San Francisco: Equal Rights Advocates, 1999), 16.

97. The Centro's clients are overwhelmingly male. I wish that I could have found women to provide me with this level of detail, but I'm grateful for this interview. A Centro volunteer provided translation for me.

98. Sam Quinones, *San Francisco Examiner*, 27 February 2000. The article explained that basketball is a particular passion of Oaxacan immigrants in Los Angeles. Introduced to Oaxaca in the 1930s and 1940s, the game has become a passion both at home and in the immigrant community in Southern California. In fact, there was a tournament in Los Angeles featuring fifty-five teams of Zapoteco Indian immigrants from Oaxaca.

99. Kibria, *Family Tightrope*, 7.

100. Ibid., 130–2.

101. These data and the quotes are contained in a communication from Jon Kangas, director of research and planning for the district, dated December 8, 1998. At that juncture, the governing board of the district included, among its seven members, three Latinos and a Japanese American. Another of its members was Richard Hobbs, director of immigrant services for Santa Clara County.

102. *San Jose Mercury News*, 8 April 1999.

103. Lien Phan, interview with the author, 17 January 1998, San Jose, California. I was able to locate this remarkable woman thanks to her daughter Rebecca, who was my student at San Francisco State University.

CHAPTER 6

1. Janet A. Flammang, *Women's Political Voice: How Women Are Transforming the Practice and Study of Politics* (Philadelphia: Temple University Press, 1997), 53. This book is an authoritative account of women's electoral success in Santa Clara County.

2. Donna Clare Schuele, "'A Robbery to the Wife': Culture, Gender and the

Marital Property in California, 1850–1890" (Ph.D. diss., University of California, Berkeley, 1999), 98, 99.

3. Cora Older, *San Jose News*, 7 September 1926.

4. See Ruth Bordin, *Women and Temperance: The Quest for Power and Liberty, 1873–1900* (Philadelphia: Temple University Press, 1981), on the importance of the temperance movement in mobilizing women's political energy.

5. This summary does not do justice to the infighting among various factions, ably discussed by Schuele in "'A Robbery to the Wife,'" chapter 3. Schuele convincingly argues that the early women's rights movement in California cannot be understood apart from the influence of Spiritualism.

6. Helen Arbuckle, "San Jose's Women," unpublished paper, San Jose Historical Museum, 1980. Barbara Babcock of Stanford Law School is working on a biography of Foltz.

7. I am indebted to the research of Willie Yaryan on this episode. Mr. Yaryan shared his work, which is part of a dissertation he is completing at the University of California, Berkeley.

8. Bertha Marguerite Rice, "The Women of Our Valley," pamphlet in the San Jose Historical Museum, 1955, 63.

9. I am the coauthor with Linda Witt and Karen M. Paget of *Running as a Woman: Gender and Power in American Politics* (New York: The Free Press, 1993). When researching our book, we repeatedly learned about this phenomenon. For example, the pioneering governorship of Ella Grasso in Connecticut is thought to have set the standard not only for women officeholders in that state, such as Congresswomen Barbara Kennelly and Rosa de Lauro, but also for women in western Massachusetts. As of 2000, Smith's own state of Maine had two Republican women senators.

10. Myra Eaton McLoughlin was the woman in the AFL cannery local leadership. Though I could not interview her, I did interview her husband, James McLoughlin, himself a leader of the Retail Clerks.

11. Flammang, *Women's Political Voice*, 172.

12. See the *Lockheed Star*, 2 May 1961 and 16 May 1961, for details about an early program. Noteworthy, too, is the fact that that same month, in John F. Kennedy's oval office, Courtlandt Gross of LMSC signed a "Plan for Progress," pledging to recruit, hire, and train minorities. LMSC was the first defense contractor to make this pledge, according to the *Lockheed Star* (13 June 1961). That same issue of the *Lockheed Star* also contained details about a commitment Lockheed had made to hiring the deaf. Lockheed Martin gave me the opportunity to read back issues of the *Star*, and the Public Relations staff also helped me locate women pioneers.

13. That other defense contractors in the Valley, too, were employing women engineers is proven by an announcement in the *Westinghouse News* (24 June 1958). The newsletter announced that a national convention of the Society

of Women Engineers had chosen Mabel Rockwell of Westinghouse, Sunnyvale, as its woman engineer of the year. With a B.S. in engineering from MIT, Rockwell performed electrical design work for the Polaris' launching equipment and had "project responsibility." (United Electrical Workers Papers, Box 9, Folder 15, Labor Archives and Research Center, San Francisco State University.)

14. Mary Ross, interview with the author, 27 August 1999, Los Altos, California. I also read about her accomplishments in the *Lockheed Star.*

15. Esther Williams, interview with the author, 21 August 1999, Menlo Park, California.

16. On August 23, 1999, I was invited to a regular luncheon meeting of retired Lockheed executives — all white men, it must be pointed out. I asked them to explain the phenomenon of opportunities for women that I was uncovering in back issues of the *Lockheed Star.* Reagan's comments came in this context. The men said that the highest reaches of the company were committed to this stance, not only because it was right, but also because it was perceived as a way of keeping the customer — the federal government — happy. They also recalled that certain male managers had a hard time with the policy. Worth noting is the fact that certain LMSC initiatives antedated any federal mandates — such as hiring the deaf in 1961. One can only infer the presence of a social conscience among one or more of the very highest executives.

17. Marlene Zimmerman, interview with the author, 19 September 1999, Los Altos, California.

18. Theresa Perea, interview with the author, 30 November 1998, Morgan Hill, California.

19. On the strength of women's organizations in the Valley, see Flammang, *Women's Political Voice.*

20. Paul Johnston, *Success While Others Fail: Social Movement Unionism and the Public Workplace* (Ithaca, NY: ILR Press, 1994), 95. This book focuses a great deal on events in the Santa Clara Valley.

21. Bob Brownstein, interview with the author, 12 July 2000, San Jose, California. Brownstein has been chief of staff for Supervisor Susanne Wilson, budget director of the city of San Jose for Mayor Susan Hammer, and a policy analyst for Amy Dean.

22. *San Jose Mercury News,* 22 February 1987.

23. Christensen, "San Jose Becomes the Capital of Silicon Valley," 217.

24. I base this generalization on interviews with people other than Wilson herself, on my archival research, and on a conversation with Professor Janet Flammang.

25. Susanne Wilson, interview with the author, 5 June 2000, San Jose, California.

26. As quoted in Johnston, *Success While Others Fail,* 94.

27. Flammang, *Women's Political Voice,* 41. In the late 1960s, I was on the

board of the League of Women Voters of the Santa Clara Valley, where I came to know and respect Hayes. I know about the television program, "Left, Right, and Center" on San Jose's Channel 36, because I was the moderator from the fall of 1968 through early 1970.

28. Flammang, *Women's Political Voice*, 41.

29. Edward O. Welles, "The Power of the County," *San Jose Mercury News, West Magazine*, 29 January 1984.

30. Flammang, *Women's Political Voice*, 186f.

31. Ibid., 50, 51.

32. Ibid., 246.

33. Ibid., 92–4.

34. Commission on the Status of Women, Santa Clara County, Annual Report, Human Relations Commission Archives, Santa Clara County Offices, September 1992.

35. Norma Mencacci, interview with the author, 20 October 1998, Santa Clara, California.

36. Wilson, interview.

37. My most important source on this subject is Johnston, *Success While Others Fail*, chapter 3.

38. Ibid., 112.

39. Ibid., 90f.

40. Connie Skipitares, "County Workers Ahead of San Jose Counterparts," *San Jose Mercury News*, 8 July 1981.

41. Johnston, *Success While Others Fail*, 55–60.

42. Ibid., 61.

43. Philip J. Trounstine and Gary E. Swan, "Job Comparison Study: How It Was Done," *San Jose Mercury News*, 8 July 1981.

44. Johnston, *Success While Others Fail*, 84.

45. Christensen, "San Jose Becomes the Capital of Silicon Valley," 223, 224

46. Joan Goddard, interview with the author, 4 June 2000, Sunnyvale, California.

47. Philip J. Trounstine, "City Workers Ratify Contract for $5.4 million to End Strike," *San Jose Mercury News*, 15 July 1981.

48. Deborah Powell, interview with the author, 4 June 2000, Sunnyvale, California. At that time, Ms. Powell was president of Local 101. I interviewed Goddard, Powell, and Rebecca Cuffman, also an AFSCME leader, together.

49. LaDou, interview.

50. Ed Sawicki, interview with the author, 1 October 1998, Santa Clara, California. Mr. Sawicki worked for Intel for seven years and now has his own consulting firm that deals with occupational safety issues.

51. Dr. LaDou offered the following explanation to me via e-mail: "Diborane is the hydride of boron. It is a toxic gas used to deposit the dopant metal boron

on semiconductor wafers. Exposure causes central nervous system effects and pulmonary edema. If exposure is continued, other symptoms occur."

52. Dee McCrorey, interview with the author, 1 June 1999, Santa Clara, California.

53. This generalization is based on interviews with Dr. LaDou and with Patricia Lamborn (interview with the author, 12 March 1999). See also Robin Baker and Sharon Woodrow, "The Clean, Light Image of the Electronics Industry: Miracle or Mirage," in *Double Exposure: Women's Health Hazards on the Job and at Home*, ed. Wendy Chavkin (New York: Monthly Review Press, 1984).

54. Baker and Woodrow, "The Clean, Light Image," 24.

55. *Monitor*, Labor Occupational Health Program, February-March 1978.

56. Baker and Woodrow, "The Clean, Light Image," 23f.

57. Lamborn, interview.

58. Baker and Woodrow, "The Clean, Light Image," 29.

59. *San Jose Mercury News*, 18 August 1979.

60. Baker and Woodrow, "The Clean, Light Image," 29.

61. *San Jose Mercury News*, 19 September 1999.

62. The first two phrases appeared in *San Jose Mercury News* stories about high tech. The third is from the *New York Times* (4 February 1999). The last was the title of a documentary about the tech revolution written and narrated by Robert Cringely.

63. See, for example, Stacey, *Brave New Families*. Three anthropologists at San Jose State University, Chuck Darrah, Jan English-Leuck, and James Freeman, have launched an ambitious research project for which they are gathering voluminous data so as to document the nature of the Silicon Valley Culture.

64. For an excellent empirical study of women in high tech as of the mid-1980s, see Strober and Arnold, "Integrated Circuits/Segregated Labor."

65. By their own admission, they played around with making a device for illegally placing long-distance telephone calls.

66. Anita Borg is the founder of the Institute for Women and Technology, located in Palo Alto. I interviewed her on March 24, 1999, and was convinced by her argument that the nerd stereotype is profoundly off-putting to women.

67. Sandra L. Kurtzig, with Tom Parker, *CEO: Building a $400 Million Company from the Ground Up* (New York: W. W. Norton, 1991), 170.

68. Judith K. Larsen and Linda Kimball, "Professional and Technical Women in Electronics," report prepared for the Santa Clara County Chapter of Women in Electronics, Cognos Associates, January 1983, 2f.

69. Everett M. Rogers and Judith K. Larsen, *Silicon Valley Fever: Growth of High-Technology Culture* (New York: Basic Books, 1984), 142, 143.

70. *Inteleads*, May 1988.

71. *Inteleads*, February 1993.

72. *San Francisco Chronicle*, 22 February 1999.

73. *Softtalk*, March 1981 (Apple Computers, Inc. Records, 1977–1997, Series 9, Stanford University Archives).

74. *Savvy*, May 1986 (Apple Records, Stanford University Archives).

75. *Apple Five-Star News*, 14 January 1991 (Apple Records, Stanford University Archives).

76. *Apple Five Star News*, 3 March 1992 (Apple Records, Stanford University Archives).

77. Stacey, *Brave New Families*, 25f.

78. Susan Brown is a made-up name. I changed it to protect her privacy, given the recency of the events she described to me. Interview, 2 June 1999, San Jose, California.

79. Barbara Wakefield, interview with the author, 29 September 1998, Sunnyvale, California.

80. Tia O'Brien, "Women on the Verge of a High-Tech Breakthrough," *San Jose Mercury News, West Magazine*, 9 May 1999.

81. Anita Borg, interview with the author, 24 March 1999.

82. Charles Piller, "The Gender Gap Goes High Tech," *Los Angeles Times*, 25 August 1998.

83. Gary Andrew Poole, "Nerds in Gilded Cubicles," *New York Times* 4 February 1999.

84. My notes from the "Life in the Fast Lane" conference, DeAnza College, Cupertino, November 13, 1998. The three anthropologists are Charles Darrah, James Freeman, and Jan English-Lueck.

85. As quoted in Keats, "It's the End of Work As We Know It," 51.

86. *San Jose Mercury News*, 8 July 1981; see also Flammang, *Women's Political Voice*, 188, and Welles, "The Power of the County."

87. Claudia Shope, interview with the author, 7 July 2000. It must be pointed out that Reed, a registered Republican, made enemies in the camp of organized labor. For example, Shope, who was part of Local 715's negotiating team for the 1985–87 contract with Santa Clara County, was quite critical of Reed. Shope singled out Supervisor Rod Diridon, who had opposed the appointment of Reed, as being the best friend of labor on the Board in the mid-1980s.

88. As quoted in Flammang, *Women's Political Voice*, 250. I have also relied on a conversation with Professor Terry Christensen of the San Jose State University Political Science Department on March 1, 1999, for my generalizations about Hammer.

89. Zoe Lofgren, interview with the author, 13 July 1994. Because Lofgren's election was so remarkable, she is discussed in Witt et al., *Running As a Woman*, 1995, 302–4.

90. Joan Goddard, Deborah Powell, and Rebecca Cuffman, interviews with the author. I gathered information about Alvarado from www.blancaalvarado.org.

91. According to the U.S. Census of 1990, women constituted 28 percent of

the self-employed managers/administrators in Santa Clara County at that time and 33 percent of the salaried ones. Women were 32 percent of the self-employed among supervisors/proprietors in sales occupations.

92. As for the San Jose Rotary Club, it began admitting women in June 1987. As of November 1998, it had 430 members, 60 of whom were women. It also had its first woman president, Mary Ann Diridon, wife of former supervisor Rod Diridon and mother of San Jose City Council member Rod Diridon, Jr. *San Jose Mercury News*, 12 November 1998.

93. Ching, interview.

94. *New York Times*, 14 November 1999, 26.

95. Terry Christensen, conversation with the author, 1 March 1999.

96. Amy Dean, interview with the author, 1 December 1998, San Jose, California. I also consulted the aforementioned *New York Times* article and the *San Francisco Examiner and Chronicle* (13 July 1997). See also Mike Weiss, "Dean of Labor," *San Jose Mercury News, West Magazine*, 28 February 1999.

97. Steve Lohr, "Setting Her Own Precedents," *New York Times*, 23 July 1999.

98. Reed Abelson, "A Push from the Top Shatters a Glass Ceiling," *New York Times*, 22 August 1993.

99. Quentin Hardy, "The Cult of Carly," *Forbes Magazine*, 13 December 1999.

100. In the spring of 2002, Fiorina spearheaded a controversial merger with Compaq, a merger that was bitterly opposed by Walter Hewlett, son of the cofounder.

CHAPTER 7

1. *Silicon Valley 2010*, 16.

2. David Friedman, "The Dark Side of the High-Tech Religion," *Los Angeles Times*, 31 January 1999.

3. *San Jose Mercury News*, 18 June 2000.

4. I do not have statistics on this point. But just within my personal acquaintance in the Valley, there are two people who have made the move into a mobile home after a divorce. I have also observed that it can be very difficult for young people who are not part of the salaried elite of the high-tech world to replicate the lives of their parents in terms of home ownership and a middle-class standard of living.

5. *Inteleads*, October 1980.

6. *San Francisco Chronicle*, 20 December 1993.

7. Joshua Cooper Ramo, "A Survivor's Tale," *Time*, 29 December 1997. This was the magazine's cover story, honoring Grove as Man of the Year.

8. Andrew Grove, "Bring Your Own Bucket," *Inteleads*, February 1986.

9. Julie Pitta, "Pain at National," *Forbes Magazine,* 29 October 1990.

10. *Varian Associates Magazine,* May 1986.

11. *San Francisco Chronicle* 20 December 1993.

12. Ibid.

13. Pitta, "Pain at National."

14. Ramo, "A Survivor's Tale."

15. Larry LeVieux, "The Historical Context of National Semiconductor: How We Got Here and Where We Are Going" (Archives of the Pacific Studies Center, Mountain View, California), 14.

16. Gary Hector, "The U.S. Chipmakers' Shaky Comeback," *Fortune,* 20 June 1988; Julie Pitta, "Rodgers' Regiment," *Venture,* April 1989.

17. *San Francisco Chronicle,* 20 December 1993; *Inteleads,* February 1988.

18. *Inteleads,* October 1980.

19. H. Garrett DeYoung, "Intel U Teaches Lessons You Never Learned in School," *Electronic Business,* 15 October 1990.

20. *Inteleads,* April 1980.

21. "San Jose: Joint Venture Silicon Valley Network," 1992, 28.

22. Sevilla, "Employment Practices," 29.

23. Tim John Sturgeon, "Turn-Key Production Networks Industry Organization, Economic Development, and the Globalization of Electronics Contract Manufacturing" (Ph.D. diss., University of California, Berkeley, 1999), 66.

24. Rogers and Larsen, *Silicon Valley Fever,* 194.

25. It is not my intention to suggest that Varian stood alone in this regard. Rather, I use the firm as an example, because I had such good access to Varian archival materials.

26. *Varian Associates Magazine,* July 1989.

27. *Varian Associates Magazine,* Spring 1992.

28. *Five-Star News,* 21 October 1993; the figure in brackets comes from *Five-Star News,* 1 November 1994 (Apple Computer, Inc. Records, Series 9, Stanford University Archives).

29. *San Francisco Examiner,* 1 October 1995.

30. *San Jose Mercury News,* 22 May 1999.

31. Siegel and Markoff, *The High Cost of High Tech,* 191, 192.

32. AnnaLee Saxenian, presentation at CEO and Minister Forum: Innovation and Entrepreneurship in Asia, sponsored by the Asia/Pacific Research Center, Stanford University, June 2, 2000.

33. The figures are from the Association of Bay Area Governments, as published in the *San Jose Mercury News,* 7 August 2000.

34. My gut feeling is that the Valley will bounce back, because there is such a staggering quantity of human talent for innovation there. But I have no crystal ball to predict when this will happen. How soon, or whether, there will be the type of superheated economy of the late 1990s is another matter.

35. Interview with David Bacon, 8 September 1998, Berkeley, California.

36. Ibid.

37. Pat Sacco Woods, interview.

38. They were members in the sense of being loosely affiliated, but not in the sense of having signed union authorization cards.

39. This account was based on interviews with David Bacon, 8 September 1998; Pat Sacco Woods, 18 October 1998; and Romie Manan, 29 September 1998.

40. Susan Yoachum, "Electronics Workers Haven't Rushed to Join Unions," *San Jose Mercury News*, 6 September 1982.

41. National Labor Relations Board, "Signetics Corporation *and* the United Electrical, Radio & Machine Workers of America. Case 32-CA-4606," *Decisions and Orders of the National Labor Relations Board* 273 (November 30, 1984–February 12, 1985), 730.

42. Ibid.; Rachel Marshall, interview with the author, 22 March 1999, Richmond, California. There is clear evidence that during the 1990s, employers were firing union organizers with virtual impunity. Either the cases take so long to be resolved that the complainant suffers from the delay alone, even if there is an eventual victory, or the penalty is so light that it is no deterrent. According to an article from the *New York Times*, reprinted in the *San Francisco Chronicle*, "A recent study of National Labor Relations Board data showed that from 1992 to 1997, employers fired or otherwise punished more than 125,000 workers for supporting a union." See Steven Greenhouse, "A Potent Illegal Weapon Against Unions," *New York Times*, as reprinted in the *San Francisco Chronicle*, 24 October 2000.

43. Rob Hof, "Union Pitfalls in Silicon Valley," *Peninsula Times Tribune*, 1 August 1988.

44. Michael Eisenscher, "Outline History of the UE Electronics Organizing Committee in the Silicon Valley," unpublished manuscript (given to me by its author), May 1985.

45. *Peninsula Times Tribune*, 1 December 1983.

46. *San Jose Mercury News*, 27 February 1980.

47. Jackson, *Inside Intel*, 152.

48. Rogers and Larsen, *Silicon Valley Fever*, 190f.

49. Bacon, interview.

50. *San Jose Mercury News*, 27 February 1980.

51. James J. Mitchell, "Silicon Valley Work Culture Gives Unions the Cold Shoulder," *San Jose Mercury News*, 4 December 1983. The insights from this writer were confirmed by what Amy Newell told me about the aspirations expressed by her coworkers. The term "Cadillac plant" is from her. Newell, interview.

52. Karen J. Hossfeld, "Why Aren't High-Tech Workers Organized?

Lessons in Gender, Race, and Nationality from Silicon Valley," in *Working People of California,* ed. Daniel Cornford (Berkeley: University of California Press, 1995), 418.

53. Beers, *Blue Sky Dream,* 269.

54. This generalization is based on anecdotal data. Yet it must be stated that when a home for which someone paid less than $100,000 is now going for nearly $1 million — more if it's in Palo Alto — then the math can be worked out rather easily.

55. *San Jose Mercury News,* 5 March 2000.

56. *San Jose Mercury News,* 28 January 2000.

57. Geoffrey Tomb, "Packing It In," *San Jose Mercury News,* 25 July 1999.

58. Ibid.; Carrasco's wife and nine daughters also worked there.

59. Geoffrey Tomb, "Fruitful Legacy," *San Jose Mercury News,* 12 September 1999.

60. Ibid.

61. Geoffrey Tomb, *San Jose Mercury News,* 10 October 1999.

62. Anne Martinez, "From Cannery to Keyboard," *San Jose Mercury News,* 18 June 2000.

63. Perez and Martinez, interviews with the author, 28 September 2000, San Jose, California.

64. Sergio Perez, telephone interview with the author, 18 September 2000.

65. *San Jose Mercury News,* 28 September 1996.

66. *Peninsula Times Tribune,* 2 September 1980.

67. In addition to the *Peninsula Times Tribune* story, see also Peter Carey and Michael Malone, "Black Market in Silicon Valley," *San Jose Mercury News,* 31 August 1980, and John Markoff, "The Sweatshop Returns: A New Subterranean Labor Market in Silicon Valley," undated manuscript, Pacific Studies Center, Mountain View, Calif.

68. The *San Jose Mercury News* of June 27, 1999, quoted Deputy Labor Commissioner Joe Razo, who handled the investigation in 1980, about the lack of fines or charges. The article then went on to explain that the investigation had been hampered by a lack of Vietnamese-speaking staff: "Moreover, the investigation came to a halt within two weeks when members of the business community met with state labor officials and local politicians and asked that they be allowed to police themselves, says Razo, who attended the meeting."

69. *San Jose Mercury News,* 27 June 1999.

70. Ibid.

71. Ibid.

72. *San Jose Mercury News,* 17 October 1999.

73. *San Jose Mercury News,* 13 December 1999.

74. *San Jose Mercury News,* 27 June 1999.

75. Sturgeon, "Turn-Key Production Networks," 189. I relied on Sturgeon's

work for my knowledge of Solectron, as well as upon conversations with Professor Boy Luethje of Frankfurt, Germany.

76. *San Jose Mercury News*, 28 June 1999.

77. *San Jose Mercury News*, 13 December 1999.

78. Melinda Ewell and K. Oanh Ha, "Working Without Contract Is Risky," *San Jose Mercury News*, 28 June 1999.

79. Chris Benner, "Shock Absorbers in the Flexible Economy: The Rise of Contingent Employment in Silicon Valley," May 1996, 17.

80. See, also, the discussion of this issue and of Mr. Conejo's plight, in Joel Kotkin, "Unions See Fertile Fields at Lower End of High Tech," *New York Times*, 26 September 1999.

81. Amanda Hawes, interview with the author, 5 June 2000; see also the editorial dealing with glycol ethers and reproductive hazards in *International Journal of Occupational and Environmental Health* 2 (January/March 1996): 73–5.

82. *New York Times*, 28 March 1996.

83. *Chicago Tribune*, 20 July 1997.

84. Dr. LaDou, interview.

85. Ricardo Alonso-Zaldivar, "Industry Opposes Study of High-tech Worker Cancers," *Los Angeles Times*, as reprinted in *San Jose Mercury News*, 6 December 1998.

86. Martinez Saldana, "At the Periphery of Democracy," 115–7.

87. *San Jose Mercury News*, 4 June 2000. Earlier, the union had lobbied high-tech firms for support in negotiations with subcontractors, with at least one, 3Com, offering support. *San Francisco Chronicle*, 20 May 2000.

88. *San Jose Mercury News*, 6 September 1999.

89. Weiss, "Dean of Labor."

90. Bob Brownstein, interview with the author, 12 July 2000, San Jose, California; *San Jose Mercury News*, 6 September 1999.

91. The quote is from www.washtech.org, a Web site created by the Washington Alliance of Technology Workers.

92. Louis Rocha, interview with the author, 16 February 2001, San Jose, California.